The Modern Element

Also by Adam Kirsch

The Thousand Wells: Poems

The Wounded Surgeon:
Confession and Transformation in Six American Poets

The Modern Element

Essays on Contemporary Poetry

Adam Kirsch

W · W · Norton & Company

New York   London

For information about permission to reproduce selections from this book,
write to Permissions, W. W. Norton & Company, Inc.,
500 Fifth Avenue, New York, NY 10110

For information about special discounts for bulk purchases, please contact
W. W. Norton Special Sales at specialsales@wwnorton.com or 800-233-4830

Manufacturing by RR Donnelley, Bloomsburg, PA
Book design by Margaret Wagner
Production manager: Andrew Marasia

Library of Congress Cataloging-in-Publication Data
Kirsch, Adam, 1976–
The modern element : essays on contemporary poetry / Adam Kirsch.
p. cm.
Includes index.
ISBN 978-0-393-06271-7
1. American poetry—20th century—history and criticism. 2. American
poetry—21st century—History and criticism. I. Title.
PS323.5.K55 2008
811'.5409—dc22

2007036461

W. W. Norton & Company, Inc.
500 Fifth Avenue, New York, N.Y. 10110
www.wwnorton.com

W. W. Norton & Company Ltd.
Castle House, 75/76 Wells Street, London W1T 3QT

1 2 3 4 5 6 7 8 9 0

To Leon Wieseltier

Contents

Introduction   9

Derek Walcott   17

Jorie Graham   25

John Ashbery   41

Geoffrey Hill   53

Frederick Seidel   79

Louise Glück   94

Charles Simic   106

C. D. Wright   113

James Merrill   125

Richard Wilbur   137

Donald Justice   148

Anthony Hecht   159

Theodore Roethke and James Wright   170

Kenneth Koch   184

Philip Larkin   192

Dennis O'Driscoll   199

Les Murray   207

Czeslaw Milosz   220

Adam Zagajewski   233

Joseph Brodsky   243

Billy Collins   257

Sharon Olds   271

Individual Talents: David Yezzi, Joe Osterhaus, Joshua Mehigan, A. E. Stallings   280

Two Modern Classics: *The Waste Land* and *Howl*   295

Yvor Winters   312

The Modern Element in Criticism   322

Acknowledgments   331

Index   333

Introduction

IN 1857, Matthew Arnold delivered his inaugural lecture as Professor of Poetry at Oxford, later published as "On the Modern Element in Literature." Like so many poets and critics since, Arnold was attempting to redefine the notion of modernness, expanding it from a merely temporal category to an aesthetic and even moral one. The modern element, he insists, is not to be found only in the poetry of the present, nor does it become increasingly evident as we approach the present. The literature of Periclean Athens, in Arnold's sense, is more modern than that of Victorian England, for it more completely meets his definition of modernness as "intellectual deliverance":

> But first let us ask ourselves why the demand for intellectual deliverance arises in such an age as the present, and in what the deliverance consists? The demand arises, because our present age has around it a copious and complex present, and behind it a copious and complex past; it arises, because the present age exhibits to the individual man who contemplates it the spectacle of a vast multitude of facts awaiting and inviting his comprehension. The deliverance consists in man's comprehension of this present and past. It begins when our mind begins to enter into possession of the general ideas which are the law of this vast multitude of facts. It is perfect when we have acquired that harmonious acquiescence of

mind which we feel in contemplating a grand spectacle that is intelligible to us; when we have lost that impatient irritation of mind which we feel in presence of an immense, moving, confused spectacle which, while it perpetually excites our curiosity, perpetually baffles our comprehension.

The immediately striking thing about Arnold's definition of the modern, to a reader a century and a half further advanced in a period that continues to orient itself around the concept of modernness (even if only in the negative form of the postmodern), is its unequivocally positive character. The artist can only become modern by mastering the civilization in which he finds himself, subduing its baffling and irritating variety through the order of art. The mark of the modern poet is his complete adequacy to a challenging world: he can, in the phrase Arnold applied to his favorite ancient modern, Sophocles, "see life steadily and see it whole."

Yet already in Arnold's lecture, it is possible to see the seeds of a later understanding of the modern, the one that T. S. Eliot would help to establish (at the expense of Arnold's own authority), and which still prevails today. It is hard to avoid the suspicion that it was the perpetual bafflement and excitement of modernity that Arnold knew firsthand, while the deliverance to which he aspired remained, like all redemption, prospective and hypothetical. Certainly, what seems modern in Arnold's poetry is not its mastery of a "copious and complex" present, but the honest confession of helplessness we find in "A Farewell": "we wear out life, alas! / Distracted as a homeless wind, / In beating where we must not pass, / In seeking what we shall not find." Even in "On the Modern Element in Literature," Arnold seems to offer a covert self-portrait, not in his paeans to Sophocles and Thucydides, but in his sketch of weary, nihilistic Lucretius:

"What a picture of ennui! of the disease of the most modern societies, the most advanced civilization! . . . Lucretius is, therefore, over-strained, gloom-weighted, morbid; and he who is morbid is no adequate interpreter of his age."

Arnold's hopeful, not to say wishful, definition of the modern would not be conclusively displaced until poets came to agree that, on the contrary, it is precisely the morbid poet who is the adequate interpreter of the modern age. This was the conclusion of Eliot, who scorned Arnold as a shallow Victorian optimist in order to conceal, even from himself, how many premises the two shared. Arnold's description of the modern world as "copious and complex" is almost identical to Eliot's in "The Metaphysical Poets." The difference is that, while Arnold sees modernness as the achieved mastery of complexity, Eliot sees it as willing surrender to complexity: "We can only say that poets in our civilization, as it exists at present, must be *difficult*. Our civilization comprehends great variety and complexity, and this variety and complexity, playing upon a refined sensibility, must produce various and complex results." The modern poet's peculiar heroism is to make himself civilization's pioneer, undergoing earlier and more intensely the spiritual experiences his contemporaries have not yet learned to articulate. The best expression of this heroism, with its strange mixture of intrepidity and passivity, may be John Berryman's in *The Dream Songs*: "I am obliged to perform in complete darkness/operations of great delicacy/on myself."

Once the modern poet has been defined in this way, not as his age's interpreter but as its exemplary specimen or willing victim, all the virtues and vices of modern poetry, up to the present day, become almost inevitable. The virtues are daring honesty, subtle self-knowledge, an intimate (if not always explicit) concern with history, and a determination to make language serve as the most accurate possible instrument of communication, even at the risk of estrangement. The vices, which correspond to the virtues and call them into question, are sentimental egotism, an obsession with staying up-to-date, and a belief that distortion of language is interesting and praiseworthy in its own right.

The best proof that these values still guide the way we read and write poetry is that a good modern poem moves us, and a bad modern poem disgusts us, more intimately and profoundly than their equivalents from previous poetic eras. Today, as for the last two centuries, it is only poets who put themselves genuinely at risk in their work who can fulfill the expectations modern poetry has bred in us. This is the risk of admitting, contrary to Arnold, that modern experience does not admit of being mastered and interpreted, only of being accurately and passionately shared. The forms this risk assumes vary as widely as poets themselves, but the willingness to take it is what unites today's best poets with their great predecessors since Wordsworth, and especially since Eliot.

To be modern in this essential sense, however, does not mean accepting the canons of modernness that previous generations have handed down to us. In fact, the major challenge for contemporary poetry is how to find its own way of being adequately and faithfully modern, without simply aping the influential techniques of the modernists of the 1910s and 1920s, or the postmodernists of the 1960s and 1970s. In contemporary poetry, it is striking how often the tools of the modernists are used to summon a factitious authority and prestige, to obscure premises that would not bear plain examination. Still worse is the use of the ludic, fracturing techniques of postmodernism, which emphasize the poem's difficult texture in order to conceal its absence of genuine insight, accuracy, and challenge. As with any moment in the history of poetry, perhaps, our own is littered with the corpses of once-vital techniques.

In writing the essays in this book over the last ten years, I did not have the question of modernness in poetry explicitly in mind; but in retrospect, it appears to me that a concern with the modern element does unite them. In reading contemporary poetry, I have usually responded to the presence or absence of the kind of risk I have suggested is genuinely modern. At the same time, I have tried to be conscious that, in a period when modernness and risk are the preeminent values, they will often be counterfeited. Fraudulent self-exposure, which makes no inner demand on poet or reader, and otiose experimentalism, which mistakes novelty for discovery, are typical of the bad poetry of our time, just as other kinds of badness characterized earlier periods. And as Arnold wrote in "The Study of Poetry," "in poetry, more than anywhere else, it is unpermissible to confuse or obliterate" the distinction between "excellent and inferior, sound and unsound or only half-sound, true and untrue or only half-true."

If the modern is an element of our poetry in the sense of the catalyst that sparks a reaction, it is also the universal element in which we move and breathe. As a result, it is impossible for us to see our contemporaries and our period as though from the outside, with an objectivity that is perhaps only another name for indifference. Over time, it has seemed less and less likely to me that criticism ought to offer disinterested assessments. Instead, I hope that these essays, by exploring the work of significant contemporary poets, will also serve the purpose of asking what poetry can and should do today, what it is for, what it and no other art can provide. Perhaps there is still no better answer to those questions than the one Arnold gave, when he defined poetry, unfashionably but wisely and truly, as "a criticism of life."

The Modern Element

Derek Walcott

EVERY POET begins as a provincial, dreaming of emigration to the city of the honored dead. "I think I shall be among the English poets after I die," wrote Keats, and the ambiguity is moving: he wants to be remembered as one of them, but also to actually walk and talk with them, like Dante with Virgil. To live on the fringes of literary society may, then, be an advantage to a poet's literary culture. He sees no reason not to converse directly with the authors he knows only from books; he does not need his passport stamped by London or New York. This is the freedom that allowed Keats, the Cockney poet, to be the direct heir of Shakespeare, and that drove Derek Walcott, as a child on St. Lucia, to envy a blind neighbor, thinking of "Homer and Milton in their owl-blind towers."

Walcott's constant theme, from his first poems to his very latest, has been the struggle to reconcile this poet's freedom with the bonds of history. He has seldom seemed to doubt his powers; his is an enormous gift, probably the greatest of any poet now alive, and his career is an almost uninterrupted progress in mastery. The doubts were rather about his place, and assailed him from both sides: the colonialist exclusivity of whites, the nationalist exclusivity of blacks. His early experience of English literature was a dissonance of sympathy and mistrust:

I had entered the house of literature as a houseboy,
filched as the slum child stole,
as the young slave appropriated
those heirlooms temptingly left
with the Victorian homilies of Noli tangere.

But Walcott's sense of mission was confirmed by the literary
world into which he exploded, still a teenager, in the late 1940s.
As the British Empire retreated, St. Lucia's native elite was
emerging into positions of authority, and they greeted Walcott's
first, self-published book, *25 Poems*, with an enthusiasm a young
poet elsewhere could hardly imagine. A newspaper account of a
reading he gave in 1951 is representative: "the lone figure of a
man standing on an intellectual promontory in the ocean of time.
A solitary figure. . . . He may be the prophet. . . . In fact, we feel
it in our bones." His work was read on the BBC's *Caribbean Voices*
program; his verse plays were performed on several islands; in
1958, when the short-lived West Indian Federation was inaugu-
rated, he was the natural choice to write the official pageant.

The dilemma that was to consume Walcott, for most of his
thirties and forties, was the smallness of the stage on which he
received such applause. It was, as he wrote in his essay "The
Muse of History," "the inevitable problem of all island artists:
the choice of home or exile, self-realization or spiritual betrayal
of one's country." There were, even in cosmopolitan Trinidad
where he lived for decades, no publishers for his books, no the-
aters for his plays, and above all no money. As a result, his self-
imposed responsibilities were crushing: Walcott was not just
writing poetry but, to a large degree, creating a culture in
which that poetry could be appreciated. "He alone would roll
the Sisyphean boulder uphill," he wrote about this phase of his
career, "even if it cracked his backbone."

Yet at the same time, Walcott has often considered himself extraordinarily lucky to be a Caribbean poet, precisely because the Caribbean lies so far away from the metropolis and its neuroses. Belatedness, that obsession of modern poetry, can be gracefully ignored by a poet who is starting from the beginning; in Schiller's terms, the Caribbean writer is not sentimental but naïve. This is the note Walcott struck in 1992 in his Nobel lecture, "The Antilles: Fragments of Epic Memory": "Visual surprise is natural in the Caribbean; it comes with the landscape, and faced with its beauty, the sigh of History dissolves. We make too much of that long groan that underlines the past. . . . The sigh of History rises over ruins, not over landscapes, and in the Antilles there are few ruins to sigh over."

The absence of the classic, in this hopeful view, makes the Antilles a richer place. Yet Walcott has been too honest to deny that it is also a hardship for the poet, for the simple reason that serious poets are besotted with allusion. Allusion is the most concrete way for a poet to assert his fellowship with the illustrious dead, and his mastery of the language to which he has fallen heir. And allusion requires, not landscape, but ruins: that is, it requires history. Walcott may proclaim the vigor and beauty that accompany the naïveté of the Antilles, but he cannot help feeling the loss of allusive possibilities that naïveté brings with it.

Thus the subject of history is always accompanied, in Walcott's poetry, by a powerfully ambivalent longing. It is evident in a poem like "Names":

and children, look at these stars
over Valencia's forest!
Not Orion,
not Betelgeuse,
tell me, what do they look like?

Answer, you damned little Arabs!
Sir, fireflies caught in molasses.

Orion and Betelgeuse, the mythological names, are denied to
the children of the Caribbean out of a sense that they are false
and foreign; yet the children's spontaneous answer, "fireflies
caught in molasses," sounds ignoble by comparison. The way
Walcott comes out with that vicious, racially tinged "damned
little Arabs"—he is both the chiding schoolmaster and the
insulted student—speaks volumes about his bitter predicament. He is drawn toward both the teacher's knowledge of formal names and the child's freedom from them.

Walcott's long struggle with Greece offers the clearest illus-
tration of this ambivalence. The Caribbean, in his poetry, is
often a version of the Aegean; his epic poem *Omeros* is nothing
less than an attempt to recast the *Iliad* on St. Lucia. But his very
insistence on the parallel implies a recognition of Homer's priority, which dashes the idea that the Caribbean is pristine territory, free from history. In "Another Life," written almost
twenty years before *Omeros*, he summed up the sources of his
epic ambition with the coldest insight:

Provincialism loves the pseudo-epic,
so if these heroes have been given a stature
disproportionate to their cramped lives,
remember I beheld them at knee-height. . . .

The poet without history, Walcott acknowledges, will find himself compelled to create a history, even a "pseudo" one. This is
because history gives places, people, and relations a content for
the mind to react against; without it, there is nothing for the
poet to write about but landscape.

Landscape, in fact, is a crucial category for understanding Walcott's verse. One of the things that makes a Walcott poem instantly recognizable is its natural ground: the star-apple and the frangipani, the ocean and the tropical rains. In part, this is because he is a painter as well as a poet—as he recounts in "Another Life," his first artistic ambition was to be a great painter—and he has a heightened sensitivity to the appearances of things, to compositions, colors, and patterns.

Yet Walcott is also drawn to the description of landscape because it is a statement of minimal historical content. He approached natural description in this spirit as early as 1948, in "As John to Patmos":

> This island is heaven—away from the dustblown blood of
>   cities;
> See the curve of bay, watch the straggling flower, pretty is
> The wing'd sound of trees, the sparse-powdered sky, when lit is
> The night. For beauty has surrounded
> Its black children, and freed them of homeless ditties.

It is a remarkable poem for an eighteen-year-old to have written, with its complex rhythm and the Shakespearean epithet "sparse-powdered." But even as Walcott's style matures, his attempt to cure the "homelessness" of the New World by claiming it as a "heaven" remains constant. It can be found fifty-two years later in *Tiepolo's Hound*:

> There was no treachery if he turned his back
> on the sun that plunges fissures in the fronds
>
> of the feathery immortelles, on a dirt track
> with a horse cart for an equestrian bronze.

There is no history now, only the weather,
day's wheeling light, the rising and setting

seasons: young Spring, with her wet hair
gone grey, the colour of forgetting.

This consistency means that the interest of Walcott's poetry is less in its ideas than in its language. Generally, Walcott's abstract ideas are a little too abstract, either too vague or too schematic; he seldom prosecutes an argument from beginning to end, and in his longer narrative poems—*Omeros*, especially—his attention wanders from the story at hand. The essentially visual organization of many poems—the willingness to slide from image to image, idea to idea, in a series of loosely connected subordinate clauses, syntax clashing with line—can baffle the reader's attention. In keeping with his painterly attitude, it may be best to read Walcott's poems as various treatments of a single subject, like Pissarro's "300 versions of visions of Pontoise" (as he writes in *Tiepolo's Hound*).

Walcott's greatest strength—a legacy, again, of his easy intercourse with the greatest poets—is his confidence to risk an elevated style. In "Ruins of a Great House," a poem from the mid-1950s that is one of his first mature works, Shakespeare's rhetoric has not been quite assimilated, but the ambition that swallows Shakespeare whole is thrilling:

Ablaze with rage I thought,
Some slave is rotting in this manorial lake,
But still the coal of my compassion fought
That Albion too was once
A colony like ours, "part of the continent, piece of the main,"
Nook-shotten, rook o'erblown, deranged

By foaming channels and the vain expense
Of bitter faction.

He also came to Auden and Eliot early on, and through them Donne and Marvell; the result was the overknotted ambiguity of *In a Green Night*. But the real breakthrough in Walcott's style arrived when he came to read (and know) Robert Lowell in the 1960s. He has said that Lowell made him drop the capital letters from the beginning of his lines, a token of a larger informality. And Walcott is perhaps the only inheritor of Lowell to equal his rhetorical force, able to combine ease with strength. With his 1984 book *Midsummer*—whose semi-sonnet form pays homage to Lowell's *History* and *The Dolphin*—Walcott came into his full powers; and it is his work of the last twenty years, including *The Arkansas Testament*, *Omeros*, *The Bounty*, *Tiepolo's Hound*, and *The Prodigal*, that makes his real stature clear. His *Midsummer* poem about the Brixton race riots shows the power of this late style:

I was there to add some colour to the British theatre.
"But the blacks can't do Shakespeare, they have no experience."
This was true. Their thick skulls bled with rancour
when the riot police and the skinheads exchanged quips
you could trace to the Sonnets, or the Moor's eclipse.
Praise had bled my lines white of any more anger,
and snow had inducted me into white fellowships,
while Calibans howled down the barred streets of an empire
that began with Caedmon's raceless dew, and is ending
in the alleys of Brixton, burning like Turner's ships.

The distance between "nook-shotten, rook o'erblown" and "Caedmon's raceless dew" is that between an imitator of Shakespeare and a successor to Shakespeare.

Walcott's constant alertness to historical injustice is the necessary complement to his nostalgia for history. But what is most
striking in his late work is the way his attitude toward history,
both its glamours and its horrors, has been transformed by a
new calm and detachment. As the title of his book-length poem
The Prodigal suggests, Walcott has become a true cosmopolitan,
which means that he is at home everywhere and nowhere. In
the Caribbean, watching a tribal sacrifice, the poet feels that
"your pale feet cannot keep time/feel no communion with its
celebrants." But he is equally suspicious of the cities of Europe:
"And why waste all that envy when they take/as much pride in
their suffering as in their cathedrals," he asks.

Finally, Walcott seems to feel that his only real home is
poetry itself. This helps to explain his fondness for metaphors
that turn the whole world into a poem: traveling in Italy, he
declares, "Blessed are the small farms conjugating Horace,/and
the olive trees twisted as Ovid's syntax." But if the whole world
is a poem, then the poet doesn't need subjects in the usual
sense. All of his poems come to seem like parts of one long
work, which is his life itself. And this is a fitting consummation
for a poet whose struggle, from his early youth, was to convince himself and the world that originality is still possible,
even at this late hour. Walcott has won his battle with history,
not by imitating the past, but by making the contemporary
classic—so that his Caribbean has become, no less than England itself, one of the original habitations of English poetry.
Walcott's victory confirms that, as he has written, "it is the language which is the empire, and great poets are not its vassals
but its princes."

Jorie Graham

AN ADMIRER once approached T. S. Eliot with a question about "Ash-Wednesday," perhaps his most obscure poem: "What did you mean when you wrote 'Lady, three white leopards sat under a juniper-tree'?" The poet replied, "I meant, 'Lady, three white leopards sat under a juniper-tree.'" This is the expected, even the necessary response; if poetry really is the best words in the best order, then no paraphrase or explication of a line can ever be as accurate as the line itself. Yet Eliot's line is sufficiently strange that it does seem to ask us to ask what it means: it announces itself as allegorical. Thinking of the leopard, wolf, and lion that accost Dante at the beginning of the *Inferno*, we are convinced that Eliot's three leopards have some symbolic meaning; and, following Dante, it is natural to take the leopards as symbols of bodily appetites, violent lusts, which have destroyed the poet ("fed to satiety / On my legs my heart my liver"). But unlike Dante's symbols—unlike the elaborate allegory at the end of the *Purgatorio*, where the "twenty-four old men crowned with lilies" are quite specifically the twenty-four books of the Old Testament—Eliot's allegory is missing its key. We cannot "read" the symbol completely.

It is this sensation of information withheld that, as much as anything, tells us we are reading a modernist poem. Our encounter with such poetry can be described in two distinct ways, what might be called the theoretical and the phenomenological. The theoretical level of communication proceeds, as it were, directly from poet to reader over the head of the poem. On this level, the opacity of the symbol is intended as a statement about the limits of communication. It demonstrates that language itself fails before the most important information, that the profoundest truths can only be gestured at.

But this kind of theoretical statement is always secondary, in our experience and in importance, to the phenomenal experience we immediately have when reading the poem. First and foremost, we respond to the poem's music and its literal meaning; these are the bedrock of any poem and must be sound if the theoretical superstructure is to hold. To put it another way, it is the phenomenal level on which we read a poem, the theoretical on which we "do a reading" of a poem, in the academic phrase. To read is to allow the poem to shine out as what it is, to take in what it presents; to "do a reading" is to apply to the poem a technique, whose product hovers above or alongside the poem itself as a ghostly presence.

This distinction is exceptionally marked in the work of Jorie Graham. More than even most modernist poetry, Graham's lives and breathes on the level of theory, with a corresponding diminishment of its phenomenal presence. Indeed, the logic of her poetry is not just allegorical but positively algebraic. In allegory, the meaning of a symbol may not be immediately evident, but the symbol must have some more or less natural relation to what it symbolizes. To take the Dantean example, men are not books of the Bible, but old men are commonly thought to be wise, to be teachers of wisdom, and the books of the Bible also teach wisdom. In algebra, by contrast, the signifier is totally arbitrary, an x; it quite literally "stands in" for something else, in that it must be removed for the equation to be solved. When, in reading Graham, we find lines like these:

opening and shutting to feel them rub against each other in
    here now (only in here),
the shut dark, the open dark—
and in between the _____ where the suspicion
    of meaning
begins. . . .

Or these:

I swear to you this begins with that girl on a day after
    sudden rain
and then out of nowhere sun (as if to expose the *what* of
    the hills—
the white glare of x, the scathing splendor of y,
the wailing interminable _____?). . . .

We know that we are being instructed to read algebraically, to
solve the poem for *x* and *y* and "_____." What may be less
obvious is that the organization of Graham's poetry on every
level, including theme, narrative, metaphor, even titles and
footnotes, is similarly algebraic. At every level, something crucial is left out, which the reader is meant to find and put back
in—or, just as significantly, to be unable to find, which failure
itself becomes part of the poem's theoretical freight.

    To understand what is involved in reading Graham, it is use-
ful to start with a characteristic passage. This is the beginning
of "The Guardian Angel of Point-of-View," from *The Errancy*:

A mourning dove. And again what you suffer
seems, ah, as if yet unlived through.
The bird keeps calling. You are in the middle
of the call.

There is thirsting in this work.
I must uphold—faultless—each outline—up—
each sloughing-off of meaning
into form. Ah . . . the bird keeps calling.
Behold—says my headless swording-in—*this*.
A gibbering, then a surprising fastness, then the opulence of
the stilled thing, seen.
There is a thirsting for ever greater aperture,
for ever more refined
beginning. Desire for a stillness that truly unfolds. Thirst,
because I'm never wholly *in* creation,
unlike these I am compelled to witness, there, everywhere. . . .
Oh to taste the limits of the single aperture.
To have that one beam burn from one's head—
the snapping of a retina—no errancy—
and starched, voracious—(plunder without narration)—
this view the very drink for whom these drinkers are
created. . . .

Clearly, such a poem requires the reader to fill in gaps, to
provide paraphrases and references—in short, to interpret, to
"do a reading"—from the very beginning. This process begins
with the first line, which mentions a bird but says nothing
explicit about its song. Thus Graham invites the reader, familiar
with the long tradition of bird-poems from Keats to Frost, to
read the presence of a song into the bare statement "A mourning dove." And the poem's third line justifies this reading, for
we are told that "the bird keeps calling"—that is, it was calling
all along, from the beginning.

So we are prepared to make a more substantial sort of cor-
rection, or interpretation, when we come upon the line "There

is thirsting in this work." The work referred to seems to be simply listening to a bird, which would in no circumstances actually make one thirsty. We take the word "thirsting," therefore, as a clue that Graham means more than just standing-there-and-hearing; thirsting implies activity, and one of her frequent themes is that perception is active, not passive. So we discount the actual word "thirsting," with its specific meanings, and replace it with something more general—"There is effort, or labor, in this work."

Similarly, in the tenth line, Graham offers a series of words relating to the birdsong: what she hears is first "gibbering," then "fastness," then "opulence." These words, too, are inapt. Perhaps a bird's voice could gibber; but to hold fast is a tactile image, and "opulent" is in still another category. So we turn from the words themselves to the progression they imply, a sort of less-more-most of perception: first a chaos of sensations, then a fixed sensation, then a richly detailed sensation.

Already the algebraic logic of Graham's poem is evident: reading it is a matter of replacing arbitrary or half-appropriate words with the concepts they stand for. (Reading Wallace Stevens is often exactly like this: when Stevens tells us that a jar placed in Tennessee made the slovenly wilderness surround that jar, we know that he means us to replace "jar" with "fixed point," "wilderness" with "chaotic space," and "surround" with something like "orient itself.") The same sort of interpretation is reprised, on a higher level, when we come to Graham's more philosophical statements: "I must uphold—faultless—each outline—up—/each sloughing-off of meaning/into form."

What can this mean in relation to hearing a bird's song, which as sound has no visual "outline"? It seems again like a statement about the active and constructive role played by the listener. Hearing is not just a matter of receiving sense data from the outside; it requires "upholding . . . each outline," that is, imposing fixity on something essentially formless. Exactly how this is connected with the description of the birdsong "sloughing-off . . . meaning into form" is not clear, since meaning and form seem to be equivalent in this context. It may express a semimystical feeling that the birdsong embodies a higher meaning, or a higher level of reality, which decays into a merely aesthetic perception of form; but this interpretation must remain tentative.

So far, then, "The Guardian Angel of Point-of-View" seems to be making a theoretical statement about perception—in particular, the desire for perfect, unlimited perception, which is impossible to satisfy. Graham writes that she longs for "ever greater aperture"—that is, openness, awareness, receptivity— so that she can really take in the birdcall, hear it completely and hold it in the mind, as though this fuller act of perception would reveal a higher truth. And this "thirst" for a more complete understanding of the material world is distinctively human, what keeps us from being "wholly *in* creation" like the complacent animals, untroubled by what surrounds them.

This interpretation offers a thread to follow through the poem's most opaque passages:

> Oh to taste the limits of the single aperture.
> To have that one beam burn from one's head—
> the snapping of a retina—no errancy—
> and starched, voracious—(plunder without narration)—
> this view the very drink for whom these drinkers are
> created. . . .

A few lines before, the poet had been asking for "ever greater aperture"; but now, in an apparent contradiction, she asks to "taste the limits of the single aperture." This seems to mean: to experience the largest receptivity possible for a single human's senses, which would mean being resigned to the limits of those senses. But this is followed by the wish for "hav[ing] that one beam burn from one's head," which implies not the consummation but the destruction, and thereby the transcendence, of the beam (the eye-beam) of an individual's "point of view" (to look back to the title). How do these two statements stand in relation to one another? Are they the same? Or does the second intentionally go beyond the first? Or must we reread the first in terms of the second—say, by reading "taste the limits" not as "enjoy the uttermost" but "devour or consume the limits"— and, in so doing, taste them as we taste food when we consume it? Similarly, is "the snapping of a retina" a snapping open or a snapping shut—or a snapping like firewood when it is burned away?

An answer to these questions may lie in the ambiguous line that follows: "this view the very drink for whom these drinkers are/created. . . ." The most natural interpretation of this phrase would be: this view, the natural world, is a drink intended to satisfy human beings, the drinkers who thirst. But the grammar suggests the reverse: that humans as drinkers are created *for the view,* the drink. The situation is further complicated by the use of "for whom" instead of "for which": "whom" suggests a personal antecedent, a human referent, but in this case it is referring to "the view," which is thus personalized. In what sense can it be said that humans are created for nature, and not vice versa?

Our interpretation can proceed with the guidance of the word "errancy." The title of the book in which this poem appears is *The Errancy*, so a passage containing the word should be of central importance. Errancy is an unusual term, and in her notes Graham illuminates it with a quotation, from a scholarly book, which points to the connection of "errancy" with the Latin *errare*, to wander (whence the phrase "knight-errant"), and thus with "error." Errancy is a wandering and an error; or, to put it another way, errancy is the region of freedom which allows for both productive wandering, as seeking, and aimless wandering-around.

To a reader familiar with Heidegger, such a sentence has a familiar sound. Heidegger is an important presence in Graham's work—she has often used epigraphs and titles taken from his writing—so it makes sense to look for clarification to one of his essays, even though it is not specifically cited in Graham's notes. This is "The Anaximander Fragment," translated by David Farrell Krell and Frank Capuzzi in the volume *Early Greek Thinking*. There we find the following passage:

> As it reveals itself in beings, Being withdraws. In this way, by illuminating them, Being sets beings adrift in errancy. Beings come to pass in that errancy by which they circumvent Being and establish the realm of error (in the sense of a prince's realm or the realm of poetry). Error is the space in which history unfolds. In error what happens in history bypasses what is like Being.

Without going too far afield, it is pertinent to mention that one of Heidegger's central concepts is that human consciousness serves as a clearing (*Lichtung*) in Being—in the sense of a clearing in a forest, an open space in which things can be seen. There is a sense, never definite, in which Heidegger implies that Being as a whole would be bereft or impaired if there were no human beings to provide this clearing. As a result, humans owe to Being the proper use of their clearing, which is to think about and protect (*bergen*) Being; this thinking is what allows

Being to appear, to be disclosed (*entbergen*). In the clearing, things are visible, "lit up," or, as the above passage says, "illuminated" by Being. But this is only possible because they are let loose into "errancy," or freedom, which also makes it possible for them to be ignored or concealed; this is how we can "bypass what is like Being." The human realm is one of error as well as of truth, of missing things as well as seeing them.

Now, equipped with this passage, we can return to Graham's problematic line. It seems that she is suggesting, in a Heideggerian sense, that "these drinkers" are really created to serve nature, or Being, by "drinking it in"—that is, eagerly and carefully regarding it, taking note of it, thinking about it. This connects back with the initial image of the birdsong, which stands in for nature or Being as a whole as one of the things which must be wholly, attentively perceived. It tells us *"Behold this,"* take care for and of Being. Perfect attentiveness would transcend errancy—"no errancy"—in that it would become impossible to "bypass" or mistake what we perceive. We would become united with Being, instead of being an "aperture" (an opening, a clearing—*Lichtung*) in Being.

This "reading," lengthy and digressive as it is, has provided one possible interpretation of one part of one poem. So one can imagine the amount of solving, substitution, and cross-referencing involved in reading a whole book of Graham's. There is no denying that this process can be a source of intellectual stimulation. But it remains doubtful whether it is a help or a hindrance to poetic communication. For even when we have done our "reading," we are left uncertain whether we have arrived at the meaning the poet intended. If we read Graham algebraically, it is always with the proviso that she alone—if even she—guards the complete solution, the master key that might unlock the poem.

There are two possible motives for this kind of withholding, which is so characteristic of modernist poetry. The first is that the poet knows that much of what she writes is unintelligible—at least at first, and sometimes at last—and consciously makes the reader's experience of frustration part of the theoretical burden of the poem. Many facets of Graham's work do seem deliberately intended to frustrate the reader. There are her titles, which are often grand ("Short History of the West") or obscurely philosophical ("What Calls for Thinking," a Heideggerian title; "Which But for Vacancy") or just obscure ("Underneath (9)"), but almost never stand in a distinct relation to the poems they name. There are her intricately unhelpful notes, which do not elucidate, but further mystify by hinting at secret references—quotations and allusions so minor that no one but the poet would know they were there, but whose presence adds another source of complication for the reader to unravel.

Take, for example, a note from *Swarm:* "David Jones's work—especially in *Anathemata* and *In Parenthesis*—provided inspiration for this work in a very general sense. 'Underneath (Upland)' is an example of his influence in terms of tone and voice." Such an acknowledgment is either fantastically scrupulous—every writer could name dozens of other writers who provided "inspiration in a very general sense"—or it is another clue: we are led to believe that reading David Jones offers another source of insight into Graham's meanings. But since so many writers are similarly invoked—in the notes to *Swarm* alone, we find Gunnar Ekelöf, Traherne, Dickinson, Anne Carson, Hélène Cixous, Susan Howe, Donald Revell, Michael Palmer, and more—to follow her leads is functionally impossible. We are left with the bare sense that if we had read everything Graham had read, we would understand her perfectly.

But this is as much as to say that if we knew what Graham thought, we could read what she writes. And this leads naturally to the second possible explanation for her obscurity, according to which it is not deliberate but a failure—or, perhaps, deliberate but nevertheless a failure. On this view, Graham's poetry demands theoretical readings and algebraic substitutions because it is not turned sufficiently outward to the public realm. Like many modernist poets, she wants poetry to serve as an evocative transcript of mental processes, rather than a finished and self-subsistent object. Instead of finding objective correlatives for inner experience, Graham attempts to reproduce that experience in a shorthand, a private idiom, which the reader is left to translate. That is why she fills her work with masses of external hints, as though to re-create in the reader, through appropriate reference, the environment in which her own thinking takes place. (This tactic is most obvious in *Materialism,* which contains dozens of long extracts from Bacon, Leonardo, Brecht, Audubon, and miscellaneous others.)

This observation seems especially pertinent when it comes to reading *Swarm,* in which Graham's obscurity takes a great leap forward. Graham's first style—the style of *Hybrids of Plants and of Ghosts* and *Erosion*—is already complex, but still comparatively lucid. From *The End of Beauty* to *The Errancy* she becomes progressively more obscure and allusive, as her lines take on the choppy, digressive quality of a transcript of consciousness. But in *Swarm* there is a reduction even more radical than the previous expansion. Instead of putting in more information, more fleeting thoughts, more images, Graham takes out virtually everything. As she writes: "I have reduced all to lower case.//I have crossed out passages.//I have severely trimmed and cleared." Indeed, words in *Swarm* are stranded in an expanse of blanks:

Mastery   scarcity   desiccation   noon
*
Owning
name of
birth
*
The gods that sleep in museums. . . .
*
(constitution   ceremony)
(take that look off   your face)

Reading a line like "mastery scarcity desiccation noon" is like encountering four points in an empty space. But since we have learned to read Graham algebraically, we can remember in this case the maxim from geometry that any two points define a line. Graham counts on the mind's natural tendency to compose a figure from points, to join the four words into a meaningful unity. In fact, the line in *Swarm* is simply a radicalization of the technique she has often used: the juxtaposition of words from different categories of discourse, with a tacit challenge to draw the connection between them. Thus, in the title poem of *The Errancy*, we find "a slippery utterly ash-free delinquency," "bloody translation," "rumorous diamond-dust," "christened bonfire," "scorched comprehension": all of them little unbalanced equations, which the reader must paraphrase and expand into meaning.

Reading *Swarm* involves performing such operations in almost every line. But again there are some guideposts, concealed and ambiguous, to help with interpretation. The title of the book uses the word "swarm" in a particular way, as Graham's note suggests. We are to read it not in the usual sense, as a chaotic mass, but in the technical sense of bees that "leave the hive . . . and fly off together in search of a new dwelling-place," or "persons who leave the original body and go forth to found a new colony or community." For "swarm," in other words, read "colonize," "begin again."

Or, by another specialized extension of meaning, "be born again." The epigraph of the book comes from St. Augustine: "To say I love you is to say I want you to be." This quotation immediately situates us in a Christian context, and encourages us to find Christian images and references throughout the text. Indeed, *Swarm* as a whole can be "read" as a record of a spiritual journey, a turning toward Christian belief. After years of struggling to impose a metaphysical order on the world, Graham may be resigning herself to the possibility that only the traditional deity can secure such an order.

The Augustine quote puts us on the lookout for Christian ideas and images. And the first poem of the book is titled "*from The Reformation Journal*": here we have another Christian word, evoking not just the historical epoch but the spiritual state of resolving to start out again (to "swarm") by reforming one's actions. As a "journal," it seems to record the poet's own experience of reformation. And the first line of this first poem sounds, at least, like a disavowal of past error: "The wisdom I have heretofore trusted was cowardice, the leaper."

Why is cowardice "the leaper"? Isn't courage what enables one to leap forward into the unknown—or, to activate another appropriate meaning, to make the "leap of faith"? This remains obscure, though one is left—as always—with the sense that a fuller "reading" might resolve what seems like a contradiction. But we can proceed on the assumption that Graham is writing about a spiritual turning point, a new beginning. So when we reach the line "A 'he' referring to God may be capitalized or not," we are confirmed in our approach; this book will evidently discuss God, though it is unsure of exactly how to address Him. This uncertainty resounds again in the poem's last lines:

> explain   asks to be followed
> explain   remains to be seen

Paraphrasing these compacted lines, they seem to be a request: "Please explain to me this idea: 'asks to be followed.'" Who or what is it that asks to be followed?

> He that loveth father or mother more than me is not worthy of me; and he that loveth son or daughter more than me is not worthy of me. And he that taketh not his cross, and followeth after me, is not worthy of me.

Jesus demands that we follow him; and yet this is difficult, because we can't be sure that Jesus was God. That "remains to be seen"—and it will be seen, when God himself is seen, at the Second Coming.

> For we know in part, and we prophesy in part. But when that which is perfect is come, then that which is in part shall be done away. . . . For now we see through a glass darkly; but then face to face: now I know in part; but then I shall know even as also I am known.

Such intimations can be found throughout *Swarm*. Many poems seem to meditate on the difficulty of belief, specifically Christian belief, even though the titles and contexts imply that they are telling stories out of Greek mythology. There are a series of poems in the book called "Underneath": "Underneath (9)," "Underneath (Upland)," "Underneath (Calypso)." (It is typical of Graham that the first poem in this sequence to appear in the book is 9, followed at intervals by 7, 1, 2, 3, 8, 11, and 13. Perhaps the misordering and omission of some numbers is significant; perhaps we are meant to rearrange them and read them in the indicated order. But perhaps not.) These titles suggest that Graham is dealing with the myth of Persephone, who descends "underneath" the earth every winter. But there are enough Christian images in the book to effectively dispel, or at least dispute, the Greek-mythical structure it announces.

To put it another way, it is possible to perform a "Christian reading" of *Swarm*. And in this reading we can make more sense of that strange line with which we began:

Mastery   scarcity   desiccation   noon

The first three words propose a series—most, less, least—which the fourth seemingly fails to continue; in its place should be something like "desolation," "destruction." It seems we are being told to solve the line, with "noon" as the variable. How, then, can "noon" be interpreted as equivalent to "desolation"?

> Now from the sixth hour there was darkness over all the land unto the ninth hour. And about the ninth hour Jesus cried with a loud voice, saying, Eli, eli, lama sabachthani? that is to say, My God, my God, why hast thou forsaken me?

The sixth hour is noon, and the time in the Passion when Jesus's degradation—from mastery through desiccation—is completed in abandonment. Here, it seems, we find the place where "noon" means not day but darkest night.

Yet no sooner has this interpretation been proposed than it begins to seem doubtful. Have we found a Christian meaning in

Swarm, or have we only introduced it by means of a "reading"? Even though this understanding of the book seems to offer a good way to navigate much of it, there is still something disquietingly unlikely, even arbitrary, about it. But Graham allows the reader no choice but to interpret, to read theoretically, because her work has so little phenomenal presence. To read her is to "read" her.

Difficulty is not, of course, a reason to reject or ignore a poem. Especially in reading the poetry of the twentieth century, one often willingly assents to Allen Tate's statement that "poetry . . . demands both in its writing and in its reading all the intellectual power that we have." There is a distinction, however, between the difficulty of obscurity and the difficulty of complexity. The latter emerges naturally from any attempt to capture a new feeling or idea for poetry. But with Graham, as with so many self-consciously modernist poets, the difficulty seems to fall into the first category. Her poems are obscure because they seem unfinished, because they reside in the privacy of the poet's mind and not in the public realm where poet and reader discuss things in common. As long as Graham asks the reader to fill in her blanks and solve for her *x*'s, she has not realized poetry's greatest and most enduring possibilities.

John Ashbery

JOHN ASHBERY, like God, is most easily defined by negatives. His poems have no plot or argument, no sustained mood or definite theme. They do not even have meaningful titles. After half a century, however, Ashbery has become such a familiar presence in American poetry that it is no longer necessary to describe his poems mainly as what they are not. To be sure, it is important not to ignore the radicalism in his work, the avant-garde playfulness that takes its inspiration from Dada and Surrealism. This is the element that defines Ashbery's voice, and makes it instantly recognizable. Yet it is equally true that Ashbery is, in other ways, a very traditional poet: he is a late Romantic, an heir to Stevens and Eliot. Like them, he uses modernist techniques to negotiate the oldest Romantic themes—most importantly, the powers and the limits of the imagination. These two inspirations, the experimental and the traditional, are equally indispensable to Ashbery's distinctive style; and our response to it must be a response to both of them.

How one feels about Ashbery's playful nonsense is perhaps a matter of taste. Consider "Daffy Duck in Hollywood":

Something strange is creeping across me.
La Celestina has only to warble the first few bars
Of "I Thought about You" or something mellow from
Amadigi di Gaula for everything—a mint-condition can

Of Rumford's Baking Powder, a celluloid earring, Speedy
Gonzales, the latest from Helen Topping Miller's fertile
Escritoire, a sheaf of suggestive pix on greige, deckle-edged
Stock—to come clattering through the rainbow trellis
Where Pistachio Avenue rams the 2300 block of Highland
Fling Terrace.

This is a fine example of Ashbery's casual, colloquial, gaudily
humorous vein. But there is also a less amiable and more abrasive
Ashbery, as in "Europe," from his first book, *The Tennis Court Oath*:

1.

To employ her
construction ball
Morning fed on the
light blue wood
of the mouth
cannot understand
feels deeply)

2.

A wave of nausea—
numerals

3.

a few berries

To read this kind of thing can be intermittently stimulating;
to read it at great length, as one is generally made to do in any

volume of Ashbery's, is mildly masochistic. Of course, such writing has an aura of transgression, and so it seems to go well with other sorts of philosophical radicalism. To drain words of their usual significance, as Ashbery does, can be seen as a way of striking a blow against the transcendental signifier, the stabilities of meaning that are the object of present-day critical mistrust. At first sight, it may seem that a powerful gift is required to evade the snares of logic, to use words the way abstractionists in the visual arts use lines and colors—not to build up an image, but as gestures in their own right.

But the fact that large swaths of Ashbery repel interest and thwart attention actually leads to the opposite conclusion. Difficulty is only possible within a system of conventions, including the convention of meaning. It is by evading and complicating rules that a poet demonstrates skill, and we are naturally attracted to displays of skill, in poetry as in music or athletics. But when a poet leaves conventions behind (which is not the same thing as playing with them or transcending them), a vast territory of verbiage is opened up, and he is left without a goal or destination. Take, for example, these lines from Ashbery's book-length poem *Flow Chart*:

> Only that one told me a
> new-laid owl's egg
> is sovereign
> against the gripes, and
> now I find you here too.
> I have found you out.
> You seem
> convinced the killer is
> one of us. Why? Did
> a drowned virgin

tell you that, or Tim the
ostler, or the one-eyed
hay-baler
with a hook for a hand?

This is not nonsense as a computer spewing out words is nonsense; it is, rather, an evasion of sense. Each phrase and line has a certain weight and atmosphere, though one might be hard put to say what it is. Yet there is something unimpressive about this kind of writing. It is too easy; too much is permitted; it is evidence of a skill that is finally worthless. For the communication of meaning is, along with the manipulation of form, one of the natural bounds of poetry. It is in the negotiation of these two demands, meaning and form, sense and rhythm, that poetic beauty is created. The need to communicate, the pressure of urgent speech, is what drives a poem forward into the open region of art, even when the difficulty of communication makes it dilate and digress. Without that forward pressure, poetry becomes merely a private language.

Ashbery's style is not exactly private, in the sense that he is using words and symbols whose meaning he understands but does not sufficiently illuminate. Even to the poet, the above passage can be nothing more than a bit of high-spirited linguistic play. But Ashbery allows this kind of play to crowd out actual communication far too often, giving long passages of his work an air of self-indulgence. His prolixity—between 1998 and 2002, he published a book a year—seems to bear out this judgment. His verse is less like an eruption of necessary speech than an adjustment of the poet's mind to a certain frequency, whose signal is then transcribed voluminously.

Yet this cannot stand as a complete or final judgment on Ashbery. For his nonsense is only one strand in his work; and the other strand, the traditional Romantic one, is more demanding and more affecting. This other inheritance explains why Harold Bloom has taken up Ashbery, vocally and insistently, as the worthiest successor to Bloom's royal line of Stevens, Whitman, and Emerson. (Eliot, too, is an important influence, especially the discursive, long-lined verse of *Four Quartets*, which echoes frequently through Ashbery's middle period. But Bloom's peculiar loathing of Eliot causes him to be deleted from the Ashbery lineage, the way deviationists were excised from Soviet encyclopedias.)

When considering Ashbery the Romantic, one is forced to look not at whole books or poems, but at passages and excerpts, often no more than a few lines long. Indeed, a brief survey of the critical literature on Ashbery shows that few passages longer than that are ever quoted, for the simple reason that his method is to drift in and out of focus, never developing any single theme or idea for very long. Yet his most interesting poems are those where the focus is sustained the longest, especially in *The Double Dream of Spring*, *Self-Portrait in a Convex Mirror*, and the title poem of *A Wave*.

Take, for instance, an unusually lucid poem, "Grand Galop," from *Self-Portrait*. In this passage near the beginning, Ashbery is writing in a slightly deflected style, where meaning is obscured but not obliterated:

> Only waiting, the waiting: what fills up the time between?
> It is another kind of wait, waiting for the wait to be ended.
> Nothing takes up its fair share of time,
> The wait is built into the things just coming into their own.
> Nothing is partially incomplete, but the wait
> Invests everything like a climate.
> What time of day is it?

> Does anything matter?
> Yes, for you must wait to see what it is really like,
> This event rounding the corner
> Which will be unlike anything else and really
> Cause no surprise: it's too ample.

The motto to this passage could be "Ridiculous the waste sad time / Stretching before and after," and indeed the rhythms and repetitions recall *Four Quartets*:

> I said to my soul, be still, and wait without hope
> For hope would be hope for the wrong thing; wait without love
> For love would be love of the wrong thing; there is yet faith
> But the faith and the love and the hope are all in the waiting.
> Wait without thought, for you are not ready for thought.

Ashbery is darker, more secular, less formal than Eliot, but the influence is clear.

The "Grand Galop" passage is unusual for Ashbery because it has something like a paraphrasable content. It is a true Romantic expression of the longing for transformation, for an inexpressible wholeness, that is inevitably disappointed by time. The poet declares his faith in the world's hidden meaning, nicely expressed in the double negative "Nothing is partially incomplete": that is to say, everything is really complete, if we could only see it properly. Yet this is impossible, since we are bound to the dimension of time, which entails the "wait" that "invests everything like a climate." And there is, further, the fear that our comprehension will be inadequate to the vision when it comes. It "will be unlike anything else," and yet "really cause no surprise: it's too ample."

To see Ashbery's whole method at work, however, we must look at what follows this passage:

> Water
> Drops from an air conditioner
> On those who pass underneath. It's one of the sights of our town.
> Puaagh. Vomit. Puaaaaagh. More vomit.

And what precedes it:

> And today is Monday. Today's lunch is: Spanish omelet, lettuce
>   and tomato salad,
> Jello, milk and cookies. Tomorrow's: sloppy joe on bun,
> Scalloped corn, stewed tomatoes, rice pudding and milk.

It is hard to know in what spirit this should be read. Is it a high-spirited kick to the shins of logic, or veiled metaphor, or just banter? All three, perhaps, to some degree. But Ashbery's refusal to follow a train of thought for very long also has another, more intelligibly poetic purpose. It is a way of indicating, by imitating, the poet's sense of the constant flux of thought. Large amounts of junk flow through the mind, Ashbery seems to say; consciousness is inconstant, reactive, essentially variable. The sensation of lucidity is rare and fleeting.

Of course, the privilege of lyric poetry has always been that the junk of consciousness is excluded from the frame of the poem, that the poet is allowed a high style because his province is the significant moment. But for Ashbery, the transient nature of poetic truth must be acknowledged within the poem itself, if its utterance is to seem authentic. We can take the measure of this innovation by comparing Ashbery with one of his Romantic ancestors. In *The Prelude*, Wordsworth describes the work of thought and memory with a water metaphor:

> As one who hangs down-bending from the side
> Of a slow-moving boat, upon the breast
> Of a still water, solacing himself
> With such discoveries as his eye can make
> Beneath him in the bottom of the deeps,
> Sees many beauteous sights—weeds, fishes, flowers,
> Grots, pebbles, roots of trees, and fancies more,
> Yet often is perplexed, and cannot part
> The shadow from the substance . . .
> · · · · · · · · · · · · · ·
> Such pleasant office have we long pursued
> Incumbent o'er the surface of past time. . . .

If Wordsworth remains "incumbent o'er the surface" of things, Ashbery's technique is rather to jump into the pond, so that vision is distorted by the bends of light and the clouds of dirt. Just as, underwater, forms swim in and out of focus, so, in Ashbery's verse, ideas and moods materialize and disappear. His swerves of tone and subject are an attempt to transcribe the way the mind works. Or else, to use Ashbery's own water metaphor, consciousness is like a wave:

> The cimmerian moment in which all lives, all destinies
> And incompleted destinies were swamped
> As though by a giant wave that picks itself up
> Out of a calm sea and retreats again into nowhere
> Once its damage is done.

"Damage" is a particularly fine ambiguity, for what Ashbery is describing is not injury but completion, the evanescent dream of wholeness that characterizes the Romantic mind. It becomes damage only because the wave then retreats, leaving us beached and isolated.

Such moments are everywhere in Ashbery's middle period, and they are the basis on which his poetry must finally stand or fall. In these passages, his vast tracts of indirection make the moments of directness seem all the more startling and true. This is another technique that Ashbery learned from *Four Quartets*. It is not enough for the poet to state his revelation; the reader must discover it by means of a difficult and lengthy process, so that the difficulty may be experienced as an integral part of the revelation. And to say that Ashbery sometimes recalls the emotional atmosphere of Eliot's great poem is high praise.

But there is also a significant problem with this sort of Romanticism, which Ashbery's work demonstrates very well. To elucidate it, we must turn back to Wordsworth, at the beginning of the Romantic tradition. Poets since Wordsworth have put great stock in the imagination's ability to transform the ordinary. For Wordsworth, the imagination worked in partnership with nature to open the human mind to the sublime and the beautiful; his famous formulation in "Tintern Abbey" describes the beauty of nature as "both what we half create / and what perceive." In the recollections of "spots of time" in *The Prelude*, we see him trying to show how this process worked in the central moments in his own life.

But after Wordsworth, in the high Romantic period of Shelley and Keats, the imagination was detached from the mundane altogether, and recast as an inscrutable, God-like faculty, which intervenes in catastrophic moments to transform the world and

our experience of it. The archetypal description of the imagination in this guise is Shelley's "Hymn to Intellectual Beauty":

> The awful shadow of some unseen Power
> Floats though unseen amongst us,—visiting
> This various world with as inconstant wing
> As summer winds that creep from flower to flower. . . .

Just as Shelley sees the imagination, or Intellectual Beauty, as
a divine being, existing independently of the human mind, so
its visitations make him act like a man possessed: "Sudden, thy
shadow fell on me;/I shrieked, and clasped my hands in
ecstasy!" This view of the imagination and its effects has the
peculiar consequence of precluding speech: it elicits not words
but a shriek. And though later poets, less excitable than Shelley,
do not speak of shrieking, there is still, in the Romantic and
modernist tradition, a tendency to remove the imagination
from the realm of the sayable. Transformation is ardently
desired, but it is conceived as being so total that it threatens to
make language, and therefore poetry, impossible. As a result,
poets devote more and more energy to diagnosing their unful-
fillment, while the idea of fulfillment becomes correspondingly
vaguer and more notional.

We may observe the same phenomenon in Stevens, the poet
to whom Ashbery is in many ways closest. Stevens can be fantastically detailed about everything relating to imaginative consummation, except what it will consist of or feel like. He
constantly maneuvers around the main point, as in "The American Sublime":

> But how does one feel?
> One grows used to the weather,

The landscape and that;
And the sublime comes down
To the spirit itself,
The spirit and space,
The empty spirit
In vacant space.
What wine does one drink?
What bread does one eat?

To which one is tempted to reply, "Well, what?" But of course
that is the point: it cannot be told. The supreme fiction "must
be abstract." Stevens's Romanticism is gestural, pointing at a
fulfillment that poetry itself cannot describe or accommodate.

Which brings us back to Ashbery, to his Romanticism and to
his nonsense. Ashbery, as a very late Romantic, is condemned
to an elephantiasis of indirection, an immense expansion of the
inessential, in order to give point to what is essential—because
the essential is itself inexpressible, no more than a vapor, a
tremor. To read Ashbery is to plod through a dismaying expanse
of trivia, jokes, bent grammar, and nonsense so that the poet
can finally bring in his five or ten lines of epiphany:

And some day perhaps the discussion that has to come
In order for us to start feeling any of it before we even
Start to think about it will arrive in a new weather
Nobody can imagine . . .
Will take place in a night, long before sleep and the love
That comes then, breathing mystery back into all the sterile
Living that had to lead up to it.

It is perfectly legitimate for the poet to make the road to his
truths a difficult one, and in Ashbery's best poems the game is

worth the candle. But the Romantic perplexity that animates his work—the dilemma of having to communicate, in words, a feeling that is beyond words—also drags it down, requiring or at least permitting a great deal that is insubstantial, inessential, insufficiently formed, tedious. Poetry has many resources Ashbery neglects or abuses, in the name of exercising one particular resource; and this is mannerism. It is therefore all too fitting that Ashbery's most famous poem, "Self-Portrait in a Convex Mirror," should be about a painting by the Mannerist Parmigianino. Ashbery, too, gives the reader a sense of exhaustion—as though, after him, there were nowhere fruitful for poetry to turn.

Geoffrey Hill

FOR A READER who cherishes the central tradition of English poetry and wants to see it extended, Geoffrey Hill is a source of great promise and great frustration. No poet writing today has been more explicit and even defiant in claiming history, complexity, and moral seriousness as his birthright. When one thinks of English poems that confront earnestly the evil of the twentieth century, Hill's "Ovid in the Third Reich" and "September Song" are among the first to come to mind. When one thinks of contemporary poets of Christian faith, in the tradition of Herbert, Hopkins, and Eliot, Hill is possibly the only one that comes to mind. By 1995, having published only five books of verse in thirty-five years, Hill had earned critical superlatives: "the strongest British poet now alive," "the major achievement of late-twentieth-century British verse."

At the same time, Hill's work to this point—it can be found in *New and Collected Poems, 1952–1992*—leaves the reader with a troubling sense that this admirably elevated poetry is lacking something crucial. Describing Hill's work in a few words, at a high level of generality, one could not avoid calling it moral and religious. But if one engages Hill more closely, it begins to seem that he writes about religion, rather than faith; about history, rather than experience; about morality, rather than conscience. That is, he addresses these things not as existential challenges, but as abstract themes and subjects.

Consider the first sonnet in Hill's sequence "Lachrimae," from *Tenebrae*. Right away, that double-barreled Latinity sounds a warning blast. This is the language of medieval Catholicism, and one knows in advance that a poet using that language in the late twentieth century must resort either to irony or to parody. Hill's verse is parody, specifically of the English poetry of the seventeenth century:

> I cannot turn aside from what I do;
> you cannot turn away from what I am.
> You do not dwell in me nor I in you
> however much I pander to your name
> or answer to your lords of revenue,
> surrendering the joys that they condemn.

The rhythms, the repetition and paradox, come straight from the Baroque. Compare, for example, Richard Crashaw's "And He Answered Them Nothing":

> Oh mighty Nothing! unto thee,
> Nothing, we owe all things that be.
> God spake once when he all things made,
> He saved all when he Nothing said.
> The world was made of Nothing then;
> 'Tis made by Nothing now again.

Crashaw's wit is licensed by surety. The paradox that God created all from nothing is beyond doubt, and so it can be varied, extrapolated, paralleled, without being undermined. But Hill's lines are actually about the absence of surety: the poet and God are severed, no matter how much the poet "panders" to God. And the borrowed language of faith is the best example of such pandering. Hill uses it to create a sense of continuity with earlier religious poetry, while acknowledging that he is actually denied religious experience.

In theory, Hill's adoption of the idiom of faith for skeptical utterance ought to move beyond parody to irony, or even mourning. But it is not affecting in such an intimate, surprising way, because the Baroque idiom Hill parodies no longer has any authority. It is literally far-fetched, something taken from the history of literature, not something that surrounds us and has the power of the nearmost. For a poet in the late twentieth century to write that he does not "dwell" in Christ is not moving as blasphemy or even as tragedy, because it is simply what we expect.

In other words, to complain of the failure of seventeenth-century ways of writing and feeling is arbitrary; and the limitation of Hill's early work lies in this kind of arbitrariness. In fact, one could say that Hill's importance is that he demonstrates, unwittingly, one of the major premises of modern poetry: the eccentricity of the canonical. In 1955, Philip Larkin made an influential statement of this alienation from the formerly authoritative, writing that "as a guiding principle I believe that every poem must be its own sole freshly created universe, and therefore have no belief in 'tradition' or a common myth-kitty or casual allusions in poems to other poems or poets, which I find unpleasantly like the talk of literary understrappers letting you see they know the right people." Four years later, Hill published his first book, *For the Unfallen*, which includes the acclaimed "Requiem for the Plantagenet Kings":

> They lie; they lie; secure in the decay
> Of blood, blood-marks, crowns hacked and coveted,
> Before the scouring fires of trial-day

Alight on men; before sleeked groin, gored head,
Budge through the clay and gravel, and the sea
Across daubed rock evacuates its dead.

Larkin's statement was perhaps deliberately exaggerated and polemical, but Hill's poem seems designed to prove his case. Can he, or anyone, really mourn the death of the Plantagenet kings, who reigned 750 years ago? Does anyone believe that a poem can or should have the ritual purpose of a requiem? Does anyone expect that on the Day of Judgment, the reanimated corpses of King Stephen and King Henry I will burst forth from their tombs? And if not, what is Hill's poem but an academic exercise, a cunning assembly of the materials of high culture?

"Requiem for the Plantagenet Kings" shows that Hill's strengths and weaknesses are inherited from the style associated with the American New Criticism. In his first book, he used an epigraph from a poem by Allen Tate, and he has written that when he was sixteen, Tate's "Ode to the Confederate Dead" "struck me like a bolt from heaven; overnight I became a modernist." The qualities of Tate's verse—the lofty guardedness, the ostentatious ambiguity, the stiffened forms—make up a large part of Hill's early ideal. Tate's way with adjectives was especially influential: Hill, too, enjoys Latinate adjectives that call attention to their own deliberateness. Tate's "Ode" has "malignant purity," "verdurous anonymity"; in *For the Unfallen*, we find "attested liberties," "abstracted menace." But Hill's Latinity is darker and more insistent, and he combines it with the Gothic, obstructed music of Anglo-Saxon roots and compounds. The height of this style, and the purpose to which he puts it, can be seen in the sequence "Funeral Music," from his second book, *King Log*:

They bespoke doomsday and they meant it by
God, their curved metal rimming the low ridge.
But few appearances are like this. Once
Every five hundred years a comet's
Over-riding stillness might reveal men
In such array, livid and featureless,
With England crouched beastwise beneath it all.
'Oh, that old northern business . . .' A field
After battle utters its own sound
Which is like nothing on earth, but is earth.
Blindly the questing snail, vulnerable
Mole emerge, blindly we lie down, blindly
Among carnage the most delicate souls
Tup in their marriage-blood, gasping 'Jesus'.

The poem is exemplary not only in its style—the dense halting rhythm, the violence of sound and image, the archaism—but also in its way of treating a historical episode. Hill is describing a battlefield of the Wars of the Roses, and at the head of the sequence stand the names of three noblemen executed for treason in the fifteenth century. But the poem doesn't treat the battle as a historical event. This is not a style suited to giving information or pursuing consecutive thought, and indeed Hill has no interest in history considered as a series of motivated human actions. Rather, the poem is a still life, a tableau; Hill sees it as the comet might, a brief glimpse of "featureless" men arrayed for battle. It is a verbal icon of violence, and what we take from it is primarily the poet's own grim satisfaction in mimicking the carnage.

Nor is it possible to credit the statement of the last two lines as a serious moral reflection. That men continue to procreate while wars rage, that they use the name of Jesus in sexual passion, is true but unshocking. Or perhaps it is better to say that this way of putting it cannot shock us, for Hill's cynical disgust is undermined by his extremely literary language. "Tup," for instance, is a word no one uses today, but that many readers will remember from *Othello* ("even now, a black ram is tupping your white ewe"). The poem has the effect, not of communicating or inspiring a moral reaction of any kind, but of impressing the reader with an artful simulation of feeling.

This sort of demurral does not imply that a poet living in 1968 can only make use of the words and things of 1968. The point must be emphasized, because there is a tendency, among Hill's admirers, to believe that the only possible reason to dissent from his techniques is philistine ignorance. One of W. H. Auden's best poems leaps back a thousand years before Hill's Wars of the Roses, to evoke "The Fall of Rome":

Caesar's double-bed is warm
As an unimportant clerk
Writes I DO NOT LIKE MY WORK
On a pink official form.

Unendowed with wealth or pity,
Little birds with scarlet legs,
Sitting on their speckled eggs,
Eye each flu-infected city.

What one admires in Auden is what Hill's poem lacks: the precision, the imaginative detail, the subtle correpondences between past and present. Hill's blatantly moralized creatures—the "questing snail, vulnerable mole"—are both less specific and less symbolically effective than Auden's ominous "speckled eggs," with their faint suggestion of disease. Auden may err on the side of levity, but that is better than erring on the side of solemnity, because it recognizes the tentativeness of any reconstruction of the distant past.

Solemnity, however, has always been Hill's besetting vice. Solemnity is to seriousness as sentimentality is to emotion: the attempt to induce a feeling that refuses to occur spontaneously. What's more, solemnity provokes a kind of resistance—mockery, or sheer disbelief—which genuine seriousness never does. And it takes courage for a poet to realize that such resistance on the reader's part may be justified, that it demands a genuine reform of his poetic methods. That is why there is something truly impressive in the stylistic evolution of a Yeats or a Lowell. Hill, however, has never embraced the kind of humility necessary for such a change. Instead, he has been the Coriolanus of contemporary poetry, proud of his refusal to compromise or condescend. This is already the case in *King Log*, in the poem "An Order of Service":

> Let a man sacrifice himself, concede
> His mortality and have done with it;
> There is no end to that sublime appeal.
>
> In such a light dismiss the unappealing
> Blank of his gaze, hopelessly vigilant,
> Dazzled by renunciation's glare.

"Sublime" must be heard with the superb contempt Hill intends. In fact, he sees it as the opposite of sublime to confess one's mortality, and all the frailties it implies. His own position—vigilant, renunciatory—may be "unappealing" to the base, but the reader can have no doubt about Hill's opinion of his own moral fineness. Yet the word "vigilant" summons, as if for its own rebuke, Lowell's beautiful phrase about Robert Gould Shaw from "For the Union Dead": "he has an angry wren-like vigilance." "Wrenlike" is a word Hill would not dare use, because it is not solemn; it does not need to be, since the moral heroism of Colonel Shaw is genuine, and can survive the precision of homeliness. Indeed, it is the homeliness that secures the grandeur, and keeps it from floating off into the untrustworthy atmosphere of rhetoric.

Ironically, one of the most admired elements of Hill's verse is his self-consciousness about the temptations of rhetoric. His poem "Ovid in the Third Reich" is often praised as a definitive statement of the moral narcissism of poetry:

> I have learned one thing: not to look down
> So much upon the damned. They, in their sphere,
> Harmonize strangely with the divine
> Love. I, in mine, celebrate the love-choir.

This is very characteristic of Hill—in the ambiguity of "look down," in the rough breaking of sentence across line. Most characteristic of all is Hill's awareness of both the attraction of such indifferentism and its danger. Similarly, in "September Song," a poem on the death in the Holocaust of a Jewish child who shares Hill's birthday, he interrupts himself to acknowledge: "(I have made / an elegy for myself it / is true)."

The solipsism and moral evasiveness of poetry are familiar themes in the last half century, and poets around the world have tried in a variety of ways to justify their violation of Adorno's prohibition against writing poetry after Auschwitz. We find it in Czeslaw Milosz:

I want not poetry, but a new diction,
Because only it might allow us to express
A new tenderness and save us from a law
That is not our law. . . .

We find it in Yehuda Amichai:

I want to sing of what happened, what has always happened,
what happened for sure. . . .

And we find it in Heaney, when he allows the ghost of a murdered Irish Catholic to reproach him:

You confused evasion and artistic tact.
The Protestant who shot me through the head
I accuse directly, but indirectly, you
who now atone perhaps upon this bed
for the way you whitewashed ugliness. . . .

What these poets have in common is that they have, in varying degrees, been personally implicated in political violence. Hill has not, and it is precisely the gratuitousness of his struggle with such violence that seems praiseworthy: it must take a poet of exceptional conscience to voluntarily take up such a burden. Yet Hill has never actually renounced the aestheticism he has so often condemned. Rather, he continues to give in to its seductions, and then berate himself for doing so. Thus, in "An Apology for the Revival of Christian Architecture in England," we find:

Platonic England, house of solitudes,
Rests in its laurels and its injured stone,

Replete with complex fortunes that are gone,
Beset by dynasties of moods and clouds.

This rich hypostasizing of England is of a piece with Hill's
tendency, in "Funeral Music," to make a tableau out of a battlefield: it is another method of abstracting history into myth. This
seems fairly inoffensive in the case of England, whose myth has
not caused the sort of carnage we associate with the myth of,
say, Germany. Yet the British, too, did violence in the name of
a national abstraction—in India, for example. And Hill's "A
Short History of British India" is torn between recognition of
this fact and a desire to continue cherishing the deadly myth:

Impound the memoirs for their bankrupt shame,
fantasies of true destiny that kills
'under the sanction of the English name'.

Be moved by faith, obedience without fault,
the flawless hubris of heroic guilt,
the grace of visitation; and be stirred

by all her god-quests, her idolatries,
in conclave of abiding injuries,
sated upon the stillness of the bride.

Hill begins by acknowledging that the British Empire was a
lethal fantasy; but then he moves immediately to the most plangent nostalgia for the faith and obedience once given to that
fantasy. This rather cancels the moral effect: one would not be
much impressed by a similar poem in praise of the faith and
obedience of the Wehrmacht, with Poland as the "bride."

Hill's book-length poem *The Mystery of the Charity of Charles*

Péguy takes up this issue at greater length, with similar results. Péguy, a French Catholic poet and polemicist, embodies the dilemma facing Hill, and any poet who feels attracted to a national myth. Purely as poetry, Péguy's "dream of France" is beautiful and moving:

> Yours is their dream of France, militant-pastoral:
> Musky red gillyvors, the wicker bark
> Of clematis braided across old brick
> And the slow chain that cranks into the well
>
> Morning and evening. It is Domrémy
> Restored; the mystic strategy of Foch
> And Bergson with its time-scent, dour panache
> Deserving of martyrdom.

But as Péguy said, *Tout commence en mystique et finit en politique*; and "their" in this passage refers to the millions of French soldiers slaughtered in World War I. They shared Péguy's dream (or so Hill suggests), and they died for it. Is the dream therefore discredited? The same question can be writ smaller, and more troublingly: Was Péguy responsible for the assassination of the Socialist prime minister Jean Jaurès, for which he had loudly called?

> Jaurès was killed blindly, yet with reason:
> 'let us have drums to beat down his great voice.'
> So you spoke to the blood.

But while Hill poses the question, his language does not seem to desire a genuine encounter with it. For most of the poem is dedicated to resuming, in limpid, lovely verse, the very dream of France which is supposed to be interrogated. Hill writes as if to say, "History is a nightmare from which I am trying to awaken—but not yet." As a result, one does not read *The Mystery of the Charity* with a sense that poetry's responsibility has been enacted; it has only been addressed as a topic. As so often in Hill's *New and Collected Poems*, one longs for the shock of recognition that comes when a poet is found in his own lines, when his questioning is not just of others but of himself. Without this audacious humility, even the most deliberately "major" verse cannot be called great.

Yet all along there were indications that Hill himself was sometimes dissatisfied with the rigorous artificiality and impersonality of his style. There has always been a vein of ingrown eroticism in his poetry, sometimes interestingly twinned with the religious, as in his translations from the Spanish baroque:

> Down in the orchard
> I met my death
> under the briar rose
> I lie slain

> I was going
> to gather flowers
> my love waited
> among the trees. . . .

The diction is plainer by far than anything Hill wrote in his own voice, and it gains a stark power by contrast. Similarly, adopting a pseudonym was a form of liberation, in "The Songbook of Sebastian Arrurruz": "One cannot lose what one has not possessed./So much for that abrasive gem./I can lose what I want. I want you."

But the greatest freedom was found when Hill cast off verse entirely, and wrote the prose poems that make up *Mercian Hymns*. In these short pieces, the voice of the poet remembering his childhood merges with that of King Offa, a figure from England's distant youth. The language is dense and heavy in the mouth, full of archaisms and compound words, and the tone is correspondingly saturnine:

> Candles of gnarled resin, apple-branches, the tacky mistletoe.
>   "Look" they said again and again "look." But I ran slowly;
>   the landscape flowed away, back to its source.

> In the schoolyard, in the cloakrooms, the children boasted
>   their scars of dried snot; wrists and knees garnished with
>   impetigo.

This has a specificity and humaneness generally lacking from Hill's verse. More precisely, it returns the customary themes of his verse to their origins in actual childhood experience, and so makes them immensely more appealing and credible. The landscape that flows away is much more moving than the "Platonic England" into which, one feels, it was transformed. Similarly, the disgusting children with their snot and rashes are a more convincing provocation for Hill's deep-rooted scorn than the tupping gaspers of "Funeral Music." It is not that the *Mercian Hymns* are to be preferred because they "humanize" Hill, or make him more lovable, or confess his weaknesses. The man we come to know in these poems is still rebarbative and bloody-minded, like King Offa. They are superior as literature because they are less literary; they have the courage to make poetry of the nearmost.

If Hill had stopped writing verse in 1995, this is where judgment of his work would have to rest: a poet of enormous gifts, usually thwarted by his own conception of poetry. But no reader of Hill could have predicted, in 1995, that in the next ten years he would publish more work than in the previous forty, that his style would be brutally remade and the whole shape of his achievement transformed. That is what happened beginning with the publication of *Canaan* in 1996, followed at short intervals by *The Triumph of Love*, *Speech! Speech!*, and *The Orchards of Syon*. Whether or not one reads them as a sequence—as the dust jacket of *The Orchards of Syon* advises— these books share obvious resemblances, and obvious differences from Hill's earlier work. Instead of form and rhyme, he employs ragged free verse; he uses the first person throughout; the properties of contemporary life are found for the first time. Most important, we feel that we are seeing the ingredients of Hill's work before they have been mixed. Pride, erudition, self-reproach, histrionic contempt and despair are thrown in the reader's face like a challenge. As these words suggest, it is not the case that Hill has become a more ingratiating poet. But in his late work one can come to grips, as never before, with the kind of poet—the kind of man—he is.

When *Canaan* appeared, more than a decade after Hill's previous book, it was clearly a departure, but it was not yet clear that it marked a transition. In many of the poems, the verse was starved and narrowed, the words sliding erratically down the page—common enough in modern poetry, but a far cry from Hill's usual sonnets and quatrains. There was also a radical indeterminacy in many poems, a sense that Hill had left out or deleted too much. This, along with the pretentious philosophical titles ("Whether Moral Virtue Comes by Habituation"), spoiled several of the poems in the book, and it is still the most inconsistent collection Hill has published.

Elsewhere in *Canaan*, however, we can see with hindsight that Hill was trying on a new voice. Briefly, he was learning to rant:

Who shall endure? What force throws off
The verdict of each day's
Idle and taunting honours,
The lottery, the trade in grief,
The outrageous quittance, the shiftless
Orders of fools?

This is from a poem "To William Cobbett: In Absentia," but one feels that Cobbett, the nineteenth-century English radical, is less its subject than its excuse. Elsewhere, the proud and contemptuous figure of Stefan George inspires a less Shakespearean rhetoric:

Contempt is in order: one
        Would give much
To see those Frankish
Rites nobly concluded.

Almost, for Childe Stauffenberg,
It fell so;
But this was tragedy
Botched, unimagined,

Within that circle.
Medallion-profile
        Of hauteur,
Caesarian abstinence!

"Childe Stauffenberg" is Hill's rather arch way of referring to Claus von Stauffenberg, the aristocratic German officer who tried to assassinate Hitler in 1944. "De Jure Belli ac Pacis," another sequence in the book, praises another of the so-called Kreisau conspirators, Hans-Bernd von Haeften. He is a figure of inevitable appeal for Hill because he opposed fascism, not out of love for democracy, but out of noble pride and Christian princi- ple; he is a nationalist on the right side of history. This allows Hill to hold him up as a chastisement of the corrupt present:

> To the high-minded
> Base-metal forgers of this common Europe,
> Community of parody, you stand ec-
> Centric as a prophet. There is no better
> Vision that I can summon: you were upheld
> On the strong wings of the Psalms before you died.

Beyond the poems addressed to or inspired by such heroes, there are a series of prophetic-denunciatory addresses "To the High Court of Parliament," in which minor British scandals of the early and mid-1990s call forth rhapsodies of Elizabethan insult: "Proud tribunes, place-men, shape-shifting nabobs," and so on. Cumulatively, these poems do not advance a coherent political or ethical vision. They are united only by a tone of voice, a pitch of superb complaint in which Hill delights. And they have the odd effect of casting doubt, retrospectively, on the Christian themes of Hill's earlier work. One begins to real- ize that Hill was entirely right when he wrote, in the Péguy poem, "We . . . honestly admire/The wrath of the peacemak- ers, for example/Christ driving the money-changers from the temple. . . ."

In other words, Hill has always remade his historical and religious subjects in his own image, turning them into objective correlatives of his choler and spleen. This in itself is no objection to Hill's work. After all, it is a familiar modernist principle that the only permanent subject for poetry is inner experience, which casts about for symbols in which to express itself. But the necessary corollary of this principle is that such correlatives must be treated ironically—there must be some recognition that they are functional and provisional, rather than absolutely valid. And Hill's refusal of this irony—his solemn insistence on taking over the paraphernalia of English Christian tradition as though it were still authoritative—is what provokes resistance in the reader.

If we cannot credit a requiem for Plantagenet kings, however, or an apology for the revival of Christian architecture, we can credit a man so dissatisfied by the world that he feels compelled to chastise it with exempla. And that is just what we find in Hill's next book, *The Triumph of Love*. The book consists of 150 free-verse sections, varying in length, composed in a style that might be called internal dialogue: Hill argues with himself, expostulates, changes his mind, explains and justifies. It is as though, after spending years admiring the wares in Hill's showroom, we are being allowed into his workshop. The forge is stoked by anger—at the ingratitude of the younger generation:

> By what right did Keyes, or my cousin's
> Lancaster, or the trapped below-decks watch
> of Peter's clangorous old destroyer-escort,
> serve to enfranchise these strange children
> pitiless in their ignorance and contempt?

At the mass murders of the twentieth century:

> Each sensate corpse, in its fatal
> Mass-solitariness, excites
> Multiples of infliction. A particular
> Dull yard on a dull, smoky day. This, and thus,
> The unique face, indistinguishable, this, these,
> Choked in a cess-pit of smoking Sheol.

At a degrading, addictive mass culture:

> Entertainment overkill: that amplifier
> acts as the brain of the putsch. The old
> elixir-salesmen had no such entourage
> though their product was superior. . . .

Significantly, however, in contrast to his earlier work, Hill no longer claims to own a historical, philosophical, or religious position from which the present might be judged. Having forsworn secular rationality, he is left with the fragments of an incredible theology, along with a reverence for art. These fragments he must try to shore against the ruins of modernity:

> But the Psalms—they remain; and certain exultant
> canzoni of repentance, secular oppugnancy. *Laus*
> *et vituperatio,* the worst
> remembered, least understood, of the modes.
> Add political satire. Add the irrefutable
> grammar of Abdiel's defiance.
> And if not wisdom, then something
> that approaches it nearly. And if not faith,
> then something through which it is made possible

to give credence—if only to Isaiah's prophetically
suffering servant. . . .

The slither of that last sentence is noteworthy. Hill seeks,
not faith, but "something" through which one might "give credence" to the prophet Isaiah—as one gives credence to an
author of fiction, perhaps. But this kind of belief is not religious, and *The Triumph of Love* dispels the illusion that Hill is a
religious poet. He is, rather, like most cultured people in this
secular age, a believer in the importance of art, thought, and
faith as related expressions of human nobility. This is a hedged
relativism: the poem praises "the Church of Newman, Wesley
and George Bell," teachers of three contradictory versions of
Christianity, because it does not fundamentally believe that
points of doctrine are important. Similarly, Hill's decision to
print the book's biblical epigraph in four languages—Old Testament Hebrew, Vulgate Latin, Luther's German, and King
James English—shows that he treats it not as a divine utterance
but as a venerable item of Western culture, accumulating prestige as it travels. The operative categories are not orthodoxy
and heresy, but civilization and barbarism.

When he acknowledges this, Hill is able to be much more
honest about the real sources of his anger. It is not just a
response to a fallen world, but also the lens through which he
sees the world:

> Is prayer
> residual in imprecation? Only
> as we equivocate. When I examine
> my soul's heart's blood I find it the blood
> of bulls and goats.

Such introspection, new in Hill's work, provides the most touching and vital moments in *The Triumph of Love*. Most remarkable of all is the admission made in section 109:

> Since when has our ultimate reprobation
> turned (*oculos tuos ad nos con-*
> *verte*) on the conversion or
> Reconversion of brain chemical—
> The taking up of serotonin? I
> must confess to receiving the latest
> elements, *Vergine bella*, as a signal
> mystery, mercy, of these latter days.

As Hill has confirmed in interviews, this means that he began in the mid-1990s to take antidepressant medication. It is impossible not to connect this fact with the simultaneous revolution in his style. The question this raises is a profound one: If misery and happiness are a function of serotonin levels, what becomes of our intellectual pride and our metaphysical cures? For once, Hill's ingrained punning carries a genuine shock. Instead of religious conversion, we are left with chemical conversion; instead of the Virgin Mary's Assumption, the "taking up" of a drug.

Yet *The Triumph of Love* does not find a way to integrate this shock into its lingering religious hope, or its eloquent denunciation. The poem remains a vexing mixture of self-righteousness, self-knowledge, and self-pity, which—like the *Cantos* that are an obvious inspiration—finally fails to cohere. Fittingly, when Hill urges himself toward a Christian affirmation, his exhortation— "*Lauda? Lauda Sion? LAUDA!*"—is immediately followed by doubt: "Incantation or incontinence—the lyric cry?"

In his next book, *Speech! Speech!*, Hill allows incontinence the upper hand. Even his most faithful readers were largely bewildered by this volume, though they differed as to whether it would improve with study or remain a piece of baffling self-indulgence. Formally, it is more regular than *The Triumph of Love*, containing 120 sections of twelve lines each. But Hill's constant self-interruptions and obscure allusions often make it impossible to say what he means on the most basic level:

> Ruin smell of cat's urine with a small gin.
> Develop the anagram—care to go psychic?
> Psych a new age, the same old dizzy spell.
> Force-field of breakdown near the edge. Now
> To work backwards not like breaking down.
> Seek modem-demo, memos to dawn-broker,
> Duty-savant. CODEBREAKERS our salvation.

Codebreakers, indeed. Matters aren't helped by the profusion of Hopkinsian accent marks, which indicate a concern for correct pronunciation of the verse far in excess of the concern for comprehensibility. At one point, Hill asks us to remember how "Shakespeare's elliptical/Late syntax renders clear the occlusions," but if he is suggesting that the same is true of *Speech! Speech!*, it is hard to agree.

Still, the poem will no doubt attract annotators—again like Pound, Hill writes with confidence in the solicitude of posterity—and in the meantime, certain themes emerge with sufficient clarity. These poems were written in the late 1990s, and events of the period turn up in sometimes baffling notation: the Clinton impeachment ("rum place for a cigar, *Herr Präsident*"), the mad cow epidemic ("beef of Old England's off"). Most surprising, we find the death of Princess Diana and the subsequent public mourning, which one might expect Hill

to have great fun denouncing as a piece of media-concocted
idiocy. But while he refers to the "outraged/hardly forgiven
mourning of the PEOPLE," he too seems inclined to mourn:

> When all else fails CORINTHIANS will be read
> by a man in too-tight shoes. No matter. You
> shall not degrade or debauch the word LOVE
> beyond redemption. As she redeems it.
> Six times this trip I have brought round my wreath
> to thy vulgar gates.

Hill is torn between admiration for Diana as a national cult
figure, a kind of saint, and disgust at the behavior of the masses
who worship her. For another major theme of the book is
mockery of the PEOPLE (as Hill writes it). The cover reproduces a Daumier lithograph of an audience of gaping, self-
satisfied fools, and that spirit—not just satire, but hatred and
ridicule—dominates *Speech! Speech!* (It has 120 sections, we are
helpfully told, "as many as the days that were of SODOM.") In
the very first section, Hill fends off his audience:

>   Imagine it great
> unavoidable work; although: heroic
> verse a non-starter, says PEOPLE. Some believe
> we over-employ our gifts. . . .
> Archaic means files pillaged and erased
> in one generation.

Later he invokes Daumier and Balzac as his tutelary spirits:

> Onto these near-Stygian sets the PEOPLE
> enters and is discovered: courtesy

Balzac, courtesy Honoré Daumier. . . .
>   Could keep this up all night
rigid with joie de vivre.

That manic rigidity is the dominant tone of *Speech! Speech!*: the sense that the poet is relieving some urgent compulsion, which the reader overhears, as it were accidentally. Most of the time, the book reads like a violent, hermetic reprise of themes from *The Triumph of Love*. The exceptions are those moments when Hill reflects on old age and the approach of death: "Go to the door. The threshold-angels/will soon come calling. Those with the gifts/have long since been and gone. You were asleep."

This tentative, homely image of self-reproach—the idea that one might miss the blessings of life just by being asleep at the wrong time—stays with the reader much longer than the trumpet blasts of insult. So, too, when Hill fetches an image of ultimate content from unlovely nature:

A pale full sun, draining its winter light,
illuminates the bracken and the bracken-coloured
leaves of stubborn oak. Intermittently
the wind spoors over salt inlets
and the whiteish grass between the zones,
apprehension's covenant. Could this
perhaps end here: a Paradiso
not accounted for—unaccountable—
eternally in prospect. . . .

This sort of redemption—unenchanted, even un-Christian—has not previously been "accounted for" in Hill's "house of solitudes," except at moments in the *Mercian Hymns*. By allowing a vision of winter sunlight to suggest Paradise, Hill also suggests that maybe Paradise was never anything more than this, an illumination that "ends here," in this world. This dialectic is an inevitable part of modern encounters with the divine, and only by incorporating it can the divine be made credible in poetry.

The Orchards of Syon is founded on this late-won insight. Its basic technique is the same as in Hill's previous two books—internal monologue, often cryptic—and there are moments of his familiar bombast ("Anarchy coheres. Incoherence coheres. Stupor animates. Chaos ordains"). But as the terminal volume of a four-book sequence—we are directed by the jacket copy to read it as "Hill's *Paradiso*"—its task is reconciliation and praise, rather than chastisement.

This would have been a perilous undertaking for Hill in earlier years, since, as readers of Dante know, an orthodox Heaven is far less credible today than an orthodox Hell. To evoke Paradise in the rhetoric of "Lachrimae" would have been ruinous. But rather than urging on himself, and the reader, a spurious transcendence—the *"LAUDA!"* of *The Triumph of Love*—Hill allows his Orchards of Syon to remain a tentative symbol of a tentative consummation.

The Orchards are Hill's emblem of heavenly beauty, but they are not always distinguishable from the earthly beauty Hill names Goldengrove, after the Hopkins poem, where the word betokens transience and mortality. The Orchards of Syon are Goldengrove's cast shadow:

> Goldengrove, even as these senses fall
> and die in your yellow grass, your landscape
> of deep disquiet, calm in its forms: the Orchards
> of Syon, sway-backed with pear and apple,
> the plum, in spring and autumn resplendent.

Such moments of splendor illuminate the poem, in two senses: they provide its lyrical beauty, and they make sense of its metaphysics. Hill has always been at his best writing about nature, but now he seems to found his whole spiritual ideal on nature's revelations. This is a far more satisfactory grounding for belief than any dogma, since it builds on an experience of undoubted validity—joy in the self-giving of nature. Such "mortal beauty" is a token of the Creator's presence and goodness, like the biblical rainbow:

> The sun, the sudden
> prism, rediscover their own time,
> whenever that is: bending to our level
> they lift us up. . . .
>   I, at best,
> conjecture divination. The rainbow's
> appearance covenants with reality.

But Hill does not insist on turning the rainbow into a symbol, or Goldengrove into Syon. Rather, he allows them to echo and blend into one another. Indeed, there is less irritable reaching after fact and reason than ever before in Hill, and his poetry benefits greatly from the change. The modulation of tone in section 43 demonstrates how much it stands to gain:

> Range
> how you will, anger, despair, are inbred
> monsters: Nebuchadnezzar's crawlingly
> bitter egress to gnaw grass; Cain's brood
> busy at Heorot. Such startings-up,
> slouchings, of self-hatred: a sullen
> belch from the ice-maker in the small hours.

Nebuchadnezzar and Cain are biblical properties of the kind Hill has been using for forty years, venerable items from the myth-kitty. But the nighttime belch as the ice-maker starts up again is a genuine poetic metaphor: surprising, accurate, witty, closely observed. It is the kind of image one does not forget. So too is the heart that "leaps fattily, apes a sexual motion/As if copulating with itself"; and the bad conscience that moves "forward, backward, across,/like a metal detector." Such moments make *The Orchards of Syon* the most appealing book of Hill's since *Mercian Hymns*. Readers familiar with his fifty years of labor will appreciate the earned simplicity that allows him his best image yet of grace:

> I've recast
> my furthest revelation; it's as much
> as you have witnessed, much as I have told:
> a massive shedding, insubstantial substance
> blurred and refocused, blurred afresh by rain.

Frederick Seidel

IT WOULD BE an interesting experiment to give Frederick Seidel's poems to a dozen different readers and ask them to describe the author. The result would be something like the fable in which blindfolded men describe an elephant by holding its legs or its trunk or its tail: one poet would fracture into a whole menagerie. Is Seidel the social climber who cranes his neck to admire "Episcopalians from the Golden Age/Of schools who loved to lose gracefully and lead"? Or the bosom friend of "Monsieur le Comte et Madame la Comtesse" de Gourcuff, his hosts at the Château of Fontenay? The professor who rides the Manhattan subway to get to his classes, or the jet-setter who takes the Concorde to Paris to buy shoes *faites sur mesure*? An elegant seducer or a violent misogynist, or both? Why does he fantasize again and again about a sexually voracious female head of state—about being in a plane crash—about space suits and spaceships?

As these examples show, the multitudes Seidel contains aren't exactly the kind Whitman had in mind. His shifting identities are more like the disguises a fugitive might use to evade Interpol. For this reason, it is not a condemnation, as it would be of other poets, to say that the major subject and interest of Frederick Seidel's poetry is Frederick Seidel. His name does not stand for a cosseted ego or a set of cherished traumas. It is more like an intersection where anyone could be passing through:

Combine a far-seeing industrialist
With an Islamic fundamentalist.
With an Italian premier who doesn't take bribes.
With a pharmaceuticals CEO who loves to spread disease. . . .

And you get Fred Seidel.

By treating his very name as an unstable signifier, Seidel approaches a kind of writing popular among younger poets today. Many poets under forty delight in writing poems where the syntax of narrative persists in the absence of meaning: the poet seems to be telling you a story about him or herself, but the story never makes sense. Where this is not simply a tic or a fad, it seems to be a theoretical statement about the way identity is constructed by discourse. A favorite device for making this point is the "I, I, I" poem, such as "Ezra's Lament" by Susan Wheeler:

I owed the baker three dollies with heads.
I owed the singer a way to recoup.
I owed the bookmaker my mother's own sauce.
I owed the outfielder plenty, plenty.

It is interesting to note, then, that Wheeler is among the poets endorsing the paperback edition of Seidel's *The Cosmos Poems*. It is not likely that Seidel was a major influence on this kind of poetry—John Ashbery and C. D. Wright are more popular role models, and John Berryman wrote the first "I, I, I" poem, in Dream Song #22. But such poets could certainly find in Seidel resemblances to their own concern for identity and incoherence. In fact, the first poem in Seidel's *Area Code 212* is an "I, I, I" poem, called "I Do":

I do pablum. I do doo-doo. I do heroic deeds.
I do due
Diligence.

I do white gloves at the dances,
But I don't dance with the fascists.
I do beat and smash their stupid wishes.
I take you to be my.

But it would be a mistake to take this for Seidel's most inter-esting or radical vein, when it is actually one of his weakest. The weakness lies in the shallow disparateness of the various things that "I do." What is noteworthy about them is the mere fact that they do not cohere, so that the poet achieves a feeble friction simply by rubbing them together. Because there is a limitless number of traits or activities that do not fit together, such a poem is all too easy to construct.

Seidel's real strangeness, however, is not so abstract or aca-demic. He is, in fact, one of the very rare contemporary poets who can be transgressive, not in the fashionable way of the seminar, but in the disturbing and baffling way of the night-mare. The reason is that Seidel is not truly interested in iden-tity at all, either as a biographical experience or as a theoretical problem. As he writes in *Life on Earth*: "He didn't talk much about himself because there wasn't much to say." For Seidel, the "self," that tediously fashionable subject, is only a pencil-thin circumference. He is more interested in what lies outside—the social and political world—and what lies inside—the uncon-scious and the obsessive.

Among contemporary poets, it is Seidel's social interest that is really unusual. This is not simply a question of being up-to-date on current events, though many of his poems can be as precisely dated as if someone were holding up a newspaper in the background. This is the mid-1980s, as seen in *These Days*:

> Unshaved men in suits walk ahead of others in masks.
> It might be the men one sees strolling
> Together outside Claridge's in London followed
> At a submissive distance by their veiled wives,
> But in Central America—hostages and their slaves
> By relay satellite.

The poem is concerned not with information but with the experience of consuming information, one of those experiences so elusive and significant that their conquest for poetry is a real achievement. Like most literary people, Seidel at least claims to look down on television: "I never watch TV. / But sometimes late at night," he deadpans in "At Gracie Mansion." But a poem like "My Tokyo," the title poem of his 1993 collection, is inconceivable without the experience of flipping channels:

> New York is an electrical fire.
> People are trapped on the top floor, smoking
> With high-rise desire
> And becoming Calcutta.
>
> Tokyo is low
> And manic as a hive.
> For the middle of the night they have silent jackhammers.
> Elizabethan London with the sound off. Racially pure with
>   no poor.

Those silent jackhammers are just the kind of factoid one might learn about Tokyo from a documentary or a *Newsweek* article, and even the syntax—"they have"—is what we use for the bored relation of novelties.

More interesting, because more surprising, are the things and people Seidel seems to know firsthand. Here we approach one of the disturbing elements in Seidel's work, his evident snobbery. He writes about his famous, rich, and wellborn acquaintances, not with the ironic distance expected of intellectuals, but with a Proustian delight. What are we to make, for instance, of "Pressed Duck," his celebration of the fashionable Manhattan restaurateur Elaine Kaufman ("Whose own restaurant would be famous soon"):

Poised and hard, but dreaming and innocent—
Like the last Romanovs—spring buds at thirty, at thirty-two,
We were green as grapes,
A cluster of February birthdays,
All "Elaine's" regulars. . . .
　　　　Elaine said, "Why do we need anybody else?
We're the world."

In this poem, Seidel eagerly participates in a complacent Manhattan provincialism. In his best work, however, his intimacy with the world of fashion and privilege is what allows him to be its effective satirist. If Seidel avidly lists his elegant tailors and shoemakers, he follows the list with: "The well-dressed man . . . /Is a sunstream of urine on its way to the toilet bowl." If he visits "The Master Jeweler Joel Rosenthal," he is reminded that "Death is loading in the van/The women and camels of King Solomon it is repossessing." And if several poems are set in the bar of the Carlyle Hotel, this is how he sees the vain, aging customers:

A man who wanted to look better
But not younger is red
Swells of raw.
Later they will remove the staples. . . .
They pull over
Their head a sock of skin.

Seidel has also written many poems in which the cast of characters, though rich and aristocratic, are effectively unknown, and thus avoid the banality of celebrity. There is "Rackets," which tells of Reginald Fincke, a "dashingly handsome" racquet-club champion of the 1910s; there is "In Memoriam," about the "Great-grandson of George Boole as in Boolean algebra." These sound like footnotes to the Social Register, but the effect is otherwise, as we can see in "Hugh Jeremy Chisholm" from *Area Code 212*:

With Jeremy Chisholm at the Lobster Inn on our way to
    Sagaponack,
Eating out on the porch in the heat, flicking cigarettes into the
    inlet.
    .   .   .   .
Billy Hitchcock landed his helicopter at a busy gas station
In Southampton July 4th weekend. . . .

Bessie Cuevas had introduced me to this fin de race exquisite. . . .
Who was as beautiful as the young Prince Yusupov

Who had used his wife as bait to kill Rasputin. . . .

Each of these is doubtless someone Seidel actually knows. But the catalogue of deracinated, faintly bizarre names seems to come, not out of *Town & Country,* but out of "Gerontion":

by Mr. Silvero
With caressing hands, at Limoges
Who walked all night in the next room;

By Hakagawa, bowing among the Titians;
By Madame de Tornquist, in the dark room
Shifting the candles; Fräulein von Kulp
Who turned in the hall. . . .

The effect in Seidel is, if anything, even more alienating than in
Eliot. We know that Eliot's people are invented, and they cannot help seeming stagy; but Seidel's are repulsively real.

This effect is greatly increased by the context in which we
read about Jeremy Chisholm and company, for in Seidel's poems
almost every narrative is seen through a glass darkly. The outer,
social world of his poetry is charged by its contact with an
extremely strange inner climate, which Seidel explores with a
boldness that is hard to distinguish from rashness. Almost
uniquely among poets, Seidel does not strategize to make himself look good in his poems. Even when Berryman's alter ego
Henry wonders if he could "end anyone and hacks her body
up/and hide the pieces," the effect is to make us feel sorry for
Berryman for having such tortured thoughts. But how should
we feel about Seidel for having these fantasies?

The most beautiful power in the world has buttocks.
It is always a dream come true.
They are big. They are too big.
Kiss them and spank them till they are scalding.
Till she can't breathe saying oh. . . .

Perhaps the only thing that could make such a poem more
explosive is the title Seidel gives it: "AIDS Days." And the

explosions start in the uncertainties, the information gaps. Who is the woman—a business executive, or (as appears possible later in the poem) the president of the United States, or a figure in a pornographic film, or an actual lover? Does she have AIDS, or is she an emblem of destructive lust? The reader has the sense of something truly private, a dark compulsion. This sense is only increased when, in another poem written more than ten years later, Seidel returns to a similar complex of images: "I am going to go public with this/Beautiful big breasts and a penis/Military-industrial complex."

Sex is seldom less ambiguous and charged than this in Seidel's poetry. Lust is a Pavlovian tic: "The old penis smells food/And salivates." Men are predators: "Every man's a rapist till he's done./The bitch relieves the dog. The wound, the gun." What's more, women secretly want them to be: "Don't stop when/I say stop" (this from a poem titled "Her Song"). The sex act is degrading and violent:

My daughter squeaks and squeaks
Like a mouse screaming in a trap,
Dangling from the cat that makes her come
When he does it to her.

These are poems without internal or external censors, and they give the sense of a man wholly inside his obsessions; indeed, the obsessions seem to be writing the poems. This is solipsism, perhaps, but not the contented solipsism of the egotist, more like the desperate isolation of the madman, or the damned soul: "God is everywhere you're not,/And you are everywhere." Images of entrapment and entombment are eerily common in Seidel's work, so that it is no wonder he would write with uncanny intimacy (in "Dune Road, Southampton") about the paralyzed Sunny von Bülow: "Locked-in Syndrome, just about the worst./Alive, with staring eyes." Perhaps the most characteristic Seidel poem—in its claustrophobia, its arbitrariness, its nightmare plot—is "Contents Under Pressure," from *Going Fast*:

> His space suit is his respirator breathing him
> From its own limited supply of oxygen. . . .
> The long tether from the mother spaceship sticks
> Straight out from his back weightlessly
> In the zero gravity of space.
> It has sheared off at the other end.
> Absolutely nothing can be done.

Seidel's mature style had a long incubation. His first book, published in 1963 when he was twenty-seven, was *Final Solutions*, a skillful anthology of effects borrowed from Robert Lowell; nearly every one of Seidel's poems can be traced to its Lowellian original. His next book, *Sunrise*, appeared in 1980, marking the first appearance of the style, voice, and persona that would be honed over the next quarter century. Perhaps that persona—worldly, depressive, overripe—could only be the creation of a middle-aged man; as he wrote in *Sunrise*, "I took for my own motto/*I rot before I ripen*." The savor of that rottenness, like an expensive cheese, grows richer and more complex over Seidel's next three books, which represent his best work so far: *These Days*, *My Tokyo*, and *Going Fast*. For the readers of the future, no poetry will give a better sense of what it was like to live in the decadent capital of American empire.

Starting in the late 1990s, Seidel's productivity accelerated rapidly, and from 2000 to 2002 he published a book a year—*The Cosmos Poems*, *Life on Earth*, and *Area Code 212*, later reissued in one volume as *The Cosmos Trilogy*. The trilogy is designed as an upside-down version of the *Divine Comedy*, beginning in Heaven and descending through earthly Purgatory to the Hell of New York City. The sour wit of that conceit is worthy of Seidel, and the structure of the poems nods at its original: each book has thirty-three poems, like Dante's thirty-three cantos, and there is a consistent (though very loose) form, eight unrhymed quatrains per poem.

But nothing about Seidel's earlier work suggested that his gifts lay in the direction of synthesis, large structure, or philosophical statement. And in fact the poems do not bear out the Dantean comparison. It does them no service to read them in search of a theology or a narrative. Often their quantity and loose uniformity seem to dilute the poisons Seidel's earlier books provide in concentrated form. Only the middle volume, *Life on Earth*, has the same proportion of successful poems as Seidel's best collections.

The Cosmos Poems is the weakest volume of the trilogy, because its celestial subjects—the Big Bang, black holes, string theory—are the farthest removed from the local realities and sullied textures Seidel has mastered. He is up on the latest cosmologies, but usually these are summarized rather than dramatized: "My friend, the darkness/Into which the seed/Of all eleven dimensions/Is planted is small." String theory tells us that there are eleven dimensions, and so does Seidel, but neither of them manages to make us really feel what this means. Only in "Forever" does Seidel use metaphor strangely and unexpectedly enough to make such creation *ex nihilo* a genuine object of experience:

The surge protector
That a spike of energy

Can't avoid,
And that the spike of energy

Destroyed,
Fires its last distress flare forever,
Which is the aftermath
Till now, and is this place.

This captures something of the paradox of how nothingness could give birth to Being: the universe is the "flare" shot out by the failure of nothingness, which is the earlier and more normal condition. Most often, however, Seidel tries to infuse the cosmological with feeling by connecting it with the sentimentally human. The childhood of the universe is equated with the childhood of the poet, and it is surprising to find the rotten-ripe Seidel so nostalgic for pristine infancy: "I hear the light. / I hear the mighty organ bellowing heaven through / The bars of my playpen. . . ."

Life on Earth is, naturally, a much more congenial theme. The modulation from the previous book occurs in the first poem, "Bali," which begins "I hear the cosmos" and descends rapidly:

The generals wanted to replace Sukarno.
Because of his syphilis he was losing touch
With the Communist threat and getting rather crazy
So they slaughtered the Communists and the rich Chinese.

The tourist island is decisively tethered to its social and political reality, its *South Pacific* aura fumigated with disease and slaughter. (It is an odd and tragic example of Seidel's contemporaneity that this poem should have been published not long before the nightclub bombing that killed dozens of tourists.)

Since the world is everything that is the case, *Life on Earth* is a good umbrella title for the travel bulletins, gossip items, news reports, nightmares, and fantasies that have always been Seidel's subjects. "Goodness" is a kind of Yeatsian great-house poem, in which an aristocratic French couple are proposed as ideal human types: "Have faith, give hope, show charity, / This is the Château of Fontenay." The alienation and irony Seidel usually brings to this milieu are notably absent, leaving us surprised by earnestness. But we are through the Seidelian looking glass once again in "Doctor Love," in which the poet tells of a movie treatment he once wrote whose heroine, a breast cancer researcher, turned out to share the name of a real breast cancer researcher. Now, there is a real Dr. Susan Love, the author of a popular guide to the disease; but it remains hard to determine whether Seidel's story is true, what it means, or whether it matters. As always with Seidel, the mystery is not just the facts but why he is telling them to us.

Still more astringently bizarre is "At New York Hospital," in which one of Seidel's odd obsessions returns: the "murderous head of state with beautiful big breasts." Here Seidel encounters her in the operating room, where she appears to be undergoing radiation therapy for brain cancer:

> a target area

> On the top of the skull will
> Be painted magenta. Her body is re-wrapped.
> Her face gets sealed off. Her crimes against humanity
> Will be lasered.

By the poem's conclusion, when the anesthesiologist "joyously / Declaims Gerard Manley Hopkins," it is clear that we are not in the real world, but the zone of the poet's reiterated fantasy. It has the disquieting, surreal calm that is one of Seidel's most effective tones.

Appropriately, *Life on Earth* ends with the subject that has always been at the center of this poet's world, "Frederick Seidel":

> My life is a snout
> Snuffling toward the truffle, life. Anyway!
> It is a life of luxury. Don't put me out of my misery. . . .
>
> I do love
> The sky above.

But misery moves center stage in *Area Code 212*, whose first poem revises that declaration of love: "I do love / The sky above / Which is black." In the Dantesque conceit of the trilogy, this volume locates the Inferno in New York; but, in fact, there is less concrete observation of the city than the title would suggest. With a few exceptions, it appears as background and incidental detail: "the steps in front of the museum" at the Metropolitan, "the center strip migraine down Park Avenue."

Instead, the most memorable poems in the book are nearly severed from plausible biographical experience. They are surreal narratives, full of dimly discerned horrors. "The Bathroom Door" is emblematic in the way it blocks the crucial events from sight, giving us only an ominous prelude and a terrible consequence:

> He hears his wife get out of their bed
> And lock the bathroom door
> That they never lock. . . .

She says I am so afraid.
She says I feel cold.
He asks her what she has done.
He makes her stand up and walk. He calls 911.

Similarly, in "Downtown," someone identified only as "it" commits a murder in an art gallery. In "Getaway," the speaker is a fugitive, a kidnapper or bank robber, who warns: "They're going to check/The trunk and find our bodies." If such poems are not as vital and unsettling as Seidel's best work, it is because he is too entirely absent from them; they don't have the unstable charge his poems carry when we can't decide whether they are invented or real. In the slightest of these poems, the artificiality seems to be a mere matter of technique, even simply of manipulating pronouns. "I Do" makes "I" the blank subject for a random catalogue of predicates; in "March," "he" refers alternately to Seidel and to Ho Chi Minh.

These are the poems most easily assimilable to current poetic trends, but they are not the most interesting or characteristic poems in the book, still less in Seidel's whole work. We hear his voice more clearly in a poem like "MV Agusta Rally," where he looks on at a motorcycle race in Italy, or "Venus," with its fantastic sexual hostility:

Venus is getting
Smaller.
Finally, she is
The size of a mouse.

A fully developed young woman
That size
Makes it difficult
To caress her breasts.

The book concludes with two poems in which the events of September 11, 2001, make an appearance, once directly, once obliquely as metaphor. As one might expect from Seidel, it is the oblique that is more powerful. The direct version, in "The War of the Worlds," is very sentimental, imagining Seidel witnessing the events as a child in "Gray flannel little boy shorts," as though he could summon the requisite emotion only by supplementing pity with self-pity. In "December," on the other hand, the image of a plane turned into a weapon seems almost spontaneous, of a piece with Seidel's usual psychic violence:

> I like the color of the smell. I like the odor of spoiled meat.
> I like how gangrene transubstantiates warm firm flesh into
> rotten sleet.
> When the blue blackens and they amputate, I fly.
> I am flying a Concorde of modern passengers to gangrene in
> the sky.

This is only the latest appearance in Seidel's poetry of the Concorde as an instrument of death. The difference here is that it has also become an instrument of purgation: "I stab the sword into the smell." But if Seidel is a moralist, he has never been the kind that wields a terrible swift sword. He has, rather, immersed himself in chaos and corruption, both public and psychic, in order to give them poetic expression. This ambiguous courage is what makes him one of the significant artists of a corrupt, chaotic time.

Louise Glück

LIKE ALL the Greek myths that remain current, the story of Persephone is valuable for its Rorschach quality, its ability to interpret its interpreters. So it proves in "Pomegranate," a poem from Louise Glück's second collection, *The House on Marshland*. For the young poet, Persephone was significant not as a cosmological emblem or as a victim of predatory masculinity, but as the archetypal rebellious daughter. In Glück's telling, she does not need to be kidnapped to be taken from Demeter, only seduced away from her mother's emotional tyranny:

> When he looked up at last
> it was to say My dear
> you are your own
> woman, finally, but examine
> this grief your mother
> parades over our heads
> remembering
> that she is one to whom
> these depths were not offered.

What makes this poem so characteristic of Glück is not just its use of myth or its dramatically narrow column of free verse, though these would continue to shape her poetry. Above all, what "Pomegranate" reveals about Glück is her fierce identification with the heroine of a family romance. Demeter may be a goddess, but by comparison with Persephone, she is shallow and passionless, a bit player in someone else's myth. Access to perilous, sexualized "depths" is the preserve of the daughter-poet, who is willing to descend to Hell in exchange for the insight, and the glamour, such an ordeal provides. That this glamour never ceased to hold Glück in thrall is suggested by the title of her tenth book, *Averno*, which refers to the crater the Romans believed was the entrance to the underworld—Persephone's departure gate.

The boast of deeper knowledge gained through deeper suffering is one of Glück's favorite rhetorical devices. She is forever flaunting this superiority before the reader: "And you who watch him/looking down in the face of death, what do you know/of commitment?" she demands in "Brooding Likeness," from *The Triumph of Achilles*. "Hear me out: that which you call death/I remember," she declaims at the beginning of *The Wild Iris*. "You, in your innocence, what do you know of this world?" she asks in *The Seven Ages*. And in the title poem of *Averno*, Glück continues to warn, berate, brag: "And I want to scream out/*you're all of you living in a dream*."

Passages like these, and there are many in Glück's work, suggest a poet who is very concerned with proving her claim to authority, and who believes that the true basis of authority is authenticity. But Glück's brand of authenticity is not, she has been at pains to insist, merely biographical. This is an important distinction for a poet who started writing in the late 1960s, when the wave of confessional poetry was beginning to crest. The polemical thrust of Glück's intelligent, serious book of essays, *Proofs & Theories*, is to discredit confessional "honesty" and "courage" as poetic values. "The truth, on the page, need not have been lived. It is, instead, all that can be envisioned," she writes in the bluntly titled "Against Sincerity."

Glück does not write confessionally about madness, suicide, and incest, as though these extreme experiences were a poet's only access to reality. But she also does not reject the ideal of extremity; she merely denies that it has to be lived in order to be written about. She insists that it is not the content of experience which allows it to rise to the grandeur of myth, but the intensity the artist brings to it. If Glück is "against sincerity," she is completely enthralled by authenticity, in just the sense that Lionel Trilling intended: an "extreme . . . exercise of personal will." Her work is a tour de force of this kind of will. Every facet of her poetry is designed to heighten its rhetorical force, to leave the reader awed and dazzled by the poet's capacity for genuine, difficult experience. Her aesthetic ideal is not delight but "candor," as she writes in "October," from *Averno*: "It is true there is not enough beauty in the world./It is also true that I am not competent to restore it./Neither is there candor, and here I may be of some use."

Candor, however, is an ambiguous concept in poetry. To be candid is to speak unpremeditatedly, thinking only of the matter, not at all of the form; but this is just the kind of speech that poetry, if it is really poetry, cannot admit. The artist is always conscious, from the beginning, of the impression her writing is going to make. Some poets convince themselves they can abjure that consideration, in the name of accurate witness or purgative confession. But Glück is too dedicated to art, in a strict modernist sense, to place any goal above the goal of writing well. One of the most appealing things about her is her commitment to poetry as a calling, an ideal she has described as "severe, strenuous, passionate—the giddiness of great discipline and great ambition." Glück is too much of a poet not to recognize that candor, in poetry, means the impression, or perhaps the illusion, of candor.

Even so, there are different kinds of illusion, different inflections the poet can choose to give to the appearance of honesty. Usually, a poet strikes us as honest when he allows us to see his weakness and confusion, since these are the experiences we are most assiduous to conceal in ordinary life. Thus Herbert's lyrics of spiritual submission, or Larkin's lyrics of worldly failure, seem remarkably honest, and we have the feeling that we know their authors intimately. But there is also another kind of poetic honesty, whose ideal is not self-exposure but truth-telling, the fierce honesty of the prophets. This kind of honesty grows not out of weakness but out of power, a self-assurance so great that it scorns our usual shifts and evasions.

In modern poetry, the most seductive example of this tone, and the one that has been most influential on Glück, is T. S. Eliot. Eliot's name is associated with many kinds of authority, critical and cultural. But Glück, in her essay "On T. S. Eliot," recognizes that his first and most enduring source of authority is his poetry—in particular, the poetic voice that seems to create "a desperate intimacy" with the reader, "as powerful as can be imagined." This is the desperation of Tiresias in *The Waste Land*, who, because he has been both man and woman, knows more than any man or woman could possibly know: "And I Tiresias have foresuffered all/Enacted on this same divan or bed;/I who have sat by Thebes below the wall/And walked among the lowest of the dead."

Glück is at her most Eliotic when she essays this Tiresian voice. And like Eliot, she finds it easiest to assume when speaking as a figure out of Greek myth. Myth is a ready storehouse of the properties a prophet needs, and which a modern, secular, democratic American finds difficult to claim: universal relevance, divine sanction, unchallengeable prestige. Over the course of her career, Glück has tried on very many costumes from the wardrobe of myth: Joan of Arc, Abishag, Circe, Penelope, Persephone. But the voice that issues from behind all these masks is recognizably the same, the voice of a poet entranced by her own dark resonance:

> Now the Queen of Carthage
> will accept suffering as she accepted favor:
> to be noticed by the Fates
> is some distinction after all.

This is Dido, from *Vita Nova*, but it might as well be Penelope, from *Meadowlands*:

> call out to him over the open water, over the bright water
> with your dark song, with your grasping,
> unnatural song—passionate,
> like Maria Callas. Who
> wouldn't want you? Whose most demonic appetite
> could you possibly fail to answer?

Or, indeed, Glück herself, speaking *in propria persona* in *Ararat*: "I was born to a vocation:/to bear witness/to the great mysteries."

Glück has never been abashed in her intercourse with the great mysteries. "The true," she writes in "Against Sincerity," "has about it an air of mystery or inexplicability. This mystery is an attribute of the elemental." In striving after this kind of mysterious, elemental truth, Glück employs a vocabulary of Romantic grandeur, making free with big, auratic, imprecise words: "the formless/grief of the body, whose language/is hunger"; "You have betrayed me, Eros./You have sent me/my true love"; "Tell me/how you live in hell,/what is required in hell,/for I would send/my beloved there." The starkness of Glück's verse—short lines, with frequent line and stanza breaks, and generous white space—is the natural expression of her belief that, as she writes in the essay "Invitation and Exclusion," "we don't follow poems as arguments, step by step. We grasp them entire, and what we first grasp is tone." But Glück's poetry also suggests that a poet who wagers everything on tone—whose poems cannot function unless they are read as urgent, reverent, hypnotic monologues—ends up losing most of the qualities that make poetic language memorable. It is as though her lines are flattened by the gravitational pull of a "mystery" so intense that it crushes adjective and metaphor.

The actual subject of Glück's poems, however, the lasting and distinctive impression they make on the reader, is not of a mind curious about mystery, but of a mind that enjoys regarding itself in proximity to mystery. Glück's sovereign egotism was already evident in her first book, *Firstborn,* which gives the style and properties of early Robert Lowell a characteristic twist, as in "Phenomenal Survivals of Death in Nantucket":

> Here in Nantucket does the tiny soul
> Confront water. Yet this element is not foreign soil;
> I see the water as extension of my mind,
> The troubled part, and waves the waves of mind. . . .

Where Lowell respected the Atlantic Ocean as a malign cosmic force, "the mast-lashed master of Leviathans," Glück swiftly reduces it to an emblem of her own interior state. It is "my mind," not "this element," that fascinates her. And this sense that the most interesting theater is the theater of the mind, where the self is always heroine, has been the most consistent feature of her poetry. The design of her books has evolved in keeping with this priority. Since *Ararat*, each of Glück's collections has been structured around a life change—the death of a father (*Ararat*), divorce *(Meadowlands)*, setting up house in a new city (*Vita Nova*), the passage to age and illness (*Averno*). Each volume is a monodrama, the lyrics working together, as in Tennyson's *Maud*, to map the protagonist's state of mind.

As this list shows, the dramas of Glück's life and poetry do not fall into the realm of abnormal psychology. In another poet, their very ordinariness might evoke a language of understated compassion—the poet suffering what we all suffer, but more articulately. But Glück's self-dramatizing impulse means that what her experience lacks in rarity she must supply in the form of rhetorical intensity. This is where the Greek myths come in. Divorce itself was grievous enough to inspire tremendously moving sequences by George Meredith and Robert Lowell, but Glück's sequence about her divorce casts the principals as Odysseus, Penelope, and Circe. Likewise, old age was a humanizing subject for Yeats, for whom it seemed to require the discarding of the "circus animals" of myth. But for Glück, in *Averno,* it can be experienced only in terms of Persephone's descent to the underworld: "What will you do, / when it is your turn in the field with the god?"

The problem with this use of Greek myth, as many contemporary poets have unwittingly shown, is that today those myths have no cultic power. They exist for us only as literature. (This is true even of biblical figures, which had a genuine mythical force in our culture far more recently than the Greek gods.) But to compare oneself to a figure out of literature is to cede to already existing literature an ontological superiority, to cast oneself as the instantiation of a law that others have already discovered. Instead of approaching literature from a position of strength, as its heir and necessary sequel, the myth-besotted poet approaches it as a supplicant—even when, as with Glück, the intoxication of myth seems to give her a factitious strength.

The one exception is when the modern writer approaches ancient myth in the spirit of satire or deconstruction. This, too, is something Eliot knew. What Tiresias sees, in *The Waste Land*, is the tawdry seduction of the typist by the "young man carbuncular," and it is the shocking juxtaposition of these registers that creates the poetic effect. It makes sense, then, that the most moving and surprising passages in Glück's work are those in which the mythological framework is violated by a disabused, merely human voice.

In *Meadowlands*, this is the role reserved for Telemachus, who serves Glück as a cool observer of the operatic passions of his parents: "My own taste dictates/accuracy without/garrulousness," she writes in "Telemachus' Dilemma." Even better, in that book, are the moments when we suddenly hear what are plainly the voices of Glück and her husband, engaged in the sort of sordid domestic quarrel that makes Odysseus and Penelope fall off their stilts: "I said you could snuggle. That doesn't mean/your cold feet all over my dick"; or, still closer to home, "You should take one of those chemicals,/maybe you'd write more./Maybe you have some kind of void syndrome."

This is the revenge of the actual on the mythical, and Glück's willingness to admit it into her poetry suggests the strong influence confessional poetry has had on her. More generally, the habits of psychoanalysis have been deeply bred in Glück. Its paradoxical encouragement of realism and narcissism at once has seldom been better demonstrated than in her poetry. She has written that psychoanalysis was her version of higher education: for seven years after graduating high school, she remembers in "The Education of the Poet," "analysis was what I

did with my time and with my mind." The brutally close inter-
rogation of family life that she performs in *Meadowlands* and
Ararat, her best books, clearly betrays a Freudian belief that
family, not character, is destiny. One of Glück's favorite subjects is her rivalry with her younger sister, which she presents
as a formative influence on her life:

> Suppose
> you saw your mother
> torn between two daughters:
> what could you do
> to save her but be
> willing to destroy
> yourself—she would know
> who was the rightful child,
> the one who couldn't bear
> to divide the mother.

This passage, from *Ararat*, is not particularly eloquent, but it
is convincing, and therefore humanly moving. Indeed, it seems
especially moving when encountered in the context of Glück's
work, where the biographical is so often inflated out of recognition. Yet it is clear that this inflating impulse, the tendency to
mythologize her own experience, is equally a product of
Glück's psychoanalytic orientation. Who but Freud, after all,
taught us to name our parents after Greek myths, and to regard
self-dramatization as a form of self-cure?

Glück suggests this paradox in "The Untrustworthy Speaker"
when she writes, "I know myself; I've learned to hear like a psychiatrist./When I speak passionately,/that's when I'm least to
be trusted." The psychiatrist is the imaginary auditor who is
supposed to be able to detect exaggeration, but whose very

presence also encourages it. Which tendency prevails depends on the character of the poet and on her conception of what poetry is supposed to be. For Lowell, psychoanalysis was a means of disenchantment, as in the savagely disillusioned portraits of his parents in "Life Studies." For Glück, it more often seems a spur to narcissism.

The enemy of narcissism is irony, for irony involves seeing one's self as if it were not oneself. And irony is the quality signally missing from Glück's poetry. Surely a saving dose of ironic detachment would have allowed her to avoid *bêtises* like the memorable anticlimax of the last poem in *Vita Nova*:

> Life is very weird, no matter how it ends,
> very filled with dreams. Never
> will I forget your face, your frantic human eyes
> swollen with tears.
> *I thought my life was over and my heart was broken.*
> *Then I moved to Cambridge.*

Ironic self-awareness would have been even more useful in *The Wild Iris*, a book admirable in its ambition and seriousness. Three voices speak in the closet drama of *The Wild Iris*: the poet, who implores God to reveal himself; God, who responds with scolding adjurations to modesty; and the flowers underfoot, which look on with detached scorn at human folly. But Glück's version of the Book of Job founders, first, on the threadbareness of her metaphysics and theodicy: her God says things like "How can you understand me/when you cannot understand yourselves?" More distasteful is the titanic arrogance of the human speaker, which cannot be dismissed as simply a commentary on the egotism of our species, since it so closely resembles Glück's voice as we know it in her other work:

If there is justice in some other world, those
like myself, whom nature forces
into lives of abstinence, should get
the lion's share of all things, all
objects of hunger, greed being
praise of you. And no one praises
more intensely than I, with more
painfully checked desire, or more deserves
to sit at your right hand, if it exists. . . .

Only our own time, perhaps, could produce a religious poem
so completely lacking in humility.

As *Averno* shows, death is no more able than God to shatter
Glück's accustomed sense of dramatic centrality. The poet is
now in her sixties, and has evidently undergone some physical
ordeal:

It does me no good; violence has changed me.
My body has grown cold like the stripped fields;
now there is only my mind, cautious and wary,
with the sense it is being tested.

But as these lines show, the chastening of the body has not
diminished Glück's pride in her mind, which has always been
the real seat of her ambitions. Her encounter with death, like
her encounters with love and sex and divorce and God, have
only confirmed her consciousness of superior insight, deeper
sensitivity, darker knowledge. "Someone like me doesn't
escape," she writes in "Thrush," as though death were not the
leveler but a doorman at an exclusive club. Thus *Averno*, despite
the change of scene and subject, marks no real evolution in the

actual substance of Glück's poetry, as is clear in these lines from "Prism":

> The self ended and the world began.
> They were of equal size,
> commensurate,
> one mirrored the other.

They may mirror one another, but for Glück, it has always been the self that comes first.

Charles Simic

IN THE LATE 1950S, Charles Simic was a self-described "immigrant with literary pretensions," recently arrived in New York by way of Belgrade, Paris, and Chicago. Like many young American poets, he was in full revolt against the "seriousness and literary sophistication" of the academically approved New Critical style. In his memoir, *A Fly in the Soup*, he captures his mood at the time in a sly anecdote: "At one of the readings at NYU given by a now forgotten academic poet of the 1950s, just as the professional lovers of poetry in the audience were already closing their eyes blissfully in anticipation of the poet's familiar, soul-stirring clichés, there was the sound of paper being torn. We all turned around to look. A shabby old man was ripping newspapers into a brown shopping bag."

To be as unrespectable and unignorable as that old man— this was the ambition of Simic's early work, and he achieved it. The poems included in his *Selected Early Poems*, written from the early 1960s to the mid-1980s, used exotic new influences to demolish the prevailing decorum of American verse. From Latin American poetry, Simic took "the mysticism, the eroticism, and the wild flights of romance and rhetoric"; from French literature and painting, the fraught dislocations of Surrealism; from Eastern European poetry, a suspicion of authority and the collective. Filter these tones through the grainy black-and-white of American film noir, and you have Simic:

This kid got so dirty
Playing in the ashes

When they called him home,
When they yelled his name over the ashes,

It was a lump of ashes
That answered.

Little lump of ashes, they said,
Here's another lump of ashes for dinner,

To make you sleepy,
And make you grow strong.

This poem, "Primer," is in Simic's most appealing vein, an allegory that invites and refuses interpretation. ("This is a tale with a kernel. / You'll have to use your own teeth to crack it," he warns in "Chorus for One Voice.") The black comedy of his fables is what makes them irresistible. "It was the love of . . . irreverence, as much as anything else, that started me in poetry," Simic has said, and he learned from Hieronymus Bosch that "there's no joy like the one a truly outrageous image on the verge of blasphemy gives":

An old man gave little Mary Magdalene
A broken piece of a mirror.
She hid in the church outhouse.
When she got thirsty she licked
The steam off the glass.

Lines like these, from "Begotten of the Spleen," however, are not just comic. They are also accusatory, the product of the poet's own childhood experience of atrocity. Born in Belgrade in 1938, Simic's earliest memories were of the Nazi occupation. What sounds like surrealism is often, in his case, simple autobiography: "It was so hot. The river was close by, but we only went to dip our feet. There were corpses in it." No wonder that his "memory is so poor that everything appears poorly lit and full of shadows," or that his poems are equally shadowy:

On the first page of my dreambook
It's always evening
In an occupied country.
Hour before the curfew. . . .
I am on a street corner
Where I shouldn't be.

Simic's best early poems, in their frightening inevitability, seem to have been dreamed, not composed. In an essay on the Serbian poet Vasko Popa, he confirms that this was almost exactly his technique: "As a young poet . . . poetry for me was still pretty much a spontaneous venting of some inner turmoil. . . . In a moment of inspiration, one somehow stumbled upon extraordinary images and metaphors—and that was that."

But this surrealist ideal gradually gave way, in Simic's later work, to an different conception of poetry. Toward the end of *A Fly in the Soup*, he defines poetry as "the re-creation of the experience of Being," a way to "let the truth of Being shine through." The idiom and the idea come from Heidegger, whose influence on contemporary poets from Jorie Graham to Adam Zagajewski has been profound. Like these and many other poets, Simic finds in Heidegger the inspiration for a distinctively postmodern poetics, which understands art in terms of preservation and caretaking, not creation and transformation.

Such a poetics represents a reaction against the heedless assertiveness of artistic and political modernism. The artist who wants to transform reality, in this view, is akin to the dictator who wants to transform society; both are examples of unleashed will to power. To avoid such hubris, the Heideggerian postmodernist dedicates himself to the intricate contingency of what is: the individual life, the powerfully present object, the fleeting instant. Thus Simic in "White," possibly his best and certainly his most philosophical early poem:

As if I shut my eyes
In order to peek

At the world unobserved,
And saw

The nameless
In its glory

And knew no way
To speak of it. . . .

This kind of poetry can succeed, even magnificently, when it preserves a sense of the radical strangeness of Being, and of our perception of it: what Simic brilliantly calls "the blossomlike / White erasure / / Over a huge, / Furiously crossed-out something." But it also has a characteristic mode of decay. When the contingent is not disclosed in its strangeness but remains closed off in its ordinariness, when witnessing devolves into epicurean appreciation, then the poem becomes an act of secular piety, complacent and reassuring.

Simic's work of the last two decades, collected in *The Voice at 3 A.M.: Selected Late and New Poems,* demonstrates the traps his own poetics laid for him. One index of his evolution as a poet is the huge increase in bookishness in his later work. The young Simic created a self-contained imaginative universe, sponsored less by literature than by pop and folk culture and the visual arts. In *The Voice at 3 A.M.*, however, we find the poet alluding casually to Jakob Boehme, Lenin, Bernard of Clairvaux, Fourier, and many more. It is a sign that he is now treating his ideas discursively, not dramatically: "Then there's aesthetic paradox/Which notes that someone else's tragedy/Often strikes the casual viewer/With the feeling of happiness."

After Simic's imagist firecrackers, this seems ploddingly prosaic. His newfound talkativeness would not be so damaging if he had not abjured, from the beginning of his career, the tools of complex discourse: argument, logic, even syntax. As a result, when his poetry attempts to conduct a discussion instead of presenting a vision, it finds itself reduced to tame, formulaic language: "How strange it all was"; "It occurred to me"; "A piercing, heart-wrenching dread." Instead of "recreating the experience of Being," many poems only refer to that experience, usually in the key of nostalgia: "The sunset sky for one brief moment/Radiant with some supreme insight,/And then it's over."

The title of this poem, "Romantic Landscape," also suggests that what once seemed the exigent mystery of Being has grown more conventional and literary in Simic's later work. Instead of the philosophically dense "blossomlike/White erasure," Simic's fleeting moments of vision are now "some supreme insight" into "What is eternally invisible." "The Old World," with its vision of the gods at an ancient Greek temple—"Oh to be one of them, the wine whispered to me"—says nothing different than Wordsworth did two hundred years ago: "I'd rather be/a pagan suckled in a creed outworn."

At the same time as mystery recedes into literature, it also makes itself too comfortable in the world. The problem with secular mysticism is that it constantly threatens to become merely praise of the ordinary—or still worse, a bourgeois appreciation of life's little pleasures. In "The Old World," Simic's divine vision comes after a nice lunch: "The olives and goat cheese tasted delicious." Even existential anxiety is delectable in the self-canceling lines from "Night Panic": "You were mulling over the particulars/Of your cosmic insignificance/Between slow sips of red wine. . . ." What is troubling is not the fact of sensual enjoyment, of course, but the suggestion that there is something religious about it:

No sooner have we made love
Than we are back in the kitchen.
While I chop the hot peppers,
She wiggles her ass
And stirs the shrimp on the stove.

"I'm crazy about her shrimp!"
I shout to the gods above.

The gods who would smile on this prayer are some distance from the Being that, in "White," "Had to get through me/On its long trek//To and from nowhere." In part, of course, the change is personal: the young unknown, writing feverishly in seedy New York hotels, has become the Pulitzer Prize–winning distinguished professor. "We bought magazines like *Poetry* in those days in order to nourish our rage," he recalls of his early days. Now the rage has mellowed, and the poetry with it.

This is not to say that *The Voice of 3 A.M.* has none of the bleakness or acerbity of Simic's best work. "Evening Chess," for instance, seems to compress a whole Kafkaesque childhood into two lines: "The Black Queen raised high/In my father's angry hand." In "Sinister Company," a gang of freaks gathers around the poet, not to menace him but to claim him:

> Blind, deaf, mad and homeless,
> Out of respect keeping their distance.
> You are our Emperor! they shouted.
> Chief executioner!

It is a reminder of his original affinities—with the refugee, the derelict, the man ripping newspapers during the poetry reading. Even though he has become a senior figure in American poetry, Simic still writes best when he and the reader are least comfortable.

C. D. Wright

THE MOST profound division in contemporary poetry is not between formal and free verse, or academic and experimental verse, though these battles are still being fought. More important than these, and in some sense underlying them, is the opposition between what might be called courteous and discourteous poetry. Poetic courtesy, of course, has nothing to do with politeness or prettiness. All modern poets have agreed in rejecting these qualities as incompatible with artistic integrity. It is, rather, a question of how the poet approaches his or her reader—the central choice from which many decisions about style and subject flow.

The courteous poet meets his ideal reader on conditions of equality. He approaches language as a medium of communication, which must be brought to a height of precision and eloquence in order to move and delight that reader. Concretely, this means that the courteous poet will try to make clear the subject or argument of the poem, its basic grammar and concepts. Reference and allusion will be used to deepen understanding, on the assumption that reader and writer share a common literary tradition. Formally, such a poet will naturally gravitate toward meter and rhyme, which knit the poem to the traditions of English verse and provide a pattern to guide the reader's expectations. All this emphatically does not mean that the experience the courteous poet offers will be inoffensively pleasant. It means simply that the poet's knowledge—even of extremity, perplexity, and tragedy—will be made available to the reader, so that it can be genuinely shared.

For the discourteous poet, by contrast, novelty and complexity are the fundamental values, both because they provide aesthetic pleasure and because they differentiate the poet from his predecessors. The reader does not need to be invited or seduced into the poem; his presence is either assumed or ignored. As a result, no effort is made to avoid confusion about the subject or argument of the poem; on the contrary, it is welcomed. The finished poem will not disclose the event or emotion that brought it into being, finding it more valuable to demonstrate the incommunicability of experience. Reference and allusion tend to be idiosyncratic and alienating, and form is conceived intellectually and theoretically rather than discursively or musically.

It is tempting to say that the first kind of poetry aspires to be a part of literature, and appeals to a generally educated reader, while the second sees itself as a part of "contemporary poetry"—almost a separate endeavor—and appeals to readers whose taste is formed on the poetry of the last hundred years. Both types of poet can produce and have produced work of the first rank. But the balance today has swung so far in the direction of discourtesy that a cautionary and probing criticism of this approach to poetry seems necessary.

One of the most influential of the discourteous poets, whose techniques can be seen everywhere in the work of younger writers, is C. D. Wright. *Steal Away*, a selection from twenty years of Wright's work, is valuable as a sort of time-lapse exposure of the development of those techniques. Wright has always been interested in narrative, and the subjects of her stories—life in the South and erotic life, especially within marriage—have remained much the same, from *Translation of the Gospel Back into*

Tongues in 1982 all the way through *Deepstep Come Shining* in 1998. But over the years, her narratives have become fractured, distended, and scumbled by discourtesy, the direct, prosy snapshots of her early work giving way to book-length riddles. Because Wright's techniques have become much more complex while her themes have remained similar, her work provides an excellent example of how the superficial challenge of discourtesy can accompany, and conceal, a fundamentally unchallenging criticism of life.

Wright's earliest poems tell stories of the working-class South, which she obviously knows well. She writes compassionately about midwives, traveling musicians, and spinsters, hard-luck cases like those in "Libretto":

Men piss in the ditch, on the toe of their shoes
thinking it must be rain or hail.

The feet of their women swell like a melon.
Their ironing boards bow
under the weight of beautiful linen
they do for other women.

But these men and women remain types, familiar representatives of a class and region, rather than individuals. Wright herself was clearly impatient with the limits of this plain, sententious style, for in her second book, *Further Adventures with You*, she began the narrative experimentation that makes her work distinctive. In "Treatment," Wright attempts to capture the fluidity of cinematic montage. The poem's headnote—"This is a 16-mm film of seven minutes in which no words are spoken" —leaves it open to question whether she is describing an actually existing film or imagining one of her own:

> A girl dresses in purple in the ·
> dark. She feels along the wallpaper to the kitchen, fixes oatmeal,
> warms coffee to which she adds globs of honey. She makes a
> sandwich for lunch. She starts to eat out of the pot on the
>   stove. . . .
>   When she
> goes back upstairs to comb her hair and make an irregular
>   part, to
> tinkle—she hears her parents. Their bedsprings. A shot of them
> under many covers.

There is nothing especially adventurous here. The continuous present tense and the accumulation of details are all well-established literary conventions for imitating film, and Wright's long and arbitrarily broken lines come so close to prose that there is no verbal rhythm to complicate the rhythm of the scenes. But "Treatment" is only Wright's first step in the defamiliarization of narrative. The storyteller's voice is further stripped down in "This Couple," where the lovers are reduced to a series of details:

> Jukeboxes
> we fed. Quarters circulating with our prints.
> Things we sent away for. Long drives. The rain. Cafes
> where we ate late and once only. Eyes of an animal
> in the headlamps. . . .

This technique, which in a later poem Wright aptly names "shining the particulars," remains well short of discourtesy, because the implied narrative is so familiar that the details slide readily into place. These are the things of which a couple's common life is built, and the homely, affectionate quality of

Wright's retelling suggests a woman shuffling through a photograph album. Indeed, marriage, or at least coupledom, is Wright's favorite theme, and she returns to it in the much-changed idiom of her later work.

But the most suggestive poem in *Further Adventures with You*, the one that shows where Wright was heading, is "Provinces." It is another essay in "shining the particulars," but this time there is a noticeable slippage between one particular and the next, so that the narrative becomes more difficult to reconstruct. The subject of the story is, presumably, the poet, but instead of a proper name or "I" or even "she," it is referred to only as "the body." This "body" is assigned characteristics and experiences that do not seem to fit together, like pieces from different jigsaw puzzles all mixed up:

> Once the body had ambitions—to be tall and remain
> soft. No more, but it enjoys rappelling to the water.
> Because the body's dwelling is stone, perched over water,
> we say the body is privileged. . . .
>   Because the body lives
> so far from others, it likes reading about checkered lives
> in the metropoli. It likes moving around at night under its dress.
> When it travels, bottles of lotion open in its bags.

Part of the strangeness of the poem comes simply from the use of "body" in place of a pronoun. At times this seems appropriate—it calls attention to the corporeal dimension of experience, such as "moving around . . . under its dress"—but elsewhere it is jarring, as when the "body" has ambitions or reads books.

More profoundly, the poem is estranging because of Wright's eccentric selection and arrangement of details. Individually, each detail is clear, even ordinary; but why is it significant that "the body's" bottles of lotion open in its bags, or that it enjoys rappelling? We can understand the primary character-istics of this body—its loneliness, its aging, its restlessness— but it remains radically underdescribed. And this withholding of the whole story, which deliberately places the reader at a dis-advantage, would become the main strategy of Wright's poetry.

Wright's next book, *String Light*, marked the key transition in her work so far. In poem after poem, a story or situation is pre-sented in a code that is left to the reader to interpret. In "King's Daughters, Home for Unwed Mothers, 1948," the scene of a young woman giving birth erupts into a swirl of details:

> Volumes of letters, morning glories on a string trellis, the job
>   at the
> Maybelline factory, the job at the weapons plant, the
>   hummingbird
> hive, the hollyhocks, her grandmother's rigid back next to her
> grandfather's bow. . . .

These are the data of the young mother's life, and they resolve into the story of her seduction and abandonment. This reduction of a human life to snapshots gives the poem a certain momentum. But it also exposes the limitations of Wright's method, for the hustle of particulars leaves little room for gen-uine intimacy with the woman whose experiences are being catalogued. One thinks of how a similar young woman in Larkin's "Deceptions" is brought to life by metaphor ("your mind lay open like a drawer of knives"), while Wright's is pinned to the page by detail. The number and variety of char-acteristics have multiplied, but this woman remains just as much a type as the characters of "Libretto," because external details cannot capture her interiority.

Elsewhere in the book, Wright's formal experiments are still more obtrusive. In "Remarks on Color," we have a numbered list:

  6. condensation off soybeans
  7. someone known as Skeeter
  8. his whole life
  9. flatbed loaded with striped melons
  10. Lopez's white car at JB's mother's house

In "Why Ralph Refuses to Dance," Wright braids two voices in alternate lines, Ralph's conversation with a woman and his internal monologue:

Who do you think I am, she said, a broom.
         looking at the moon's punched-out face
No, he mumbled, saxophone.
         think about Lily coming down the staircase
At the tables they whispered about him
         her crushed-velvet chairs. . . .

And in "More Blues and the Abstract Truth," punctuation does the work of estrangement:

         Again. And. Again.
With the wine. And the loaf.
And the excellent glass
of the body. And she says,
Even. If. The. Sky. Is. Falling.
My. Peace. Rose. Is. In. Bloom.

These are discourteous narratives, in which Wright violates the usual rules of storytelling and grammar, though still only moderately. The reader can quickly ascertain the key to each poem—montage, alternation, punctuation—and reassemble the story it encodes. But what we discover after performing this operation is a disappointment: a point of view, an understanding of life, that is considerably less novel and challenging than the technique with which it is expressed. Wright's words of wisdom in "More Blues"—"even if the sky is falling, my peace rose is in bloom"—amount to an exhortation to love the little things, or even to stop and smell the roses. In other poems, this encouraging word is spoken still more clearly: "The machine's vocation was to type, but its avocation / was to tell everyone up before light, I love you, I always will; to / tell the sisters waiting on their amniocenteses, Everything's going to be fine."

This affirmation is Wright's most characteristic note. We are left with the paradox that a discourteous poet can be warmly sentimental, while a courteous poet can be genuinely tragic. The paradox is taken still further in *Just Whistle*, whose subtitle—"A Valentine"—points again to Wright's essentially affirmative erotics. This book-length poem alternates between fulsome grandiloquence and cryptic minimalism, with the governing plot thoroughly buried, if it exists at all. On the one hand, there are hymns to the concrete of a kind common in contemporary poetry:

> the panties, which
> the body had not really noticed so used was the body to the
> cloth, the plight of their facticity, the elastic in the legs and the
> waist not being felt, the discoloration having blended them
> perfectly with the flesh, no line or hair, neotenous, and there
> being very little moisture, except for the thinnest issue of
> piss. . . .

It is possible to feel awe at the "facticity" of the ordinary; but the reader is not made to share in this awe merely by an extended description of the ordinary. Wright's method of surrounding an object with details, rather than capturing its essence with one sure stroke of image or metaphor, leads to orotundity, as in this panegyric to the vagina:

> Hole of Holes: world in the world of the os, an ode,
> unspoken, hole in its infancy, uncuretted, sealed, not yet
> yielded, nulliparous mouth, girdle against growth, inland
> orifice, capital O, pore, aperture to the aleph. . . .

Yet side by side with such genial rhapsody we find the most angular and extreme discourtesy, poems whose action, situation, grammar, and purpose are completely veiled. It is one thing when Wright plays cut-and-paste with a famous Hopkins poem:

> No. It. Worst. Destroys. None. Possibility. Pitched. Of.
> Friendship. Past. With. Pitch. Others. Of. It. Grief.

As in "Why Ralph Refuses to Dance," reading this poem is a matter of separating out the alternating voices. This operation yields Wright's gloss on Hopkins's sonnet "No Worst, There Is None": "It destroys possibility of friendship with others," and so on. Wright has simply interleaved the brilliant despair of Hopkins's poem with her own, considerably less brilliant, expression of unhappiness, a maneuver that allows her to borrow Hopkins's eloquence while signing it with her own technique.

But this is downright perspicuous compared with "A Brief and Blameless Outline of the Ontogeny of Crow." "Crow" threads its way through *Just Whistle* as a code word—often, it

seems, for the female genitalia—but its meaning is not elucidated by this poem:

Tonight one said	Bluets the other said
Goosefoot one said	Hungry the other said
Hangnail it said	Spanish bayonet it said
Daylilies it said	Hotel it said
Matches it said	Sickle senna it said. . . .

In this extremely discourteous poem, everything that might
orient the reader has been withdrawn: the identity of the
speakers, their tone of voice, the real subject of their conversation. Yet the grammar of dialogue is retained, inviting us to try
to hypothesize some situation in which this exchange might
take place. It is a prime example of what Donald Davie called
"syntax as music": "The whole play of literal meaning, in fact, is
a Swedish drill, in which nothing is being lifted, transported, or
set down, though the muscles tense . . . as if it were."

Some twenty pages later, however, Wright gives us a clue to
"A Brief Blameless Outline" in a passage of prose: "Everywhere
were bluets and Spanish bayonets, goosefoot, morning glories
and daylilies, purslane and clotbur and panic grass and fever-
few. Especially in a circle at the center, sickle senna grew in
extraordinary regeneration. . . ." We recognize that the plant
names from the earlier dialogue have now taken their place in
a description, but we still have no idea of what is being
described or why. A reader of the original edition of this poem
would be permanently at a loss. But in *Steal Away*, Wright has
surrendered her obscurity to the extent of adding an introduc-
tory note, in which she mentions "borrowing descriptive terms
of the teeming botanical aftermath of the bombing of Japan
from John Hersey's shattering book *Hiroshima*." Since this

seems to be the only passage to which the note could refer, we can finally "solve" the reference. Wright has taken over Hersey's description of regrowth after destruction as a symbol of the emotional regrowth her poem charts.

Yet this use of allusion, especially in its original, unannotated form, entirely defeats the function of allusion, which is courteous: allusion exists to remind the reader of precedents and to establish an orientation for reading. But the Hersey passage is not one that any reader could be expected to identify. Nothing in Wright's poem suggests its origins or tone, and the permutation to which she subjects it estranges it still further. If a name is dropped in the forest and there is no one to hear it, does it make a sound?

Tremble, the collection of lyrics that followed *Just Whistle* (and the last book substantially represented in *Steal Away*), extends and confirms Wright's technique of elliptical narrative. A reader familiar with her work to this point knows what to expect: implied stories that cannot be elucidated, but that revolve around the celebration of sexual intimacy. In "Sonic Relations," we do not expect that "she mentioned ralph and fire / twice mentioned ralph / and the fire" will not be followed by any further information about "she," Ralph, or the fire. It is a brazen example of what Yvor Winters categorized as "pseudo-reference," specifically "reference to a nonexistent plot." Even if the plot exists for the poet, it remains nonexistent for the reader.

Nor will we flinch at the inconsequence and eccentricity of the list in "Autographs":

Weather: late ozark spring
Soft entry: it can be done
Strangest device: cock rings

Preferred intervention: human hand
Source of common terror: retina
Wish: to never know unhappiness again
State flower: bearded iris

But it is unnecessary to multiply examples. As this last passage shows, whatever the surface confusion, the essence of
Wright's poetry is reassurance and affirmation, especially as
these are found in sex. In a poet usually difficult, it is significant
that her clearest statements bring news to which no one could
possibly object:

> It is
> just so sad so creepy so beautiful.
> Bless it. We have so little time
> to learn, so much. . . . The river
> courses dirty and deep. Cover the lettuce.
> Call it a night. O soul. Flow on. Instead.

That final "instead" may be a mystery, but when it is proceeded
by so much "blessing" and "beauty," it cannot be a challenge. As
Wright's poetry shows, difficult form and ingratiating matter is
a far less interesting combination than difficult matter and
courteous form.

James Merrill

PROUST'S MADELEINE has become the popular shorthand for his novel, the Atlantis of memory resurfacing after a single taste of a cookie dipped in tea. In fact, Proust's metaphor for remembering is much more arduous than that:

> I place in position before my mind's eye the still recent taste of that first mouthful, and I feel something start within me, something that leaves its resting place and attempts to rise, something that has been embedded like an anchor at a great depth; I do not know yet what it is, but I can feel it mounting slowly; I can measure the resistance, I can hear the echo of great spaces traversed. . . . Ten times over I must essay the task, must lean down over the abyss.

It is instructive to compare James Merrill's rival metaphor for the process that turns life into art, in his poem "For Proust":

> What happened is becoming literature.
> Feverish in time, if you suspend the task,
> An old, old woman shuffling in to draw
> Curtains, will read a line or two, withdraw.
> The world will have put on a thin gold mask.

The poet has made the novelist over in his own very different image: not an anchor but a mask, not the depths but the surface. So perfectly does the metaphor of gilding capture Merrill's artistic goals that he resorts to it, or versions of it, many times in his poetry: "A changing light is deepening, is changing/To a gilt ballroom chair a chair/Bound to break under someone before long"; "under water all/Becomes a silvery weightless miracle"; "I saw the parents and the child/ At their window, gleaming like fruit/With evening's mild gold leaf."

Reading lines like these, it is easy to see why Merrill has sometimes been dismissed as a merely decorative poet. The charge seems all the more credible because of his great wealth: in the old American contest between paleface and redskin, Merrill's money and status place him firmly in the first camp. The son of a founder of Merrill Lynch, he was the closest thing his time could show to an American aristocrat. (It is suggestive of his family's social position that, in "Days of 1935," he remembers fantasizing, as an eight-year-old, about being held for ransom like the Lindbergh baby.)

Merrill passed unscathed through a Depression childhood, and as an adult he enjoyed the fruits of his father's labor: leisure, travel, beautiful homes. In her memoir of Merrill and his companion David Jackson, Alison Lurie remembers the air of moneyed ease that surrounded the pair in the 1950s: "I loved visiting Stonington. To go to 107 Water Street from a house cluttered with shabby, worn furniture and toys and dirty laundry and the cries of children was like being transported to another world: one not only more attractive, but more luxurious, calm, voluptuous; more free and leisured—a world in which the highest goods were friendship, pleasure, and art."

"Luxurious" is also an apt description of Merrill's poetry, which is superficial in the most deliberate sense: it is profoundly concerned with surfaces. This fact of Merrill's art is often euphemized by calling him a comic or Mozartian poet.

But such appellations are misleading if they suggest that Merrill was artistically happy, that his gifts found free and ideal expression in his chosen forms and subjects. In fact, Merrill only intermittently gives the sense of a complete achievement. Like a fresco painter, he often seems to lay his brilliant colors onto a weak and crumbling material; his themes are rarely equal to the language in which he clothes them. He presents the spectacle, rare in modern poetry, of a serious writer whose style outstrips what he has to say.

To appreciate the limits of Merrill's achievement, it is necessary to understand the substance of that achievement. We might begin with one of the most notable features of his work, his love of puns. Merrill tied hundreds of comic knots in the English language:

> My father, who had flown in World War I,
> Might have continued to invest his life
> In cloud banks. . . .

> On the one hand, the power and the gory
> Details. . . .

> The god at last indifferent
> And she no longer chaste but continent.

In life, the pun receives the tribute of a groan; we feel that there is something cheap about drawing attention to the arbitrary resemblances and double meanings of words. "Continent" means both a "landmass" and "sexually controlled," but we learn nothing about the world from this accidental fact. Yet it is just this arbitrariness that makes Merrill's puns genuinely poetic: they willfully divert the reader's attention from the signified to the sign, to the materiality of language. If language were entirely transparent, if there were one word per object, there could be no poetry. It is in the resistance or the excess of the medium that poetic felicity resides.

In this sense, the pun is really just an extreme case of the playfulness at work in all verse. As the eighteenth-century poet John Dennis wrote, "Rime may not so absurdly be said to be the Pun of Harmony." Rhyme asserts that two words do sound the same, just as puns remind us that one word does have two meanings, regardless of logic. When rhyme-words are extremely disparate in meaning or etymology, they come to seem like puns on one another, as in *Don Juan*. Or as in Merrill, where we find "peacocks/Orthodox," "sacerdotal/Aristotle," "one of us/homunculus." He is so much under the spell of sound that his poems occasionally lose themselves in little rhapsodies of assonance, as in "Flying from Byzantium":

> Up spoke the man in the moon:
> What does that moan mean?
> The plane was part of the plan.
> Why gnaw the bone of a boon?
>
> I said with spleen, "Explain
> These nights that tie me in knots,
> All drama and no dream,
> While you lampoon my pain."

Merrill takes an almost mischievous pleasure in showing that sonic patterning can be taken to such an extreme while still making sense. His metrical repertoire is extraordinarily wide, from the elaborate stanzas of his early work to sonnet sequences, short epigrams, and narrative couplets. (Almost the

only thing Merrill did not write was actual songs—an interesting difference from Auden, whom he otherwise resembles in
this respect.) He gives the reader a sense of linguistic riches so
vast that he can strew them carelessly about.

But Merrill's very liberality can be a flaw if we begin to suspect that, like a Weimar fortune, it is a result of the cheapness
of the currency. A poet gives the impression of strength only if
his linguistic powers seem to meet and overcome the challenge
of significant statement. Simple things said simply are graceful;
difficult things said with difficulty are impressive; but simple
things said with difficulty are merely showy. At times, Merrill
consciously tests this imbalance, as when he describes urinating
in *The Book of Ephraim*:

> When the urge
> Comes to make water, a thin brass-hot stream,
> Sails out into the updraft, spattering
> One impotent old tree that shakes its claws.
>
> The droplets atomize, evaporate
> To dazzlement a blankness overdusts
> Pale blue, then paler blue. It stops at nothing.

The passage is carefully constructed, from the striking adjective
"brass-hot" to the concluding ambiguity. What it lacks is any
kind of surprise, any sense that the poet is urging his subject
beyond itself; and absent this pressure, it is just an unusually
elegant description of urinating. The elegance is even complacent: the word "dazzlement" here seems too pleased with itself,
with the mild frisson of being applied to something so trivial.

To object to such a style is not to object to beautiful writing.
The distinction must be maintained, because Merrill himself

often elided it, writing as though the only argument to be made against his conception of style were a plebeian political attack. We find such a self-defense in section "W" of *The Book of Ephraim*, the first part of his Ouija-inspired epic, *The Changing Light at Sandover*. In terza rima, Merrill relates a Dantesque meeting with Wendell, a painter whose subjects are "ill-knit/ Mean-mouthed, distrustful" faces. Merrill asks why he creates such ugly portraits:

> "I guess that's sort of how I see mankind,"
> Says Wendell. "Doomed, sick, selfish, dumb as shit.
> They talk about how decent, how refined—
> All it means is, they can afford somehow
> To watch what's happening, and not to mind."
> Our famous human dignity? I-Thou?
> The dirty underwear of overkill.
> Those who'll survive it were rethought by Mao
> Decades past, as a swarming blue anthill.
> "The self was once," I put in, "a great,
> great Glory." And he: "Oh sure. But is it still?"

Merrill presents himself here as the defender of aristocratic humanism against the modern tide of ugliness, brutality, and mass mind. As he writes in another poem, "Form's what affirms."

Yet if we ask what Merrill's form affirms, the answer can only be: form itself. His idea of art is a throwback, it often seems, to the 1890s and art for art's sake. It is not surprising to read, in "Days of 1941 and '44," that his first literary enthusiasms were for Wilde and Baudelaire:

> But viewed from deep in my initial
> Aesthetic phase, brought like a lukewarm bath to

Fizzy life by those mauve salts,
Paradises (and if artificial
So much the better) promised more than Matthew
Arnold. Faith rose dripping from the false.

This "initial phase" passed in time, but Merrill continued to think of the beautiful as though it were an iridescence that can be peeled off any art object. There is a revealing moment in his prose memoir, *A Different Person*, when he writes of visiting the early Christian mosaics in Ravenna:

> The profusion of motifs, their vigor by now a reflex long past thought, gives out a sense of peace and plenty in the lee of history's howling gale. It isn't the creeds or crusades they tell of, but the relative eternity of villas, interior decoration, artisans. . . . While empires fell offstage, these happy solutions to the timeless problems of scale and coherence stretched, like flowers to the light, wherever a patron beckoned.

It is not the history, or the symbolism, or indeed the meaning of the mosaics that interests Merrill, but their "solutions" to technical "problems."

But to defend the aesthetic in these terms is, ironically, to abandon what is most genuinely beautiful in poetry. The particular heroism of modern poets since Wordsworth lies in the courage of their self-scrutiny, and their boldness in expressing what they have discovered. To this end, what F. R. Leavis called "heuristic poetry" uses form in a destructive-creative way, breaking down conventional or received modes of expression in order to build up new, more accurate modes. Merrill is not a poet of discovery, in this sense. His idea of beauty is static, exterior, and therefore basically conservative.

He provides a perfect emblem of this sort of beauty in "Charles on Fire," where a glass of "amber liquor" is set aflame:

> A blue flame, gentle, beautiful, came, went
> Above the surface. In a hush that fell
> We heard the vessel crack. The contents drained
> As who should step down from a crystal coach.
> Steward of spirits, Charles's glistening hand
> All at once gloved itself in eeriness.

This, of course, is another version of the "thin gold mask," a surface glamour. It is significant that Merrill describes the flame as "beautiful," a word that has been steadfastly avoided by most modern poets, on the assumption that real beauty does not need an epithet. But the tag is necessary in this case, because the phenomenon described is inherently nugatory: it means nothing, it discovers nothing. That is, it is not truly beautiful, with the exigent beauty of the best poetry; it is only "interesting."

When the valuable is identified with the rare and the precious, rather than with the common and the profound, it makes sense that the poet will see himself as addressing a select audience. Merrill was an exceptionally generous person (Lurie writes that "no one will ever know the extent" of his benefactions), but in his poetry he has an exaggerated sense of his own particularity, his separation from the rest of the world, which can border on snobbery. In "Tony: Ending the Life," he writes of

> The longing to lead everybody's life
> —Lifelong daydream of precisely those
> Whom privilege or talent set apart:
> How to atone for the achieved uniqueness?

Nothing could be more alien to the self-conception of the "heuristic" poet, who is essentially representative of mankind, even if he lives among them as a stranger. In lines like these, one suspects that the idea of material privilege has infected the idea of artistic talent, which is not a privilege but a responsibility.

Nowhere is this attitude more evident than in *The Changing Light at Sandover*, which purports to document metaphysical truths communicated by a Ouija board to Merrill and Jackson. As Merrill began "talking" with a spirit named Ephraim, Alison Lurie looked on with dismay: "From the beginning I didn't care for Ephraim. He was a part of David and Jimmy I hadn't met head-on before, and instantly felt estranged from. He was foreign, frivolous, intermittently dishonest, selfishly sensual, and cheerfully, coldly promiscuous." Indeed, *The Book of Ephraim* presents a depressingly narcissistic vision of the world to come.

Merrill allows that Ephraim might have been "a projection/ Of what already burned, at some obscure/Level or another, in our skulls." But it is hardly reassuring to think that passages like the following are addressed by Merrill to himself:

> take our teacher told us
> from sensual pleasure only what will not
> during it be even partly spoiled by fear
> of losing too much. This was the tone
> We trusted most, a smiling Hellenistic
> Lightness from beyond the grave. Each shaft
> Feathered by head-turning flattery:
> Long b4 the fortunate conjunction
> (David's and mine) allowed me to get through
> may I say weve had our eyes on u
> —On our kind hearts, good sense, imagination,
> Talents!

The Book of Ephraim contains some of Merrill's finest writing, but the system it is meant to expound is intellectually unacceptable and imaginatively complacent. It is not necessary, of course, to write a long poem in order to be a major poet. But there are qualities of the major poet whose absence from Merrill's work is confirmed in his long poem.

Still, Merrill is an undisputed master of certain modes. The aristocratic irony that freezes his largest statements is very rewarding when he writes about his childhood or his love affairs, subjects on which many poets are grimly humorless. Indeed, it is not his style, but the tone his style creates, that is Merrill's greatest achievement. The man we come to know in the *Collected Poems* is witty, clever, and cool, meeting suffering with self-mocking fortitude. The resigned *"Ja, ja"* of Strauss's Marschallin is Merrill's characteristic response to tragedy:

> Change of scene that might, I thought, be tried
> First, instead of outright suicide.
> (Looked back on now, what caused my sufferings?
> Mere thwarted passion—commonest of things.)

In fact, some of Merrill's best poems are about opera. As he relates in the sequence "Matinees," attending a performance of the *Ring* was the beginning of his aesthetic education. Opera taught him that emotion can be performed, that it can be simultaneously sincere and parodic. The artistic consciousness is inevitably a double consciousness: "The point thereafter was to arrange for one's / Own chills and fever, passions and betrayals, / Chiefly in order to make song of them."

Merrill's autobiographical sequences—"Matinees," "The Broken Home," "The Thousand and Second Night," "Lost in Translation," the series of poems titled "Days of . . . ," "Clearing the Title," and a few others—are the height of his art. In them, he finds in his own life a subject important enough to compel interest but not so important as to resist irony, and the pressure of narrative restrains his tendency to the baroque. Perhaps the best of these sequences is "Family Week at Oracle Ranch," from *A Scattering of Salts*. It recounts the poet's trip to a New Age recovery facility to visit his lover, who is a patient there. Here the disparity between complex language and primal feeling becomes Merrill's explicit subject:

> Simplicities. Just seven words—afraid,
> Hurt, lonely, etc.—to say it with.
> Shades of the first watercolor box
> (I "felt blue," I "saw red"). . . .
> While the connoisseur of feeling throws up his hands:
> Used to depicting personal anguish
> With a full palette—hues, oils, glazes, thinner—
> He stares into these withered wells and feels,
> Well . . . sad and angry?

For a poet so enamored of eloquence, therapeutic language represents a radical deprivation. Yet this very loss allows Merrill a way around the ironic self-awareness his usual style enforces. It is one of the rare moments when Merrill appears discomfited by language, by the disjunction between eloquence and communication.

Reading Merrill's *Collected Poems* leaves no doubt that he was one of the most talented American poets of the last half century. His achievement was all the more valuable because he was strong in areas where most of his contemporaries were weak. Yet the book also leaves the suspicion that Merrill's major work was left unwritten. How glad we would be to have, instead of

The Changing Light at Sandover, his verse autobiography. It would probably not have been a profound exploration of memory, like *The Prelude*, or like Proust; but it would have been sparkling and sociable, like Pope.

Indeed, the Augustan Age would have been the perfect setting for Merrill's gifts. He was meant for an era in which the poet could take much for granted—his audience, his principles, his forms—and could devote himself to the perfection of what he received. One can easily imagine Merrill going to Court and to the coffeehouses, writing witty verse epistles, and turning his couplets to a dazzling polish. There would have been no question, in those days, of his poetry being too beautiful to be great.

Richard Wilbur

IN 1953, literary history—acting through the good offices of Edna Ward of Boston, Massachusetts—brought together two of the most gifted, and least similar, American poets of the postwar era. Mrs. Ward was the mother-in-law of Richard Wilbur—at age thirty-two, the author of two acclaimed books of verse—and a friend of Aurelia Plath, whose twenty-year-old daughter, Sylvia, had just endured the hellish summer she would go on to chronicle in *The Bell Jar*. Wilbur was invited, as he wryly recalls in his poem "Cottage Street, 1953," "to exemplify/The published poet in his happiness,/Thus cheering Sylvia, who has wished to die." Of course, Wilbur's goodwill could not make a dent in Plath's hermetically sealed misery: he describes himself as "a stupid lifeguard" who finds "a girl . . . immensely drowned." But the meeting was productive in another way. Decades later, after Plath had written, died, and become a myth, it offered Wilbur a test and an emblem of his own, very different poetic calling.

In his poem, Wilbur slyly turns Mrs. Ward's polite inquiry about tea—"if we would prefer it weak or strong"—into a literary and moral question. Plath, of course, preferred it strong, in art and in life. She would go on, in Wilbur's words, "to state at last her brilliant negative/In poems free and helpless and unjust." But where does this leave Wilbur himself, whose poems are brilliantly affirmative, and who enjoyed all the blessings Plath eschewed or was denied—longevity, reputation, worldly success? Does the very fact that he was destined for happiness condemn his poetry to be weak, the tepid "milk" to Plath's acrid "lemon"?

The question Wilbur asks in "Cottage Street, 1953" has been posed by critics since the beginning of his career—starting with Randall Jarrell, whose review of Wilbur's second book, *Ceremony,* complained that Wilbur "never goes too far, but he never goes far enough." And it echoes from beginning to end of the *Collected Poems, 1943–2004* that will be Wilbur's monument. How does a poet who feels himself, in the words of an early poem, "Obscurely yet most surely called to praise," practice that calling in an age when poetry is overwhelmingly drawn to crisis, confession, and complaint?

This is more than just a matter of literary fashion, though in Wilbur's public statements one can often sense his impatience at being typecast as the straight man to his wilder contemporaries—above all, Robert Lowell. Lowell and Wilbur made their poetic debuts in the same postwar moment: Lowell's *Lord Weary's Castle* won the Pulitzer Prize in 1947, the year Wilbur's *The Beautiful Changes* appeared. And it was Lowell, much more than Plath, whom critics perpetually used as a foil when describing Wilbur. In a 1964 interview, Wilbur ruefully recited the standard contrast: "I'm all grace and charm and short gains, and he's all violence and . . . Well, he's Apollo and Dionysus locked in a death grip."

Lowell, like Plath, John Berryman, and countless lesser poets, wrote about and out of a spiritual turmoil that amounted to, or resulted in, madness. In "Waking in the Blue," Lowell insisted on the dangerous and pathetic majesty of the mad: he writes of "Stanley" with his "kingly granite profile," of "Bobbie," "a replica of Louis XVI/without the wig." In his poem "Driftwood," however, Wilbur declares his opposite allegiance to "emblems/Royally sane,"

> Which have ridden to homeless wreck, and long revolved
> In the lathe of all the seas,
> But have saved in spite of it all their dense
> Ingenerate grain.

Wilbur has always been conscious that his particular poetic gifts—accurate vision, copious eloquence, spiritual resilience —and his great subject—the richness and adequacy of the natural world—were untimely. Indeed, he started writing, as he later recalled, "for earnest therapeutic reasons during World War II," in an effort to bring the sanity of art to bear on "a personal and an objective world in disorder." The poems of his first book treat his experiences as a frontline infantryman in a style so elaborately formal that the most awful subjects are sublimated into irony, or even black comedy. There is something deliberately, monstrously cartoonish about "Mined Country," where "Cows in mid-munch go splattered over the sky." The persistence of the mines—"Danger is sunk in the pastures. . . ./ Ingenuity's covered with flowers!"—is clearly Wilbur's way of writing about persistence of the war itself, with all its psychic casualties: "it's going to be long before/Their war's gone for good," he soberly predicts.

But in this poem, as throughout *The Beautiful Changes*, Wilbur's style—influenced by the estranging precision of Marianne Moore and the courtly ironies of John Crowe Ransom— makes disorder almost parodically articulate. Surely there has never been a more aestheticized vision of K.P. than Wilbur's in "Potato":

Scrubbed under faucet water the planet skin
Polishes yellow, but tears to the plain insides;
Parching, the white's blue-hearted like hungry hands.

All of the cold dark kitchens, and war-frozen gray
Evening at window; I remember so many
Peeling potatoes quietly into chipt pails.

Jarrell, whose experience of military life was much milder than Wilbur's (he served as a Stateside flight instructor), was far more willing to admit the sorrow and pity of war into his poetry. There is nothing in Wilbur that resembles Jarrell's defiant matter-of-factness in "The Death of the Ball Turret Gunner": "When I died they washed me out of the turret with a hose."

But then, as Jarrell wrote, "The real war poets are always war poets, peace or any time"; and the same holds true of peace poets, in whose company Wilbur confessedly belongs. In "Up, Jack," he looks to Falstaff as a tutelary spirit for the postwar world, "a god/To our short summer days and the world's wine." While Wilbur's refined epicureanism is far removed from Falstaff's grossness, the poet dares, like the fat knight, to make an ethic of enjoyment. There is something quietly but unmistakably polemical about Wilbur's proud adoption-by-translation, in *Ceremony*, of La Fontaine's "Ode to Pleasure":

For games I love, and love, and every art,
Country and town, and all: there's nought my mood
          May not convert to sovereign good,
Even the gloom of melancholy heart.
Then come; and wouldst thou know, O sweetest Pleasure,
What measure of these goods must me befall?

Enough to fill a hundred years of leisure;
    For thirty were no good at all.

Such praise of mundane joys defies the whole trend of English and American poetry since Eliot, if not since Wordsworth.
Against the potent myth of the Romantic *poète maudit*—the
glamorous lineage of Chatterton, Shelley, Keats, Rimbaud, and
Hart Crane, fatally revived in Wilbur's own time by Plath, Lowell, and Berryman, among others—Wilbur sets the unfamiliar
ideal of the *poète bénit*. In a 1977 *Paris Review* interview, he
specifically rejected the tragic glamour of a Berryman, who had
compared writing to surgery ("I am obliged to perform in complete darkness/operations of great delicacy/on myself"). "John
Berryman," Wilbur said, "was such a very hard worker that he
lived almost entirely within his profession. . . . The impression
one is left with is of a man who is working desperately hard at
his job. Well, I admire that, but I think it can break your health
and destroy your joy in life and art."

Throughout his long career, Wilbur has remained committed
to that ideal of "joy in life and art"—alert to its shortcomings,
but faithful to its possibilities. He is a poet of fruitful activity,
not barren speculation; of artful enjoyment, not suffering
purity. Against the seductive whisper of Whitman's "When
Lilacs Last in the Dooryard Bloom'd"—"Come lovely and
soothing death,/Undulate round the world"—Wilbur sets
what he calls, in "In the Field," "the heart's wish for life, which
. . . is ourselves, and is the one/Unbounded thing we know."

Wilbur's position was often a lonely one, however, in a
period that tended to view all affirmation as mere bourgeois
complacency. One can get a good idea of the climate of literary
opinion in which Wilbur began to write from Lionel Trilling's
great study *Sincerity and Authenticity*, published in 1972. Trilling

suggests that all of English literature, from Shakespeare to Henry James, had explicitly or implicitly agreed on an ideal of earthly life, on the reward that awaits characters who live "happily ever after." This is the worldly felicity promised by the goddess Juno in *The Tempest*: "Honour, riches, marriage blessing, / Long continuance and increasing." "It has to do," as Trilling says, "with good harvests and full barns and . . . affluent decorum." But "in the literature of our own day," Trilling goes on to insist, "the visionary norm of order, peace, honour, and beauty has no place." Both writers and readers instinctively meet it with "bitter contemptuous rejection," whether out of "despair over the impossibility of realizing the vision," or out of a profoundly modern disbelief that any earthly happiness could satisfy the needs of the spirit. Rather than worldly completeness, the twentieth-century mind seeks in literature "the disintegration which is essential if it is to develop its true, its entire, freedom."

Strangely enough, the whole course of Trilling's argument— right down to the image of "good harvests and full barns"—was anticipated, and disputed, by Wilbur in a poem from his 1956 collection, *Things of This World*. In "Sonnet," Wilbur offers his own characteristic response to the problem of the "happily ever after":

> The winter deepening, the hay all in,
> The barn fat with cattle, the apple-crop
> Conveyed to market or the fragrant bin,
> He thinks the time has come to make a stop,
>
> And sinks half-grudging in his firelit seat,
> Though with his heavy body's full consent,
> In what would be the posture of defeat,
> But for that look of rigorous content.

Worldly satisfaction, Wilbur acknowledges, can have the look of defeat, because it means that there is nothing more to aspire to; and aspiration, rather than achievement, is the noblest ideal of Faustian modernity. Wilbur insists, however, that what looks like defeat should really be understood as "content," the only content available in this world: of labor completed, tasks achieved, the future secured. Still, in the last lines of "Sonnet," he acknowledges that the weary, satisfied farmer must always remain haunted, and in some degree reproached, by another figure—the scarecrow that stands in the field, "floating skyward its abandoned hands/In gestures of invincible desire."

Wilbur is too honest a poet to deny the persistent glamour of the scarecrow's aspiration, but his instincts are all on the side of the farmer's satisfaction. Throughout his work, he is generally uncomfortable when he tries to imagine what Trilling called "disintegration." From time to time, Wilbur has written poems of comprehensive moral statement, which attempt to do justice the horror of the modern world while still winning through to the optimistic composure that is his instinctive disposition. But these poems are among his least convincing, because his invocations of evil seldom avoid seeming merely dutiful. Certainly this is the case in "On the Marginal Way," from his 1969 collection *Walking to Sleep*. The poem begins with a walk on a beach that becomes a scene of horror:

> The rocks flush rose and have the melting shape
>   Of bodies fallen anyhow.
> It is a Géricault of blood and rape,
> Some desert town despoiled, some caravan
> Pillaged, its people murdered to a man.

It is typical of Wilbur, however, that this murderous vision should be, precisely, a vision, a mirage. Indeed, what Wilbur sees is twice removed from reality: the rocks remind him, not of "blood and rape" themselves, but of "a Géricault," an already aestheticized violence. And while Wilbur goes on to invoke "Auschwitz' final kill," the poem does not take account of that evil in a truly dialectical fashion, in such a way that the memory of evil would affect the imagination of good. Instead, in its last stanzas, "On the Marginal Way" turns away from evil altogether, in order to receive an unaccountable consolation:

> And like a breaking thought,
> Joy for a moment floods into the mind,
>   Blurting that all things shall be brought
> To the full state and stature of their kind. . . .

This kind of joy is not the conclusion to an argument but a complexion of the mind, which Wilbur cannot finally evade or disguise. As he explained in the *Paris Review* interview, "To put it simply, I feel that the universe is full of glorious energy, that the energy tends to take pattern and shape, and that the ultimate character of things is comely and good. I am perfectly aware that I say this in the teeth of all sorts of contrary evidence, and that I must be basing it partly on temperament and partly on faith, but that is my attitude."

If Wilbur's essentially hopeful, joyous temperament leaves him ill equipped for certain kinds of moral inquiry, however, it is also the source of his enormous poetic gifts. No twentieth-century American poet, with the possible exception of James Merrill, demonstrates such a natural talent for the writing of verse, or such pleasure in exercising it. This is partly a matter of formal mastery: Wilbur has written the best blank verse of any American poet since Frost. Yet Wilbur's formal poetry never has the slightly defensive, belligerent tone that afflicts many writers of formal verse in this era of free verse. That is because, just as his spirit takes naturally to "rigorous content," so his musical imagination takes naturally to contented rigor. "I have no quarrel at all with Emerson," he has remarked. "He said, 'not meter, but a meter-making argument makes poetry,' and I think that's true. I simply write a kind of free verse that ends by rhyming much of the time."

This seeming paradox is actually a profound truth about Wilbur's genius: for him, the conventional *is* organic. More than a matter of verse technique, this is the theme and argument of some of his best poems. In "A Baroque Wall-Fountain in the Villa Sciarra," Wilbur contrasts two Italian fountains that are also two ways of being in the world. The Baroque fountain of the title is a triumph of fantastic ingenuity, all shells and fauns and cherubs: "More addling to the eye than wine, and more//Interminable to thought/Than pleasure's calculus." But the poet is haunted, even here, by the suspicion that art should be more than just delightful: "Yet since this all/Is pleasure, flash, and waterfall,/Must it not be too simple?" Maybe, he wonders, there is more truth and more honesty in "the plain fountains that Maderna set,/Before St. Peter's," whose simple aspiring jet is a legible emblem of Romantic yearning and disappointment, "struggling aloft until it seems at rest/In the act of rising, until/The very wish of water is reversed. . . ."

There is no doubt which of these two fountains appears more modern, in Trilling's sense. But Wilbur finally declares his preference for the Baroque fountain, whose fauns, "at rest in fulness of desire/For what is given," seem to promise that a complete happiness is possible on earth. And in poem after poem, Wilbur finds new metaphors with which to assert that—to quote the title of his best-known poem—"Love Calls Us to the Things of This World." In "A Black November Turkey," he praises "the cocks that one by one,/Dawn after mortal dawn, with vulgar joy/Acclaim the sun"; in "After the Last Bulletins" the garbage collectors, "saintlike men,/White and absorbed, [who] with stick and bag remove/The litter of the night"; in "The Beacon" "the beacon-blaze" that "turns/The face of darkness pale/And now with one grand chop gives clearance to/Our human visions. . . ." The most famous of these emblems is the clean laundry of "Love Calls Us," in which the sight of sheets and smocks calls forth a secular prayer: "'Oh, let there be nothing on earth but laundry,/Nothing but rosy hands in the rising steam/And clear dances done in the sight of heaven.'"

The profusion of such emblems in Wilbur's *Collected Poems* is more than just a proof of his talent for metaphor. It is the poetic fruit of Wilbur's distinctive metaphysics, which deserves the quaint name of Transcendentalist. The condition of metaphor is the capacity of things to be likened to one another; and for Wilbur, as for Emerson, this very capacity suggests that all things share the same essential nature. "I think that all poets are sending religious messages," he once declared, "because poetry is, in such great part, the comparison of one thing to another; or the saying, as in metaphor, that one thing *is* another. And to insist, as all poets do, that all things are related to each other, comparable to each other, is to go toward making an assertion of the unity of all things." This faith in what he calls, in a late poem, "the dove-tailed world" is clearly inspired by Emerson's "The Poet": "Things admit of being used as symbols because nature is a symbol, in the whole, and in every part."

This doctrine—or, better, this intuition—provides Wilbur with his motive for metaphor: "What should we be without/The dolphin's arc, the dove's return,/These things in which we have seen ourselves and spoken?" The happiest of Wilbur's gifts is his confidence that we do indeed see ourselves in nature, that the human being is profoundly at home in this world. That confidence is what makes possible the hundreds upon hundreds of brilliant images and observations that light up Wilbur's *Collected Poems*:

> a still crepitant sound
> Of the earth in the garden drinking
> The late rain. . . .

> Slow vultures kettling in the lofts of air.

> the shucked tunic of an onion, brushed
> To one side on a backlit chopping-board
> And rocked by trifling currents, prints and prints
> Its bright, ribbed shadow like a flapping sail.

Whether the golden world of Wilbur's poetry is the real world, it is up to the "temperament and faith" of each reader to decide. What is certain is that Wilbur has given his vision the permanence, the immediacy, and the conviction of major poetry. His *Collected Poems* has the same moving and ambiguous power he ascribed, in an early poem, to yet another fountain, this one in "Caserta Garden":

> A childhood by this fountain wondering
> Would leave impress of circle-mysteries:
> One would have faith that the unjustest thing
> Had geometric grace past what one sees.

Donald Justice

When he died in August 2004, just twelve days before the publication of his *Collected Poems*, Donald Justice seemed to be posing one last time, in grievously concrete terms, the question he asked so often in his work: What survives of a life dedicated to poetry? Justice lived to be seventy-eight, but he was already imagining his death more than thirty years before, when he wrote "Variations on a Text by Vallejo":

> I will die in Miami in the sun,
> On a day when the sun is very bright,
> A day like the days I remember, a day like other days,
> A day that nobody knows or remembers yet. . . .

The poem is clearly a kind of spell, a way of gaining power over death by inviting it into the realm of language, where the poet is all-powerful. In this sense, it enacts in miniature the lifelong ambition of a poet who believed that posterity was the necessary dream of the serious artist. Though he taught in universities for many years, like most poets of his generation, Justice retained a severe and noble sense that being a poet is not a profession or a credential, but a vocation: "The vows may not be codified and published, but they are secretly known and one does take them."

Yet Justice was the least vaunting of poets. Compared to older contemporaries like Robert Lowell or Theodore Roethke, who bid loudly for eternity, he was positively reserved about the possibilities of art, and of his own art. The afterlife he imagined was not a matter of fame but a kind of Platonic ideal. It was not the poet who endured, but the poem, as he wrote in "Poem": "Even while you sit there, unmovable, / You have begun to vanish. And it does not matter. / The poem will go on without you."

Such metaphysical certainty, however, is unusual for Justice. More often, he does not make claims but asks questions, even wistful questions. His book of criticism is called *Oblivion*, and the title essay pays tribute to three poets who died almost forgotten: Weldon Kees, Henri Coulette, and Robert Boardman Vaughn. Vaughn, a friend of Justice's who led a life of Hart Crane–like dissipation—according to rumor, he was beaten to death in a Manhattan alleyway—published only a handful of poems in magazines. If it were not for Justice, he would be completely unknown. But for that very reason, he stands as the ultimate test case of poetic dedication. Does his failure of achievement refute his sense "of belonging to an elect, though doomed"? After all, as Justice was well aware, far more celebrated poets than Vaughn—finally, even the most celebrated— will one day be just as forgotten.

What remains is the mysterious sense that such a failure is itself a victory: "Persistence in the face of such certitude of oblivion is in its small way heroic, or so my romantic spirit commands me to believe." This is the persistence of Dante's Brunetto Latini, who even in Hell seemed like one who wins, not one who loses. In his poem "Hell," Justice gives to Vaughn's ghost a speech of Brunetto-like dignity: "Say this: / I sought the immortal word." The poem ends with Justice implicitly declaring himself one of Vaughn's company: "So saying he went on / To join those who preceded him; / and there were those who followed."

The romance of oblivion, and of everything allied to oblivion—transience, longing, regret—is what gives Justice's poetry its melancholy beauty. It is the ground note of all his work, helping to determine the fine texture of his perceptions no less than the composure of his language. Long before even the premonitions of "Vallejo," he felt the charm of mortality. "To shine is to be surrounded by the dark,/To glimmer in the very going out," he wrote in "Ladies by Their Windows," from his first book, *The Summer Anniversaries* (1960). The extraordinary assurance of that collection is partly owed to its long gestation: Justice was thirty-four when it was published. But still more, it is a sign that he already recognized the nature of his gifts. One of the distinctive pleasures of reading Justice is the constant evidence of his poetic intelligence, his complete understanding of his own methods and goals. This is especially rare and valuable in an age that admires eccentricity and authenticity more than mastery.

In *The Summer Anniversaries*, Justice's own masters are still occasionally in evidence. Wallace Stevens, who would remain a fertile influence throughout Justice's career, appears in the dandyish suavity of the blank verse, as well as in a few explicit echoes: "And chimes, and tinkles too, *fortissimo*." More pervasive is John Crowe Ransom, whose style, studded with courtly archaisms, is taken over wholesale in several poems: "I publish of my folk how they have prospered," Justice writes in "Tales from a Family Album."

Yet this Southern Elizabethan dialect—bedecked with "aught," "whereat," "in special," and other grace notes—is at odds with Justice's explicit disclaimer of any Cavalier ancestry. "The family tree," he declares, is "a simple chinaberry/Such as springs up in Georgia in a season." In his later work, Justice would continue to write affectionately about his Southern childhood, while making it clear that Miami in the 1930s was not Charleston in the 1830s. His model would no longer be Walter Scott but Sherwood Anderson, whose brevity, homeliness, and compassion Justice emulates in his narrative poems. "If Sherwood Anderson, one of my favorite writers, seems never to have had an idea longer than thirty or so pages," he declared in the preface to *A Donald Justice Reader*, "my own ideas come up even shorter."

Even in his early work, however, it is evident that what really draws Justice to the South as a poetic subject is not its grandeur but its decline. "Beyond the Hunting Woods" indulges in a Yeatsian fantasy of plantation life, imagining a "great house" where "dame and maiden" consort with "men after their red hounds." Yet Justice's authentic note is struck only when he asks, "What charm was in that wine / That they should vanish so?" Likewise, in "Southern Gothic," he "Conjures a garden where no garden is / And trellises too frail almost to bear / The memory of a rose, much less a rose."

As these lines show, the constellation of feeling that appears in Justice's early work, and survives almost without alteration into his last poems, is unashamedly Romantic. Loss and nostalgia, solitude and regret are his magic subjects. The emotional atmosphere of his poetry is close to that of nineteenth-century Romantic music, which he learned to love as a child. As he writes in "The Pupil," one of several late poems about his musical education, he immersed himself in "Chopin or Brahms, / Stupid and wild with love equally for the storms / Of C# minor and the calms of C." For a time he even studied composition with Carl Ruggles, and wrote in a memoir that "had I met Ruggles earlier I wonder if I might not now be writing music, very happily." What survives of this training in Justice's poetry is less any specific technique than an ambition to re-create or recollect in verse the emotional intensities of music—"this throbbing/Of the piano's great exposed heart."

Such an ambition naturally carries with it the potential for sentimentality. But Justice's poetic intelligence, honed by his New Critical apprenticeship, allows him to avoid this pitfall almost completely. One of the most impressive things about his poetry is the way it allows the reader to enjoy its self-delighting inwardness, its conscious delectation of emotion, without embarrassment. For when Justice takes the risk of sentimentality, he is always aware that he is taking it, and the awareness enforces a compensating strictness of form and irony of perspective.

This balance is struck in "Anniversaries," the first poem of his first book, when Justice remembers his ecstasy at the piano: "Keys of Chopin! I sat/All afternoon after school,/Fingering his ripe heart." The slightly repellent word "fingering" marks the poet's judgment on, and distance from, his own childish voluptuousness. Other early poems channel intense emotions into rigid forms, such as "Sestina on Six Words by Weldon Kees," whose recurrent end-words—"burden," "others," "silence," "harm"—form a lexicon of self-pity: "Each is alone, each with his burden./To others they are always others,/And they can never break the silence."

But Justice's most valuable technique of objectivity is the intellectual surprise of the conceit. His best early poems temper their vulnerability with Metaphysical wit. In his well-known sonnet "The Wall," the hoary theme of paradise lost is given new life:

> They had been warned of what was bound to happen.
> They had been told of something called the world.
> They had been told and told about the wall.

They saw it now; the gate was standing open.
As they advanced, the giant wings unfurled.

The sudden concrete detail of the angels' wings, appearing for
the first time only when they can no longer be seen, turns what
could have been a static lament into a miniature drama. Such
ingenuity is needed to keep Justice's potentially inundating
emotions in check: "It is not a landscape from too near," he
warns in "Variations on a Theme from James." "Like sorrows,
they require some distance/Not to bulk larger than they are."

The need for distance also helps to account for the elegant
formality of Justice's verse. Like Yvor Winters, Justice believed
in form as a token of poetic self-control:

The writer in meters, I insist, may feel as deeply as the non-
metrical writer, and the choice whether or not to use meters
is as likely to be dictated by literary fashion as by depth of
feeling or sincerity. Nevertheless, they have become a conventional sign for at least the desire for some outward control; though their use cannot be interpreted as any guarantee
of inner control, the very act of writing at all does usually
imply an attempt to master the subject well enough to
understand it, and the meters reinforce the impression that
such an attempt is being made and perhaps succeeding.

This Wintersian credo is only admirable, however, if there is
actually something there to be controlled; otherwise, it
becomes merely a paean to repression. Only a poet, like Justice, who is susceptible to great emotion knows the importance
of disciplining that emotion. Surrendering to it remains a perpetual temptation, one that he describes ironically in "To Satan
in Heaven": "Satan, who, though in heaven, downward

yearned,/As the butterfly, weary of flowers,/Longs for the cocoon or the looping net."

Yearning and longing would continue to be Justice's subjects for the rest of his life. A poet of his sensibility, who is provoked to write only by a certain rare and intense kind of experience, could never be prolific. After his debut he published just three full-length collections, all with crepuscular titles: *Night Light* (1967), *Departures* (1973), and *The Sunset Makers* (1987). Smaller groups of new poems were added in selections of his work published in 1979 and 1995. The *Collected Poems* includes all of that previously published verse, as well as ten new poems.

The book helps to reveal the striking consistency of Justice's inspiration. A few poems venture political statements, but the sophistication and obliquity of Justice's style leaves a poem like "To the Hawks"—subtitled "McNamara, Rusk, Bundy"—rather too indirect to be effective. Neither is he suited to the explicit self-exposure that attracted the best poets of a slightly older generation, like Lowell and Berryman. The closest he comes to it is the obviously unhappy archness of "Heart":

> Only think
> What sport the neighbors have from us, not without cause.
> These nightly sulks, these clamorous demonstrations!
> Already they tell of thee a famous story. . . .

"Clamorous demonstrations" were not Justice's natural terrain—indeed, he doesn't make them sound very clamorous—and as early as 1957 he wrote irritably about the fashion for "those orgies of public confession or self-expression—vulgarly known as 'getting it out of your system'—upon which absolution, or perhaps merely health, is expected to follow." But in attacking confessional sincerity—"Sincerity so conceived, as a kind of equation between the life and the work, seems to me possibly not a measure of literature at all"—Justice is really defending his own quieter version. He cannot write about the wildness of parties—his poem "Party" resorts to invoking "Lord Bacchus"—but he writes intimately about the loneliness of parties:

> And when you go
> It is there, towards music.
>
> Your shadow, though,
> Stays with me. . . .
>
> It is a dark rock
> Against which the sea beats.
>
> This is that other music, to which
> I embrace your shadow.

Not surprisingly, Justice enters middle age like a monarch coming home from exile: it is the phase of life he was born to write about. Already as a young man he had been acutely conscious of time's passage. Now, in poems like "Men at Forty," "The Thin Man," and "The Missing Person," he captures perfectly the pathos, and the self-conscious self-pity, of the aging man:

> There was no storm coming
> That he could see.
>
> There was no one out walking
> At that hour.

Still,
He closes the windows
And tries the doors.

He knows about storms
And about people

And about hours
Like that one.

This poem, "The Man Closing Up," is from *Night Light*. By the time of *Departures*, six years later, Justice had already moved beyond middle age and begun to dwell on death. He does this without terror or melodrama, rather with elegiac calm. When this feeling is given dramatic form, Justice produces some of his best poems, such as "An Elegy Is Preparing Itself":

There are pines that are tall enough
Already. In the distance,
The whining of saws; and needles,
Silently slipping through the chosen cloth.

The poem's double perspective on death—as a fatality in the indefinite future, and as a process that has already begun— offers an intellectual surprise strong enough to bear its emotional weight. "Variations on a Text by Vallejo" is a product of the same period, as is "Presences," which is characteristically a poem about absences: "Clouds out of the south, familiar clouds—/But I could not hold on to them, they were drifting away,/Everything going away in the night again and again."

In his late work, Justice continues to record and mourn those disappearances. But he also tries to stave them off through recollection, especially of his childhood. A series of poems return to his early piano lessons, sometimes in narrative form—as the title of "After-school Practice: A Short Story" suggests. Other poems preserve instants or, especially, images: the sequence "My South" replaces the Southern legends of his early work with domestic snapshots, "On the Porch" and "On the Farm." Justice's late work is visual, above all, in its attentiveness to light. He writes about a train window where "little lights / Glitter like lost beads from a broken necklace," a parlor where "the sunlight spilled like soda / on torporous rugs." The title poem of *The Sunset Makers* invokes Bonnard: "Impressions shimmering: broken light. The world / Is French, if it is anything."

Naturally, it is the shimmering, broken, evanescent quality of light that captures Justice's imagination. Light effects are nostalgic almost by definition, since they can hardly be appreciated before they have passed. In this they are like childhood itself, and it is the light of childhood that Justice finds most beautiful: in "Vague Memory from Childhood," he remembers a lamp "Printing a frail gold geometry / On the dust." In his best late poems, Justice defuses the threat of nostalgia with an irony learned in part from Jules Laforgue. Several of Justice's late poems pay homage to that great poet of self-consciousness— most explicitly "Nostalgia and Complaint of the Grandparents," whose Laforguean title simultaneously mocks and defends its own sentiment: "But where, where are they now, / All the sad squalors / Of those between-wars parlors?"

It is this capacity both to enjoy and to criticize his own emotion that makes Justice's best poems possible. In "Childhood," he can unguardedly remember, "coming and going in waves, / The stupid wish to cry." But at the same time, in his "Tremayne" sequence—which features an author-surrogate rather like Kees's "Robinson"—he can wryly admit that it's

nard not to be reconciled/To a despair that seems so mild."
Indeed, despair, as Justice implies, is not the right word for his
inspired bittersweetness. Better to say that Justice will be
remembered—and there is no doubt that he will be remembered, and read—as his generation's best poet of sadness:

> Sadness has its own beauty, of course. Toward dusk,
> Let us say, the river darkens and looks bruised,
> And we stand looking out at it through rain.
> It is as if life itself were somehow bruised
> > And tender at this hour; and a few tears commence.
> > Not that they are but that they *feel* immense.

Anthony Hecht

ONE OF Anthony Hecht's best-known poems, "More Light! More Light!," is an anecdote of the Holocaust:

> We move now to outside a German wood.
> Three men are there commanded to dig a hole
> In which two Jews are ordered to lie down
> And be buried alive by the third, who is a Pole.
>
> Not light from the shrine at Weimar beyond the hill
> Nor light from heaven appeared. But he did refuse.
> A Luger settled back deeply in its glove.
> He was ordered to change places with the Jews.
>
> Much casual death had drained away their souls.
> The thick dirt mounted toward the quivering chin.
> When only the head was exposed the order came
> To dig him out again and to get back in.
>
> No light, no light in the blue Polish eye.
> When he finished a riding boot packed down the earth.
> The Luger hovered lightly in its glove.
> He was shot in the belly and in three hours bled to death.

When the Pole offers a glimmer of resistance, the Jews willingly become his executioners; his momentary bravery saves no one and results in his own murder. The exclusion of moral light from this episode is insistent—the phrase "no light" is repeated four times. But what makes the atrocity especially dark to Hecht is that it occurs just outside Weimar, the "shrine" of Goethean humanism, and represents the denial of Goethe's dying plea.

The dramaturgy of culture versus barbarism is a familiar one. What makes it unusual in Hecht's poetry is that, at the same time that he reflects on the shattering of humanism, his own language continues to pay homage to it. The contrast with, for example, Paul Celan could not be greater. Hecht's regular meter and rhyme, his formal diction and clear expository sentences betray none of the uncertainty or extremity his subject seems to demand. He is like the courtier of a deposed monarch, punctually attending the shrunken levees of reason.

For more than fifty years, Hecht's poetry maintained this disciplined disjunction between form and subject. He often wrote about the forces of dissolution—evil, chaos, lust, slovenliness—but always in a decorous, ornate style, as though these subjects were explosive chemicals that could only be handled with tongs. "Goliardic Song," a small poem about "Venus Pandemos," deliberately exaggerates this decorum to the point of archness:

> We, who have been her students,
>   Matriculated clerks
> In scholia of imprudence
>   And vast, veneral Works,
> Taken and passed our orals,
>   Salute her classic poise:
> Ur-Satirist of Morals
>   And Mother of our Joys.

This is donnish and satirical. But in *The Darkness and the Light*, Hecht's last collection, the poem "Elders" is an earnest portrait of the sources and consequences of lust:

> As a boy he was awkward, pimpled, unpopular,
> Disdained by girls, avoided by other boys,
> An acned solitary. But bold and spectacular
> The lubricious dreams that such a one enjoys. . . .
>
> And so it went year by tormented year,
> His yearnings snarled in some tight, muddled sensation
> Of violence, a gout of imperiousness, fear
> And resentment yeasting in ulcered incubation.

It is characteristic of Hecht that this description, however personal its source, is meant to apply to one of the "elders" who watched Susanna bathe, in the biblical story. The self-disgust of the poem is tamed by giving it a respectable frame, by turning it into an allusion. The language itself conspires in this taming: though the words are violent, the lines are not. The rhyme scheme, the rhythm, the Latinate diction, even the cliché of the pimpled adolescent, all ward off real violence of feeling. Nor does Hecht attain such violence even when his language is deliberately coarse:

> I have been in this bar
> For close to seven days.
> The dark girl over there,
> For a modest dollar, lays.
>
> And you can get a blow-job
> Where other men have pissed

In the little room that's sacred
To the Evangelist.

This could have been a monologue by any drunk, but in fact it
is spoken by "The Man Who Married Magdalene," in Hecht's
book *The Hard Hours*. To most of Hecht's readers, however,
Mary Magdalene is not a vital symbol but merely an allusion,
and invoking her only makes the poem feel remote and literary.
While there is a moment of genuine scabrousness in these
lines—the fleeting suggestion that the prostitute's mouth is
"where other men have pissed"—the poem's other elements
work against the potential shock. There is the odd use of the
word "lays," which is usually not transitive; there is the far-
fetched joke about the Evangelist (the "John"). These things
conspire to separate the author of the poem—ill at ease with
slang, but familiar with the Bible—from its degraded speaker.

The only reason to create such a speaker in the first place,
of course, is to allow the poet to express a part of his own
nature. Hecht is never prudish or self-regarding when dealing
with vice; the man we come to know in his work is highly
prone to lust and anger. In "Poppy," he identifies anger as
another powerful foe of the light:

It builds like unseen fire deep in a mine,
This igneous, molten wrath,
This smelting torture that rises with the decline
Of reason, signifying death.

But in Hecht's work, the man who suffers these vices is usually kept at a strict remove from the poet who writes about
them. This is the cost of Hecht's defensive posture with regard

to the values of civilization. He identifies form with reason and reason with goodness, so that his poems, even when they are about evil and degrading things, are always formal, reasonable, and good. But this means that they do not really engage with evil and degrading things. They do not allow them to rise to speech, only to be spoken about.

The allure of such strictness is easy to understand, for Hecht's writing life—his first book was published in 1954, his last in 2001, three years before he died—coincided with a universal abandonment of strictness, not least in the poetic sphere. In an essay on Richard Wilbur, Hecht writes of "this poetic era of arrogant solipsism and limp narcissism—when great, shaggy herds of poets write only about themselves, or about the casual workings of their rather tedious minds." In such times, an erudite, sensitive, and earnest poet such as Hecht might well feel the burden of tradition lying heavily on his shoulders. Apollo demands much, too much, from his disciples, since the rest of the world has gone over heedlessly to Dionysus.

In "An Orphic Calling," Hecht finds a symbol of Apollonian clarity in the music of Bach, which he compares to the currents of a stream:

And from deep turbulent rapids, roiled and spun,
They rise in watery cycles to those proud
And purifying heights where they'd begun
On Jungfrau cliffs of edelweiss and cloud,

Piled cumuli, that *fons et origo*
("Too lofty and original to rage")
Of the mind's limpid unimpeded flow
Where freedom and necessity converge. . . .

An Orphic calling it is, one that invites
Responsories, a summons to lute-led
Nature, as morning's cinnabar east ignites
And the instinctive sunflower turns its head.

The metaphor of the stream rising from turbulent depths to purifying heights might seem like an orthodox account of creative sublimation. But Hecht extends the image further, and so reverses its logic. The stream itself, in this poem, begins as rain from the "piled cumuli" of Heaven: the depths begin in the heights. "The mind's limpid unimpeded flow" is the beginning and the end of art, leaving the terrestrial world as only a way station. The myth of Orpheus appears in the poem in a similarly one-sided fashion. Hecht has in mind the Orpheus who awakened Nature with his song, not the Orpheus who descended into Hell. And the poem's refusal to acknowledge this second, more famous Orphic myth is so complete that it returns with the force of the repressed, reminding us of all that is missing from Hecht's conception of art.

As "An Orphic Calling" suggests, Hecht's idea of the beautiful is of something brachiated, gemmed, baroque. His poems abound in golden descriptions, as in "Somebody's Life":

He gazed down at the breakneck rocks below,
Entranced by the water's loose attacks of jade,
The sousing waves, the interminable, blind
Fury of scattered opals, flung tiaras,
Full, hoisted, momentary chandeliers.

Perhaps because the human world is so corrupt, Hecht turns to this sort of inanimate splendor with a religious attentiveness, as he explains in "Devotions of a Painter," from *The Transparent Man*:

Cool sinuosities, waved banners of light,
Unfurl, remesh, and round upon themselves
In a continual turmoil of benign
Cross-purposes, effortlessly as fish. . . .
I am an elderly man in a straw hat
Who has set himself the task of praising God
For all this welter by setting out my paints
And getting as much truth as can be managed
Onto a small flat canvas.

As the lines themselves acknowledge, however, there is a limit to the truth that can be captured in this way. It really does require a painter to make such scenes come to life, in all their detail and individuality. It is hard to distinguish one description of light from another; language drives toward abstraction, and in spite of itself makes what is seen into a symbol. This fact presents less of a problem to a poet, like Dante, for whom light is explicitly symbolic of the divine. In that case, it is less necessary that we see the light than that we understand it. But Hecht, like many other poets of his time, adopted a sort of Flemish-painting spirituality, in which the detailed observation of nature is itself a kind of prayer, a way of "praising God" for the sheer fact of existence. And in this form of attention, whose whole reason for being is detail, the inability of poetry to capture visual detail is a serious impairment.

Hecht's best and most original poems, in fact, have not been still lifes but long dramatic monologues, especially those in his 1979 book *The Venetian Vespers.* The title poem of that book, spoken by a dying man in Venice, is perhaps Hecht's best. His elevated language, slowly unrolling in blank verse, is entirely appropriate to the atmosphere of elegance run to seed. Hecht's Venice, which is the sordid city of Aschenbach, provides an

objective correlative for the darkness the poet usually holds at
a distance:

> Returning suddenly to the chalk-white sunlight
> Of out-of-doors, one spots among the tourists
> Those dissolute young with heavy-lidded gazes
> Of cool, clear-eyed, stony depravity
> That in the course of only a few years
> Will fade into the terrifying boredom
> In the faces of Carpaccio's prostitutes.

One can see the difference between observing "depravity"
and merely attacking it by comparing this convincing portrait
of the "dissolute young" with the lampoon against them in "To
L. E. Sissman, 1928–1976":

> Dear friend, whose poetry of Brooklyn flats
> And poker sharps broadcasts the tin pan truths
> Of all our yesterdays, speaks to our youths
> In praise of both Wallers, Edmund and Fats,
>
> And will be ringing in some distant ear
> When the Mod-est, last immodesty fatigues,
> All Happenings have happened, the Little Leagues
> Of Pop and pop-fly poets disappear. . . .

Here, the younger generation, its fashions and behavior, are
irritably dismissed in a way that sounds close to old-fogeyism.
What the narrator of "The Venetian Vespers" can observe and
communicate, Hecht writing in his own voice must isolate and
oppose. Of course, this is a smaller, more jocular poem. But
there is a distinct souring of Hecht's tone whenever he defends

the old against the new, tradition against fad. In *The Darkness and the Light*, "Rara Avis in Terra" is similarly marred by its attacks on English-department feminists:

> The ladies' auxiliary of the raptor clan
> With their bright cutlery,
> Sororal to a man.
> And feeling peckish, they foresee
> An avian banquet in the sky,
> Feasting off dead white European males,
> Or local living ones, if all else fails.

In general, it may be said that Hecht's impersonal narrative poems are his best. (This makes him exceptional among contemporary poets, whose excursions into narrative are usually failed experiments.) In *The Darkness and the Light*, there are no poems on the scale of "The Venetian Vespers," but "A Fall," "A Brief Account of Our City," and "1945" are in the same category. "1945" reports an incident from World War II, in which a French family seems willing to sacrifice their son's life in order to keep their bicycle hidden from a German officer. As in "More Light! More Light!," Hecht is calling our attention to human evil, and his remote, objective tone is that of a judge admitting an exhibit into evidence:

> It wasn't charity. Perhaps mere prudence,
> Saving a valuable round of ammunition
> For some more urgent crisis. Whatever it was,
> The soldier reslung his rifle on his shoulder,
> Turned wordlessly and walked on down the road
> The departed German vehicles had taken.

This narrative is especially strong in contrast to the other two parts of the sequence, "Sacrifice," to which it belongs. These are monologues by Abraham and Isaac about the sacrifice of Isaac, averted by God at the last minute. The story is so well known that it demands some original interpretation or striking new idiom to make it live again. But Hecht's language here is sedate and literary: "Youthful I was and trusting and strong of limb,/The fresh-split firewood roped tight to my back,/And I bore unknowing that morning my funeral pyre." The diction and the inversions make this sound like the speech, not of any actual person or period, but of Poetry itself.

This is a persistent temptation in Hecht's verse, another facet of his desire to defend and continue a tradition, for it is always difficult for a poet to be sure when he is renewing tradition and when he is only echoing it. For the same reason, allusion is problematic in Hecht's poetry. His work is saturated with reference, especially to Shakespeare, but the effect is often to make it seem as though texts have replaced things as the objects of thought. "I had the gift, and arrived at the technique/That called up spirits from the vasty deep," says the speaker in "The Witch of Endor." But the second line is so instantly recognizable as Glendower's, in *Henry IV*, that it works against its context. Glendower's claim is meant to be vain and boastful, quickly parried by Hotspur: "But will they come when you have called for them?" Yet Hecht does not seem to wish to undermine the reader's faith in the witch's powers. It is rather that his mind moves so much in the Shakespearean realm that the idea of conjuring immediately calls forth the quotation. And this opens a gulf between the poet's mind and that of the witch whose voice he is attempting to assume. Allusion becomes another way in which the poet keeps his subject under moral quarantine.

Hecht's strengths—seriousness, intelligence, formal discipline—are all rare in contemporary American poetry. He expressed, as well as any writer of the last fifty years, the resolve of the cultured mind faced with the enormous barbarism of the modern world. But that very stance is also what set the limit to his poetic achievement. It is not necessary for a modern poet to take chaos as his theme; but if he does, it may be necessary for him to accede to that chaos, to allow it into his very speech, as Lowell and Berryman and Plath did in their various ways. It is to them, rather than to Hecht, that future readers will turn for a sense of what it was like to live, and suffer, in the late twentieth century.

Theodore Roethke and James Wright

ON AUGUST 22, 1957, Pete Rademacher fought Floyd Patterson in Seattle for the world heavyweight championship. In the crowd that day were two boxing fans who were also members of the English Department of the University of Washington: Theodore Roethke, a forty-nine-year-old professor, and James Wright, a thirty-year-old graduate student. Roethke had bought the tickets to celebrate Wright's taking his Ph.D.; the same year also saw the publication of Wright's first book of poems, *The Green Wall*, which had been chosen by W. H. Auden for the Yale Younger Poets series. Roethke, meanwhile, had won the Pulitzer Prize for his last book, *The Waking*, published in 1953.

The crowd that day could not have suspected that they had in their midst the leading American poets of two generations. But neither Roethke, the son of a greenhouse owner from Saginaw, Michigan, nor Wright, the son of a factory worker from Martins Ferry, Ohio, regarded a prizefight as an incongruous setting for poets. On the contrary, they imported the vocabulary of boxing—its masculine swagger, its perpetual ranking—into their discussions of poetry, or at least of that less sublime thing, the "poetry world." "Allen Tate," Wright assured Roethke later that year, "certainly seems to think you're the Heavyweight Champion of contemporary American poetry." It must have been music to the ears of the older poet, who approached his rivals in a fighting crouch: "Those limp-pricks," he bragged to the critic Kenneth Burke, "I can write rings around any of them." Meanwhile, Wright defined his own view of poetry, in a letter to James Dickey, by saying that without "the high joy which is all that matters . . . poetry is considerably less interesting than boxing."

But as is so often the case, these growls and verbal fisticuffs were the most fragile of carapaces. For there are few American poets more acutely tenderhearted, more genuinely and at times dismayingly sensitive, than Roethke and Wright. Roethke wrote about the secret life of flowers, plants, and children, while Wright allied himself with the dispossessed and the outcast of American society. Both were deeply sentimental about women, especially after each found happiness in a late marriage. And they were still more vulnerable on the subject of fathers—the harsh, unemotional fathers they strove to resemble and defy, and about whom they wrote some of their best poems.

In their correspondence, however, Roethke and Wright stepped gingerly around the obvious paternal element in their relationship. "I've spent practically the whole of three sessions with my doctor yacking about you," Roethke wrote Wright in 1958. "Apparently you're more of an emotional symbol to me than I realized: a combination of student–younger brother—something like that. (I even shed a tear or two.)" Wright was equally careful to avoid the father-son metaphor. "I've never directly told you what I think of you," he had written earlier the same year, "because I'm afraid you would think I am turning you into a father. I swear I never have thought of you as a father." Wright's praise for his teacher finally relaxes into more comfortably masculine territory: "I myself feel funny about writing it down on paper. It's as though I were reminding myself that I am breathing, or that I am happy, or that I just won a fist-fight."

It makes sense that these sensitive, taciturn men, battered by their demons and their ambitions, dreamed of a communion of souls beyond or below the level of language. In their poetry, they attempted to forge a new kind of speech, for which literary sophistication was unnecessary and even inimical. At a few precious moments, they even managed to achieve it. But in the long run, both Roethke and Wright paid a high price for their hope that earnestness could do the work of eloquence.

The idea that modernist poetry had gotten too difficult—too remote from ordinary language and subjects, too hard to understand, too hard even to write—was by no means limited to Roethke and Wright. It was practically the only thing that united American poets of the middle third of the twentieth century—academic and populist, New York and San Francisco, the students of John Crowe Ransom and the students of Allen Ginsberg. It was the thirst of these poets—those born, roughly, between 1905 and 1930—for an alternative to the strenuous complexities of high modernism, as defined by the example and precept of Eliot and Pound, that led to the explosion of new schools in mid-century American poetry: the Beats, the confessionalism of Lowell and Berryman, the projective verse of Charles Olson, and the "deep image" poetry with which Wright and Robert Bly would be associated. In their different ways, each of these groups sought to break through what had become the obstacle of modernism, though none of them could or wanted to abjure the immense resources of language modernism had opened up.

Like so many poets of their time, both Roethke and Wright had to violently dislocate their own early styles, in order to escape what came to seem a glib, received facility. Each of them started out as a conventional, formally accomplished poet—Roethke in his 1941 debut, *Open House*, Wright in *The Green*

Wall—before achieving the breakthrough that made his name. But these two poets were unusual in their deep and early mistrust, not just of modernism, but of the whole idea of poetic sophistication. The products of working-class families, the only budding writers in their towns, Roethke and Wright remained wary of the seductions of fluency, abstraction, art for art's sake. To justify or redeem their calling, it seemed, they had to insist that it was not an elite pastime but something primal, and therefore essentially, if not actually, democratic.

This anxiety can be seen in remarkably parallel statements made by each poet when still in his teens, long before the two had met. In 1926 or 1927, when he was a sophomore at the University of Michigan, Roethke turned in an essay for a writing course in which he defensively announced his "sincerity—that prime virtue of any creative worker. I write only what I believe to be the absolute truth," he insisted, "even if I must ruin the theme in so doing. In this respect I feel far superior to those glib people in my classes who often garner better grades than I do. They are so often pitiful frauds—artificial—insincere. They have a line that works. They do not write from the depths of their hearts. Nothing of theirs was ever born of pain. Many an incoherent yet sincere piece of writing has outlived the polished product."

Of course, Roethke would move far beyond the provincial defensiveness of this essay, to become one of the boldest and most erudite of American poets. (His course on verse writing, which he taught for decades at a series of colleges, was legendarily thorough. "Here was an assignment," Wright remembered many years later; "he wanted us to go to the library and find ten or maybe even twenty iambic trimeter lines that had a caesura after the first syllable.") But he clung to the belief that "sincerity" and "polish" are finally opposing values—a dichotomy that, in the work of the greatest poets, simply fails to arise.

In the luckiest phase of his career, Roethke did succeed in making magic out of "incoherence," inventing a suitable language for the shapeless urgency of the id. "One belief: 'One must go back to go forward,'" he wrote to Burke in 1946. "And by back I mean down into the consciousness of the race itself not just the quandaries of adolescence, damn it." In *Open House,* Roethke's verse was constrained by the neo-Romantic neatness of his early influences—especially Louise Bogan, who was briefly Roethke's lover and, more durably, his mentor and friend. Even in those early poems, however, Roethke was drawn to images that could not help seeming Freudian and Jungian, to metaphors of subterranean forces and painful hidden blockages. "The teeth of knitted gears/Turn slowly through the night,/But the true substance bears/The hammer's weight," he wrote in "The Adamant"; or, in a more overtly Freudian vein, in "My Dim-Wit Cousin": "The cost of folly is forever mounting,/Your bed collapses from imagined sins."

Like most talented poets, Roethke had wandered into his true subject before he invented a style that could accommodate it. The creation of that style in the mid-1940s was an arduous triumph, requiring him to descend to the primeval sources of the English language, and to the primal scenes of his own childhood. His biographer, Allan Seager, records that, while working on the poems of what would become his best book—*The Lost Son*, published in 1948—Roethke sometimes went around the house naked, a token of a larger stripping down.

The first fruit of this effort was the famous "greenhouse poems," in which Roethke evokes the scenes and locales where his childhood was spent. It was a poetic windfall for Roethke that his father owned one of the largest greenhouses in Michigan, allowing him to fill his poems with immediately legible symbols of psychic growth—roots, stems, blossoms. But it

took his talent for powerfully indirect evocation to make the
greenhouse not just a metaphor, but an eerily living presence,
as in "Root Cellar":

And what a congress of stinks!—
Roots ripe as old bait,
Pulpy stems, rank, silo-rich,
Leaf-mold, manure, lime, piled against slippery planks.
Nothing would give up life:
Even the dirt kept breathing a small breath.

A century and a half after Wordsworth, Roethke manages to
invent an entirely new kind of nature poetry, in which the earth
is not reassuringly earthy, but teeming and alien. At times,
Roethke's greenhouse becomes an uncanny phantasmagoria:
"So many devouring infants!/Soft luminescent fingers,/Lips
neither dead nor alive,/Loose ghostly mouths/Breathing."
Lines like these, from "The Orchids," show just how much
Sylvia Plath learned from Roethke about how to make the
reader shiver.

It is a sign of Roethke's talent and seriousness as a poet that
the greenhouse poems, which were miles beyond anything he
had written before, did not exhaust his inventiveness, but
refreshed it. Already in *The Lost Son*, he began the sequence of
poems he would wrestle with for the next several years—what
he described as "a series of longer pieces which try, in their
rhythms, to catch the movement of the mind itself, to trace the
spiritual history of a protagonist (not 'I' personally but of all
haunted and harried men)." If poems like "Weed Puller" had
shown the poet pressing himself as close to nature as he could
get—"Me down in that fetor of weeds,/Crawling on all

fours"—Roethke's next major sequence attempted to vault the barrier of sentience, to speak with nature's own voice.

From *The Lost Son,* through his next book, *Praise to the End!* (1951), all the way to the Pulitzer Prize–winning *The Waking* (1953), Roethke would extend and experiment with this new style. But he never accomplished more with it than in "The Lost Son," the first poem in the sequence. Like *The Waste Land,* whose influence is profound but seldom obvious, "The Lost Son" dispenses with plot and argument for the sake of a more powerful impressionism. The poem charts the emotions of a man grieving the death of his father, and it progresses not through a series of events but through a chain of moods: grief, nostalgia, regression to childhood terrors, and finally a tentative reawakening to adulthood. Appropriately, Roethke draws from the deepest wells of English literature—Mother Goose, Shakespeare, the Bible—in order to create a new idiom for primal experiences:

> All the leaves stuck out their tongues;
> I shook the softening chalk of my bones,
> Saying,
> Snail, snail, glister me forward,
> Bird, soft sigh me home,
> Worm, be with me.
> This is my hard time.

"The Lost Son" is the peak of Roethke's inventiveness as a poet. But his attempt to extend its discoveries into a series of poems exposed the limitations of this style: without the momentum of narrative, it quickly grows static. There are wonderful passages in Roethke's next book, *Praise to the End!*, which manage to capture childish orality and sexuality with a disturbing vividness. But by the time of "O, Thou Opening, O," from

The Waking, the poet himself is clearly sick of his own style: "And now are we to have that pelludious Jesus-shimmer over all things, the animal's candid gaze, a shade less than feathers. . . . I'm tired of all that, Bag-Foot."

Yet when Roethke tried to return to a more explicit and formal style, the limits of his sensibility were harshly exposed. Roethke had none of the interest in the outside world—in history and human relations, metaphysics and morality—which poets must increasingly bring into their work if they are to develop. ("Ted had hardly any general *ideas* at all," Auden reportedly said.) And his late poems, from *The Waking* through *The Far Field*, are crowded with limp, quasi-mystical abstractions: "I learned not to fear infinity,/The far field, the windy cliffs of forever,/The dying of time in the white light of tomorrow." When Roethke died in 1963, of a sudden heart attack, his enduring work was a decade behind him. What is most shocking is the way Roethke fell back into direct imitation of other poets, especially Yeats and the Eliot of *Four Quartets*. Imitation as direct as Roethke's of Yeats, in "The Dance," is usually found only in very young poets, not accomplished masters. It was as though, having spent his windfall, Roethke tried to keep up appearances by echoing those brilliantly authoritative voices.

The truth, however, is that Roethke's only real subject was his own inwardness. He wrote best when he could dislocate language into a nearly private idiom, evoking shades of feeling that could never be paraphrased or systematized. "Much of the style," he acknowledged, "is based on shifts in association. Now, either these are imaginatively right or they're not." It is a return, decades later, to his teenage opposition of "sincerity" and "polish." If the poet feels intensely enough, Roethke holds, that feeling will spill over to the reader; if not, no amount of artifice will heal the breach.

This is why Roethke was always at a loss when confronted with readers' inquiries about what his poems meant. They could not be elucidated, he felt, only intuited. "Believe," he adjured the reader; "you will have no trouble if you approach these poems as a child would, naïvely, with your whole being awake, your faculties loose and alert." From there, it is only a short step to insisting that the poet's failure of communication is actually the reader's failure of sensitivity, or even of goodwill. "Poetry is written for the whole man; it sometimes scares those who want to hide from the terrors of existence, from themselves," Roethke wrote in 1953. But it is exactly the whole man who does not appear in Roethke's poetry, as it does, for example, in Lowell's or Auden's. Those poets know many parts of human experience, while Roethke knows only one. Yet that one is exceptionally difficult to capture in words; and the fact that Roethke did capture it, in a handful of poems, guarantees him a permanent place in American poetry.

Almost two decades after Roethke wrote his student essay defending sincerity against polish, the eighteen-year-old James Wright took up the same issue, in a letter to an encouraging professor who had agreed to read his poems. "As you read them," Wright warned, "you will be conscious of the absence of a syllable here and there, and even of the discarding of iambics altogether. I would rather sacrifice technical skill than sincerity. And I have let the rhythm of emotion govern many of the lines rather than the rhythm of Milton." Throughout his career, Wright, even more than Roethke, would gamble on the obvious intensity of his emotions—his loneliness, compassion, wonder—to accomplish more than mere technique ever could.

Wright's revulsion against the whole idea of "technical skill" was all the more extreme thanks to his early proficiency as a writer of traditional verse. In his first book, the poet Dudley

Fitts noted in a review, Wright "work[s] quietly. If audacity is what you're after, there's not much of it." Instead, there was a polished, traditional literary language: "For who could bear such beauty under the sky?/I would have held her loveliness in air." Yet Wright had emerged from a still less literary milieu than Roethke. "My mother had to leave school when she was in the sixth grade, my father had to leave when he was in the eighth grade," Wright recalled near the end of his life. "He went into the factory when he was fourteen and my mother went to work in a laundry." Wright would often honor his father's lifetime of manual labor in his poems: "one slave/To Hazel-Atlas Glass became my father," he wrote in "At the Executed Murderer's Grave," one of his best early poems. But already in that poem, from Wright's second collection, *Saint Judas* (1959), he was moving beyond the pastoral elegance of his earliest work, straining to incorporate the real atmosphere of working-class Ohio:

> I waste no pity on the dead that stink,
> And no love's lost between me and the crying
> Drunks of Belaire, Ohio, where police
> Kick at their kidneys till they die of drink.

The real crisis in Wright's development, however, came in July 1958, a time of violent transition that is fascinatingly documented in his correspondence. The stylistic revolution that was to produce his best poetry was provoked by a passing insult in a review, by James Dickey, of the famous anthology *New Poets of England and America*, edited by Donald Hall, Robert Pack, and Louis Simpson. In that volume, Wright took his place alongside many of the poets who were to dominate late twentieth-century poetry—Richard Wilbur, Adrienne Rich, Anthony Hecht, and Geoffrey Hill were all included. But Dickey was not

the only reader to find the anthology, in his words, "representative of a generation that has as yet exhibited very little passion, urgency, or imagination." Among the poets to come in for
a scolding was Wright, whose work was dismissed in just two
words—"ploddingly sincere."

After Dickey's essay appeared in the *Sewanee Review*, Wright
wrote him an extraordinarily defensive letter. "Since you both
think and feel that my verses stink, it is your responsibility as
well as your privilege to say so in print. But even if my poems
are bad," he pleaded, "I am asking you to believe, purely on
faith, that I do indeed care about poetry in *some* sense." He went
on to describe Dickey's critical technique in a way that could
not fail to give offense: "Sometimes students have cautiously
and tentatively brought verses to me, under that somewhat silly
impression of very young people that my having had something
in print made me a valid judge; when their verses were sentimental and inept, I believe that I have criticized them honestly
and severely; however, I have never greeted a student by telling
her to go fuck herself and shove her hideous poems up her ass."

But when Dickey replied angrily to this attack from out of
the blue, Wright did not stick to his guns; instead he launched
into an orgy of contrition and self-reproach. "As I sit here," he
admitted, "I think I know why I was hurt. You simply said that I
was not a poet. This remark of yours only confirmed what—
obviously enough—is a central fear of mine, and which I have
been deeply struggling to face for some time." Wright's doubts
about his highly praised work were only compounded by
another shock he received the very same week, when he read
the first issue of Robert Bly's new little magazine, *The Fifties*.
The motto on the magazine's inside front cover—"The editors
of this magazine think that most of the poetry published in
America today is too old-fashioned"—gives a good sense of its

missionary impishness, and it made a huge impression on the vulnerable Wright. Just two days after his mea culpa to Dickey, Wright wrote to Bly, entirely renouncing his early work: "My book was dead. It could have been written by a dead man, if they have Corona typewriters in the grave."

In the space of a week, Wright had been converted to what Bly called, in an essay in the second issue of *The Fifties*, "the new poetry." Bly insisted that the "old style, with the iamb, its caesuras, its rhymes, its thousands of rhythms reminding us of other poems and other countries . . . is like a man speaking who gestures too much. . . . But in the new poetry, the contrary is true—there is no necessity in the form itself for continual gesture, by rhyme, etc.—therefore, if you raise your little finger once, slowly, it has tremendous meaning."

This metaphor perfectly describes the technique of the first volume Wright produced after his conversion: *The Branch Will Not Break*, published in 1963. The book contains much of Wright's best writing, which indeed wagers everything on the effectiveness of small, dramatic gestures. The most famous example comes in "Lying in a Hammock at William Duffy's Farm in Pine Island, Minnesota," a favorite specimen for workshops in free verse. Duffy was Bly's coeditor on *The Fifties*, so it is fitting that his farm was the site of Wright's demonstration of "the new poetry," or what would come to be called "deep image" poetry.

The poem is a catalogue of meticulously observed natural details—"the bronze butterfly / Asleep on the black trunk," "The droppings of last year's horses"—which concludes with a sudden, seemingly unjustified swerve: "A chicken hawk floats over, looking for home. / I have wasted my life." The last line indicates how "deep image" poetry differs from the Imagism of the 1910s: it is not the visual composition that matters to Wright, but the way things seen mysteriously provoke an inward experience. And for Wright—as for Roethke, who declared that his leaps of association "either . . . are imaginatively right or they're not"—the link between things seen and things felt cannot be artfully prepared. "I think, in the new style, where the tension and density of the emotion is everything, you have to, like a good gambler, agree to stake everything on one throw," he wrote to Bly. If the reader doesn't agree that the poet has rolled a seven—if, like Thom Gunn, he regards that famous last line as "a general observation that may well have occurred to the poet after he perceived the images, but is for us connected with them by neither logic nor association"—there is no way of convincing him otherwise.

Still more than Roethke, then, Wright is tempted to turn his poems' aesthetic gamble into a moral test. Increasingly, after his quasi-religious conversion to Bly's principles ("I . . . feel as if I had risen from the dead"), he would evaluate his own and other people's poetry on ethical grounds. As he wrote to Donald Hall, "Whatever a poet has been in the past, right now he is defined, to me, as a man who has both the power and the courage to see, and then, to show, the truth through words. If I'm a bad poet, that means a liar."

The effects of this principle on Wright's own work, however, were decidedly mixed. In his work of the 1960s, Wright's determination "to show the truth" can give his voice a taciturn credibility, as in "Speak": "To speak in a flat voice/Is all that I can do.//I speak of flat defeat/In a flat voice." But often in his later work, up to his death in 1980, Wright strips from his poetry the very artifice that can turn a private experience into a shared work of art. In his quest to make poetry an instrument of communion, he descends to melodramatic reporting on his own emotions: "I feel lonesome,/And sick at heart,/Frightened,/And I don't know/Why." And he wards off any doubts

about this style—his own or his readers'—with a kind of truc-
ulent sincerity:

> This is not a poem.
> This is not an apology to the Muse.
> This is the cold-blooded plea of a homesick vampire
> To his brother and friend.
> If you do not care one way or another about
> The preceding lines,
> Please do not go on listening
> On any account of mine.
> Please leave the poem.
> Thank you.

But the job of the poet is to make the reader want to care,
not to demand his sympathy as the price of admission to the
poem. Wright's and Roethke's aesthetics of sincerity not only
leave no room for some of the greatest English poems—
masterpieces of artifice like "Lycidas," or "The Eve of Saint
Agnes." They end up allowing the poet to be too easy on himself, to believe that right feeling is more important than good
writing. In a 1961 essay, Wright made this denigration of
artistry explicit: "It should be unnecessary to say that gentle-
ness and courage in dealing with a subject matter very close to
life as the creatures who live it are primarily matters of personal character; and that, where the character is lacking, no
amount of literary skill can substitute for it." But it should be
equally unnecessary to say that the reverse is also true: gentle-
ness and courage, unfortunately perhaps, are unavailing without the colder virtues of the artist.

Kenneth Koch

No LESS than the politicians, the American poets of the 1950s knew that they were living through the United States' Augustan moment. Most of them looked on anxiously as a putative republic was translated into a frank empire. But the poets of the American Century were never immune to its dark glamour. Delmore Schwartz fantasized about the role he would be invited to play in an Adlai Stevenson administration; others pinned their hopes on JFK. Even those who felt called to resist American power recognized that it was power that called them. None of the great modernists of the 1920s would have chosen the ancestors Robert Lowell claimed in "Beyond the Alps":

> Rome asked for poets. At her beck and call,
> came Lucan, Tacitus and Juvenal,
> the *black republicans* who tore the tits
> and bowels of the Mother Wolf to bits. . . .

But if New York was to be the new Rome, it needed celebrants as well as satirists—not just its Juvenal but its Ovid and Horace and Catullus. It found them in the New York School poets, whose sensibilities were forged in the city of the early 1950s. Frank O'Hara, John Ashbery, James Schuyler, and Kenneth Koch are poets of very different gifts and attainments, but all their best work retains something of the period: its amphetamine jumpiness, its abstract-expressionist bravery. They resemble the Latin and English Augustans not so much in their verse, which is the opposite of classical, as in their easy assumption of their own and their city's centrality. The egotism and in-jokes of the New York School are warranted, if at all, only by the instinctive confidence of an atomic-age *jeunesse dorée*.

Frank O'Hara's "Personism" may have been a rebellion against modernist impersonality; but still more, it was a product of the same metropolitan ease that allowed Catullus to make his poems a running conversation with friends he might meet in the Forum. We don't need to know who O'Hara is talking about to know that we want to know them, or ought to:

> Where is Mike Goldberg? I don't know,
> he may be in the Village far below
> or lounging on Tenth Street with the gang
> of early-morning painters (before noon)
> as they discuss the geste or jest
> of action painting. . . .

The New York School poets incarnated this kind of glamour, but among them, only Kenneth Koch made it his explicit theme. His *Collected Poems*, which includes all his shorter poems from 1952 until his death in 2002, breaks decisively in two around 1975. Before *The Art of Love*, published in that year, Koch is buoyant, clowning, exclamatory—a rhapsode of friendship and love, the very heaven of being young in the Cold War dawn. Afterwards, he becomes the elegist of that dawn, writing with nostalgic plainness about the experiences that once inspired his insouciant surrealism.

What remains constant in both phases of his poetry is Koch's civilized and civilian spirit, his belief in pleasure as the highest good:

> Oh the pleasures of Peace are infinite and they cannot be
>   counted—
> One single piece of pink mint chewing gum contains more
>   pleasures
> Than the whole rude gallery of war!

This poem, "The Pleasures of Peace," provided the title of a collection published in 1969—a year when most poets would sooner have seen peace as a moral imperative. Koch's refusal to join them—"To my contemporaries I'll leave the Horrors of War,/They can do them better than I," he half jokes—is brightly subversive, as is his choice of emblem. Chewing gum is as pure a product of America as one could hope for, but it is not the kind American literature usually likes to celebrate.

Similarly, in "Thanksgiving," what Koch gives thanks for is the disappearance of the very Indians whom that holiday sentimentally honors. Without European civilization, Koch reminds us, there would be no place for delights that are artificial, unnutritive, "modern":

> there were a New York
> It would be a city of tents, and what do you suppose
> Our art and poetry would be like? For the community! the
>   tribe!
> No beautiful modern abstract pictures, no mad
>   incomprehensible
> Free lovable poems!

This slightly hysterical frivolity is not just the natural register of Koch's New York. It is also a form of rebellion against the conspicuous seriousness of his poetic elders. In a couple of late, anecdotal poems, Schwartz, in particular, emerges as the stifling modernist superego to Koch's rollicking postmodern id. Koch had been a student of Schwartz's at Harvard—he attended on the G.I. Bill, after serving in the Pacific during World War II—and he found the older Jewish poet an impossible role model:

> In the old days a good place to publish a poem was the *Partisan Review*. Heady—among those thick, heavy pages—one felt ranked by the rankers, a part of the move, a part of the proof—toward what? of what? To find out, you had to read countless *Partisan Review*s. Then you would see what it was. You could be as serious as Delmore Schwartz, as serious as anyone who ever lived. He consistently turned down my poems.

Only against this particular poetic background does the dandyism of the early New York School poets make sense. Rather than be "as serious as anyone who ever lived," Koch aspired to be a breath of "Fresh Air"—the title of his celebrated rant against the academic poetry of the 1950s:

> At the Poem Society a black-haired man stands up to say
> "You make me sick with all your talk about restraint and
>   mature talent!
> Haven't you ever looked out the window at a painting by
>   Matisse. . . .
> Did you ever glance inside a bottle of sparkling pop,
> Or see a citizen split in two by the lightning?"

To be as fizzy as pop ("You're that famous COKE, aren't you?" he puns) was Koch's early ambition. At the very beginning, in fact, he was so carbonated as to be indigestible. The *Collected Poems* opens with the Dadaist poems Koch wrote between 1952 and 1954, which makes sense chronologically but feels like an editorial mistake. Even Koch didn't collect this work until near the end of his life, in the volume *Sun Out*, and then with a kind of disclaimer: "a way of using language that was very stirring to me and seemed to mean a lot." Whatever these strings of words meant to their author, their actual purpose was to wave a placard labeled "Avant-Garde": "Ocean of Nibelungenlied! Romulus/ Satie Mellon canard shoeflex Greene/Dairy farmer. Virus."

This is an unpleasant introduction to the *Collected Poems*, though there is no doubt a type of reader, even today, who will find it fruitfully daring. With his first published book, *Thank You and Other Poems* (1962), Koch made a large step toward coherence. Because his late work often reads like a guide, or even a poem-by-poem gloss, to his early work, we even know what provoked the change: falling in love with a married Russian woman, whom he calls "Marina" in several poems. In his first, undergraduate poems, Koch remembers in "To Marina," he "had been thinking about songs which were very abstract./Language was the champion. . . ." Love gave him the pressure of a subject for the first time: "And in the heat/Of writing to you I wrote simply."

But not too simply. The Koch of *Thank You* is close to Ashbery in his ability to sound like sense without always making it. He advertises this elusive, wavering style in "On the Great Atlantic Rainway," the first poem in the book:

And that is the modern idea of fittingness,
To, always in motion, lose nothing, although beneath the
Rainway they move in threes and twos completely
Ruined for themselves, like moving pictures. . . .

Yet always beneath the rainway unsyntactical
Beauty might leap up!

That leaping beauty, however, is more a matter of willed mood than of achieved language. Koch cultivates the New York School's trademark wide-eyed zaniness, which can be charming in small doses, as in his best love poems—"To You" or "In Love with You." But Koch's range is more limited than his colleagues. There is nothing in his work to match the occasional plangency of O'Hara or sublimity of Ashbery. All of these poets employ wit, in the Johnsonian sense of yoking unlike things forcibly together, but with Koch this yoking often comes to seem rote.

In fact, many of his comic poems rely on repeating, with diminishing returns, a simple formula announced in the first lines. This is the case with one of his best-known poems, "Taking a Walk with You," where the joke is the variety of things the poet "misunderstands": "I misunderstand generally Oklahoma and Arkansas, though I think I understand New Mexico. . . . / I misunderstand Renaissance life," and so on. Koch relied on this technique throughout his career: three decades after "Taking a Walk with You," in the 1994 volume *One Train*, he is doing similar riffs, this time on a railway sign that declares "One Train May Hide Another" ("In a family one sister may conceal another").

Here, as in other aspects of his work, Koch displays that lack of moderation, of tact, which is so important a part of the New York School's aesthetic. All of them believed in writing often and at length, in a way that comes to seem self-indulgent and even a little bullying. Fluency, of course, was another part of their revolt against the costive New Critics, as Koch suggests in "The Art of Poetry," one of the essay-poems in *The Art of Love*: "'If I can write one good poem a year, / I am grateful,' the noted

Poet says, or 'six' or 'three.' Well, maybe for that Poet,/But for you, fellow Paddler, and for me, perhaps not." More immediately, it was an effect of their coterie coziness. They celebrated one another with a consciously excessive, "gratuitous" enthusiasm, as O'Hara wrote in "3 Poems About Kenneth Koch": "Under the careful care of our admiration his greatness/ appears like the French for 'gratuitous act,' and we're proud/of our Hermes, the fastest literary figure of his time."

In the first half of Koch's writing life, these friendships were the background to his poetry; starting in the mid-1970s, they became his explicit subject. The autobiographical turn is announced in "The Circus," in *The Art of Love*, which returns to an earlier poem of the same title and reveals the circumstances of its composition: "I remember when I wrote The Circus/I was living in Paris. . . ." In this phase, Koch writes prosily about the dramatis personae of his glorious youth:

> I never mentioned my friends in my poems at the time I wrote
>   The Circus
> Although they meant almost more than anything to me. . . .
> John Ashbery Jane Freilicher Larry Rivers Frank O'Hara
> Their names alone bring tears to my eyes

Those names make increasingly frequent appearances in his late work, which sometimes takes on a definite chimes-at-midnight quality. This is entirely in keeping with the professorial persona that emerges from the prankster's chrysalis—the don who amuses himself by constructing a very long parody of Thomson's "The Seasons." In an essay-poem like "Some General Instructions," Koch's sunniness has mellowed into a tired humanism, reminiscent of the late Auden's, which expresses itself in deflationary maxims: "You should be glad/To be alive. You must try to be as good as you can."

The *Collected Poems* still has one pleasure in store, however, thanks to the late flowering of Koch's wit in *New Addresses* (2000). Here again Koch relies on a comic formula, but it is a happy one: each poem is cast as an address to some unlikely concept or object. This allows Koch to compose a wittily fragmentary memoir, in poems like "To Psychoanalysis," "To My Twenties," and "To Stammering." More important, by transforming every subject into a "you," it allows Koch to approach them with the enlivening ease he always found in his friendships. This makes *New Addresses* a fitting consummation of the limited ideal that always drove Koch's poetry: "an ideal/Of conversation—entirely about me/But including almost everything else in the world."

Philip Larkin

IN THE MID-1990S, Maeve Brennan—a colleague of Philip Larkin's for thirty years, and his lover for nearly half that time—mentioned to a new acquaintance that she used to work at the Hull University Library. Immediately the woman cried: "You don't mean to say you worked for that ABOMINABLE man!"

That abominable man had been known, until his death in 1985, as England's greatest poet. But in 1993, after the publication of Larkin's selected letters and a biography by Andrew Motion, he suddenly became—in the gleeful rhetoric of Britain's book-page pundits—"rancid and insidious," "repellent, smelly, inadequate," "a petty-bourgeois fascist." What mattered most about Larkin, it seemed, was not that he wrote some of the best English poems of the twentieth century— "Church Going," "The Whitsun Weddings," "Faith Healing," "Aubade"—but his taste for pornography, and his occasional use of racial slurs. As Martin Amis wrote at the time, "The word 'Larkinesque' used to evoke the wistful, the provincial, the crepuscular, the sad, the unloved; now it evokes the scabrous and the supremacist."

Even worse, it seemed that Larkin's poetry would become a casualty of the scandal. One prominent professor of English editorialized (under the headline "Philip Larkin's letters have exposed him as a misogynist and racist—defending him is despicable") that he had been "edged . . . from centre to margin" of English literature. A columnist for the *Library Association Record* demanded that Larkin's books be banned from libraries. The whole sordid episode seemed to confirm, with a vengeance, what Larkin once told an interviewer: "I think it's very sensible not to let people know what you're like."

Yet in 2003, when the Poetry Book Society commissioned a poll of Britain's favorite poets of the last fifty years, Larkin came in first, above T. S. Eliot, W. H. Auden, Ted Hughes, and Seamus Heaney. It appeared that what he called, admiringly, "the cash customers of poetry" had not forgotten Larkin the writer. And in 2004, as if to symbolize Larkin's rehabilitation, his literary executor, Anthony Thwaite, produced a new edition of his *Collected Poems*.

The symmetry was perfect, for it could be said that the publication of the first Collected Larkin, in 1988, marked the beginning of his posthumous slide. Almost all of Larkin's important poems are found in three slim books, published at long intervals: *The Less Deceived* (1955), *The Whitsun Weddings* (1964), and *High Windows* (1974). He was a rigorous judge of his own work, waiting years to publish some poems, and refusing to let others ever see the light of day. What's more, he carefully planned the order of his collections. "I treat them like a music-hall bill," he told an interviewer, "you know, contrast, difference in length, the comic, the Irish tenor, bring on the girls." Yet the 1988 volume included almost everything Larkin wrote—not just the uncollected poems, but the unpublished and even the unfinished. And since the book was arranged chronologically, the delicate sequences of Larkin's collections were destroyed, masterpieces jumbled up with squibs.

The second version of the *Collected Poems* is the book that should have been published in the first place. Smaller than its predecessor by some hundred pages, it reproduces each of Larkin's collections in their original order, with an appendix of poems that were published in magazines but never included in books. Thwaite's only questionable decision is to start off the volume, not with *The Less Deceived*, but with *The North Ship*, a collection of juvenilia that appeared in 1946. While Larkin did allow the book to be republished later in life, he also wrote that "I could never contemplate it without a twinge, faint or powerful, of shame compounded with disappointment." If these poems have any value, it is the light they shed on the origins of Larkin's poetic personality. For that personality was remarkably consistent, from the beginning of his writing life to the end; and it is only by understanding the poet that we can make sense of the unlovelier aspects of the man.

The central fact about Larkin is that he accepted, with harrowing seriousness, the challenge of W. B. Yeats: "The intellect of man is forced to choose/Perfection of the life or of the work." In 1944, at the age of twenty-one, he wrote to a friend: "I feel that myself & my character are nothing except insofar as they contribute to the creation of literature. . . . To increase one's value as a pure instrument is what I am trying to do." Every great poet essentially feels the same way, but Larkin was unusual in the extent and ferocity of his renunciations. While writing his poems, Yeats got married, had children, ran a theater company, and served in the Irish Senate. Larkin, for reasons he himself never claimed to understand, could not write without a nearly monastic isolation and routine.

In "Round the Point," a dialogue he wrote in 1950, we can see Larkin trying to convince himself that such loneliness is his unavoidable lot in life, that "a writer's development is a slow approximation to his fated position." In the sketch, which was not published until long after his death, he divides himself into two alter egos, the brutally direct Miller and the earnest, naïve Geraint. Miller argues that the writer must erect "a crustacean barrier between himself and the rest of the world to protect the shrinking membrane that registers every sensation so appallingly." Geraint is shocked by this notion, but Miller insists: "Once and for all, get it into your head that you cannot be a complete writer without being a complete cad."

It was only by embracing Miller's ruthlessness that Larkin attained his poetic maturity. In the poems of *The North Ship*, one can already discern his great themes—loneliness, sexual deprivation, fear of death—but he writes about them in a borrowed Yeatsian diction, and with the misty self-pity of adolescence. In "Ugly Sister," however, he begins to suggest that his lovelessness is not just a curse, but the necessary price of his gift:

> Since I was not bewitched in adolescence
> And brought to love,
> I will attend to the trees and their gracious silence,
> To winds that move.

Larkin became a great poet only once he had confronted the full implications of this bargain. In the three years after he left Oxford, he was precociously prolific, publishing two novels, *Jill* and *A Girl in Winter*, in addition to *The North Ship*. Then, as he later recalled, "There came a great break in about 1948 when I finished—I thought I'd finished writing. I knew I'd finished writing novels, and I thought I'd finished poetry." By the time the crisis was over, he had broken off an engagement (to Ruth Bowman, his first love), renounced fiction, and begun to write the poems of *The Less Deceived*.

It was, however, an ironic triumph. Larkin, one might say, immolated his life in order to write poetry, and then found that the true subject of his poetry was the immolation of his life. Just as Yeats fell hopelessly in love with Maud Gonne so that he might write "The Folly of Being Comforted," so Larkin buried himself in provincial bachelordom in order to write "Mr. Bleaney," "Talking in Bed," and "Dockery and Son":

> Life is first boredom, then fear.
> Whether or not we use it, it goes,
> And leaves what something hidden from us chose,
> And age, and then the only end of age.

As Larkin himself once wrote about John Betjeman, "he was holding off with an instinctive obstinate wisdom anything that might hinder contact with the factors that were to form his particular nature." And because this is an instinct, or a destiny, it is beyond the poet's deliberate choice. "To have acted differently," he wrote to Brennan, "I should have needed to have *felt* differently, to have *been* different." As in life, so in art: "One no more chooses what one writes," he explained, "than one chooses the character one has or the environment one has."

It is for this reason that the posthumous indignation about Larkin's character was so shallow and hypocritical. Of course, his avidity for pornography is ugly, and his use of racial slurs is a shameful moral failure. But when the critics declared themselves shocked to discover a "rancid" or "repellent" Larkin, one wonders which Larkin they had been reading all along. Surely not the poet who imagined the inside of his head, in "If, My Darling," as "Monkey-brown, fish-grey, a string of infected circles," and described his face, in "Send No Money," as "The bestial visor, bent in/By the blows of what happened to happen." To read Larkin's poems is to know the worst that his letters reveal, and then some.

But it is also to know the best. For while journalism reduces people to foolish formulas ("the little Englander porn fiend," as one writer put it), poetry is a universal charity. And an intelligent one: what makes Larkin's verse appealing, even at its darkest, is the uncomplacent wit of his self-portraits. He always includes himself in his own satire. "Toads" starts out with a comic attack on work—"Six days of the week it soils/With its sickening poison"—but ends by acknowledging, "something sufficiently toadlike/Squats in me too."

At times, Larkin rises to a self-exposure of extraordinary courage, putting himself at risk in a way few poets dare. "Love Again"—perhaps the only poem whose absence from the revised *Collected Poems* is to be regretted—has drawn a lot of fire from Larkin's detractors, with its use of words like "wanking" and "cunt." But you would have to be blind, or malicious, not to see that the violence of Larkin's language—as in "The Old Fools," a poem about mortality that begins by mocking the aged—is meant as a symptom of his own pain, grief, and fear:

Isolate rather this element

That spreads through other lives like a tree
And sways them on in a sort of sense
And say why it never worked for me.

If suffering honed Larkin's savagery, it also bred his remarkable compassion. Many poets might write on the subject of "Faith Healing," and even rival Larkin's sharp eye for the unctuous, fraudulent preacher, "Upright in rimless glasses, silver hair." What is unique is Larkin's pity for the women who flock to be healed, a pity secured against condescension by his own experience of lovelessness:

In everyone there sleeps
A sense of life lived according to love.
To some it means the difference they could make
By loving others, but across most it sweeps
As all they might have done had they been loved.
That nothing cures.

Lines like these remind us what it really means for a poet to sacrifice himself for his art. It has nothing to do with ambition, vanity, or even material deprivation, though many poets' lives include all of these. It means hollowing out one's self, in order to allow all the bitterness and joy of life to take up residence there and find expression. In this sense, even a misanthropic poet is bewilderingly generous; as Larkin said, "The most negative poem in the world is a very positive thing to have done." It is this rare generosity, not his common failings, that will secure Larkin's reputation for posterity. As he wrote in "An Arundel Tomb," "What will survive of us is love."

Dennis O'Driscoll

IN AN ESSAY on Seamus Heaney's poem "The Biretta," Dennis O'Driscoll calls attention to Heaney's fondness for the word "credit": "he prefers to 'credit' things rather than discredit them." This is a diplomatic way of putting what could be a serious criticism. After all, "credit" seems closer to credulity than to belief; one only needs to extend credit to customers, or ideas, that can't pay their own way. O'Driscoll contrasts this indulgent tendency with "Philip Larkinesque disillusion and scepticism," which instinctively regards tenderness for the things of this world (and the next) as pretentious or hypocritical.

O'Driscoll the critic (whose work is collected in *Troubled Thoughts, Majestic Dreams*) has written warmly and intelligently about Heaney; but O'Driscoll the poet (whose *New and Selected Poems* appeared in 2004) leaves no doubt that he is on Larkin's side of this temperamental divide. The traces of Larkin in his poetry are sometimes on the surface, as when a line from "Talking Shop" ("Seven days, he takes his place behind formica") draws on the memory of "Toads" ("Six days of the week it soils"). But the deeper similarity is found in the subject of those two poems, the miseries and consolations of work. For O'Driscoll is the poet after Larkin who has made the most of his day job, both as a subject for verse and as a part of his poetic identity.

The jacket of each of O'Driscoll's books informs the reader that he has worked for the Irish Civil Service since the age of sixteen. It is hard to parse the exact tone of this announcement: is it a boast, a demurral, a warning? Certainly O'Driscoll takes pride in not making his living as a poet. He has been an acute diagnostician of the poetry world's *déformations professionelles*: provincialism, careerism, dishonesty. (He is especially scathing about Irish poets who "try to export their produce to America and spend time marketing it there.") His criticism could hardly be so scrupulous and nonpartisan if he were a full-time resident in that world.

But more fundamentally, O'Driscoll's proud embrace of his office job seems connected, as with Larkin, to a tacit despair about the possibilities of human life. For a certain kind of poet, there are really only two activities, poetry and everything else. Poetry must supply the true satisfactions—the sense of worth, mastery, possibility, control. Everything else is, in T. S. Eliot's words, "the waste sad time stretching before and after." To spend that time in an office is no worse than any other option. In a sense, it is better precisely because the office is confessedly tedious, thus allowing the poet to draw a clear line between life and work, or between "work" and the real work of writing (which is, of course, what the outside world sees as unreal play).

This kind of depressive lucidity about everyday life is the keynote of O'Driscoll's best poetry. This is not to say that he is noisily unhappy, demanding attention for his personal suffering. At the bottom of such narcissistic displays one always finds sentimentality, a belief that the world has let the poet down; by definition, grievances seek redress. In O'Driscoll's poetry, there is no redress (and compare Heaney once again: "The Redress of Poetry"). There is only insistent observation:

And listen to the sound
your life makes

flowing down the waste-pipe,
the stifled noises as it drains away.

Running through O'Driscoll's poetry is this sense, not just of the nearness of death, but of the way death nullifies life. Because life is just a brief vacation from death, it can seem unimportant whether one is actually alive or dead. O'Driscoll makes the point with characteristic wit in "Either":

They are either alive and well or decomposing
slowly in a shroud; I could either call them up
and chat, or confirm that they are ex-directory now.
It is a matter of life or death.

A matter of life and death is the most important matter of all; by changing "and" to "or," O'Driscoll implies that it is negligible, a choice between six and half a dozen. His poetry is drawn again and again to the leveling memento mori: "It is only for now," as he writes in "Only." But his attitude toward death seldom rises to Larkin's pitch of ashamed terror. Rather, O'Driscoll displays a cool resignation, shading into bemusement whenever he or the reader tries to forget the unforgettable. "How easily pleased we are," he laments in "Weather Permitting"; "remind me how bad/things might—will—be," he requests in the characteristically titled "Churchyard View: The New Estate."

O'Driscoll's poetry reminds us why, for the Metaphysical poets, mindfulness of death was the most fertile mother of wit. If wit is shocking juxtaposition—the bracelet of bright hair about the bone—there is no more shocking juxtaposition than that of death and life. And it takes a witty dislocation of language to make us feel death's nearness, which we spend so much time trying to forget. That is why the best and most surprising moments in O'Driscoll's poetry are the darkest, as in "Beauty and the Bag," from the sequence "Back Roads":

> She holds the bag
> —NECTAR BEAUTY PRODUCTS—
> in perfectly manicured hands.
>
> The small print reads:
> *This bag is biodegradable.*
> *It will decompose*
> *when buried in soil.*

Without saying a word, O'Driscoll transfers the description, and the prognosis, from the product to the woman. An equally swift and daring metaphor transforms "Votive Candles":

> what is left
> of inflamed hopes
>
> is a hard waxen mass,
> a host;
>
> the shard of soap
> with which
>
> God washes
> His spotless hands.

By punning wax candles into waxy soap, O'Driscoll turns God into Pilate—a brilliantly economical piece of wit.

If death is the major theme of O'Driscoll's poetry, his favorite subject is work. In his verse, the routines and impedimenta of the office exemplify the standardized, globalized, pampered, and otiose life led by the middle classes in the West—in Ireland no less than Britain or America. Indeed, the most striking thing about O'Driscoll, to the American reader, is his refusal to make use of the literary glamours of Irishness. In his essay "Foreign Relations: Irish and International Poetry," he throws cold water on the "romantic view that Ireland is awash with inspired and instinctive poets whom even the gentlest of critical tools would wound." Instead, he embraces what John Montague called the "global-regionalist" perspective: "This attitude is alert to the political, economic, and environmental upheavals which uproot people and force them into new imaginative relationships with their native places. . . . The global village casts light on the deserted village."

When applied to Ireland in particular, such alertness cannot help sounding like debunking. O'Driscoll's Ireland is equally distant from the mythos of Yeats and the mythos of Heaney; his Dublin sounds like a version of Dallas or Detroit. In his prose memoir "Circling the Square," he gives his own sly account of Heaney's famous bogs:

> In summer, those in search of casual employment could turn to the bogs a few miles from the town. "Footing" turf quickly exhausted the townies and most of us had to draw on fictional resources to conjure up the early start, the twittering lark, the blue sky, the implements, the back-breaking labour, the compensatory lunch-bag of wholesome country food, as we struggled to satisfy our teachers' perennial appetite for an essay about "A Day on the Bog."

But if O'Driscoll is alert to the hypocrisy of that compensatory lunch-bag, he is equally alert to the deracinated pretension of what has replaced it: "Time now, however, for the lunch-break/orders to be faxed. Make yours hummus/on black olive bread. An Evian." These lines from "The Celtic Tiger" suggest that O'Driscoll's careful inventory of modern urban life is another expression of the same detachment we see in poems like "Beauty and the Bag." In writing about what people like him—people like us—do with their days, O'Driscoll seems always to be asking incredulously, "You mean you *care* about that?" Do you genuinely feel proud of your "tooled-leather/and buffed teak, hands-on management/techniques, line logistics, voice-mail"? Can you take pleasure in your "charge-card orders/or own-brand bargains/in suburban shopping malls"? In "Looking Forward," O'Driscoll offers his final sardonic endorsement of such vanities: "Lose no time in enjoying earthly goods,/for tomorrow (in a manner of speaking,/at least) we die. . . ."

As in Dorothy Parker's bleak jingle, you "might as well live"—but don't think it's any better than the alternative. O'Driscoll's irony toward "earthly goods" is exactly parallel to his larger irony toward work itself: work, too, is at best a minor distraction from mortal truths, at worst a complacent substitute for them. He is always aware that "We are wasting our lives/earning a living," and he notes the grim way we hand on that waste: "Ferrying the kids to school in style/imbues them in the long term with/some gainful aspirations of their own."

Because O'Driscoll is a member of the urban bourgeoisie, his cold eye takes in the characteristic illusions and properties of that class: no contemporary poet has written more accurately about the life actually led by his readers. But O'Driscoll is not simply satirizing a class, which would imply that he finds true virtue located in some other class, whether higher or lower. Take, for example, "Them and You":

They get drunk.
You get pleasantly inebriated.

Their wives have straw hair.
Yours is blonde. . . .

They use loose change, welfare coupons.
You tap your credit card impatiently on the counter.

Of course, the obvious irony is directed against "You," the bourgeois reader, for thinking that you are better than "Them," the poor. But really, O'Driscoll is not a bit kinder to Them: both classes are engaged in futile pastimes, they simply use different euphemisms. The office is O'Driscoll's subject only because it is the local habitation of his real theme, our willfully ignored progress to the grave. That is why his best poem about having a job is really a poem about Job, leaving the title momentarily suspended between the two senses. In "Job" O'Driscoll rehearses Job's curse of the day he was born:

And why is my mother
yielding to his whim?
And why do I
(my future cursed)
rush breathlessly to win?

Could they not have turned over
or taken more care
to leave me
in my element,
part of their gulped air?

The amazing literalness of that last stanza—if his parents had turned over while making love, a different sperm would have reached the egg and the poet would not have been born—is O'Driscoll at his best. And at his best, his dark intelligence and serious comedy make him one of the most appealing of contemporary poets.

Les Murray

LES MURRAY, born in 1938, has been one of Australia's foremost poets for decades. In recent years he has become a familiar presence to American readers as well, to the point that he can be considered—with Walcott, Brodsky, and Heaney—one of the non-Anglo-American poets who have been at the center of English poetry in the last twenty years. Yet there is nothing international about Murray's poetry, in style or intention. In fact, it would be hard to think of a contemporary poet more insistent on his rootedness, his tribal loyalties.

The battery of Murray's art is charged by the positive and negative legacies of Bunyah, the rural town where he was born: love for its landscape, its people and vernacular and working-class ethos, and hostility bordering on hatred for citified pretension. Such a conflict can easily slide into a simple binarism, a war of the healthy low against the corrupt high, and Murray is not always averse, in his poems and public statements, to this caricature. (A literary eminence on three continents, he has declared that "I've no time for the exclusiveness of high culture, anything that excludes my people.") At their extremes, Murray's praise and condemnation can sour into piety and resentment. But in the broad median of his art, where ambiguity is allowed to flourish, he is a poet of great linguistic power and moral energy.

Murray appears in many of his lyric poems as a character, in both senses of the word, and the character has a recognizable literary parentage. In his desire to encompass and give moral meaning to the idea of Australia, he can suggest Whitman, and Whitman certainly echoes in the psalmlike rhythms of "The Buladelah-Taree Holiday Song Cycle":

> It is good to come out after driving and walk on bare grass;
> walking out, looking all around, relearning that country.
> Looking out for snakes, and looking out for rabbits as well;
> going into the shade of myrtles to try their cupped climate,
>   swinging by one hand around them,
> in that country of the Holiday. . . .

But the comparison can very easily mislead. Murray does not have Whitman's endless erotic adhesiveness; indeed, his erotic feelings are deeply troubled, as can be seen particularly in his verse novel *Fredy Neptune*. He is not open, universal, inviting; he excludes with rigor, defining himself and his people in large part through opposition. Murray is closer to Frost in his admiration of the farmer's and worker's hard, suspicious manliness, as in an episode from the same "song cycle":

> The warriors are cutting timber with brash chainsaws; they
>   are trimming hardwood pit-props and loading them;
> *Is that an order?* they hoot at the peremptory lorry driver, who
>   laughs; he is also a warrior. . . .
> Addressed on the beach by a pale man, they watch waves
>   break and are reserved, refusing pleasantry;
> they joke only with fellow warriors, chaffing about try-ons
>   and the police, not slighting women.

It is easy to imagine one of Murray's "warriors" impulsively trying to kill a "pale," condescending outsider, as a farmworker does in Frost's "The Code": "Never you say a thing like that to a man, / Not if he values what he is. God, I'd as soon / Murdered him as left out his middle name." And as with Frost, Murray's code of silence and honor sometimes sounds like mere hatred of the loquacious and overeducated: "Snobs mind us off religion / nowadays, if they can. / Fuck them. I wish you God."

This tone, unfortunately, grows more rather than less obtrusive in Murray's later work. His early poems condemn less and praise more; they have some of the intense vitalism of Dylan Thomas, who is affectionately parodied in "Vindaloo in Merthyr Tydfil" ("I sang for my pains like the free"). "The Burning Truck," the first poem in *Learning Human*, Murray's selected poems, turns a freak wartime event—a truck, machine-gunned and set afire, continues to speed down the street—into a symbol of liberation:

> And all of us who knew our place and prayers
> clutched our verandah-rails and window-sills,
> begging that truck between our teeth to halt,
> keep going, vanish, strike . . . but set us free.
> And then we saw the wild boys of the street
> go running after it.
>
> And as they followed, cheering, on it crept,
> windshield melting now, canopy-frame a cage
> torn by gorillas of flame, and it kept on
> over the tramlines, past the church, on past
> the last lit windows, and then out of the world
> with its disciples.

Here is a carefully worked-out contrast between the types Auden called "reader" and "rider." Those who know their place, hemmed in by verandahs, spectators at windows, long to be set free; the "wild boys" actually achieve freedom, by violating the boundary of tramline (which echoes the "rails" of the verandahs) and church (thus becoming a new set of "disciples," apostles of the truck). The phrase "gorillas of flame" shows Murray's ability to conjure up a strange, seemingly hyperbolic image, which on reflection is both thematically and descriptively exact.

In its mature form, however, Murray's ideal type is not quite as "wild" or destructive as "The Burning Truck" suggests. He comes to recognize that his ethos of forceful, taciturn masculinity lends itself easily to violence, and in a series of poems outlining his key ethical concepts, he takes care to disavow mere aggression. Those poems—especially "First Essay on Interest," "Equanimity," "The Quality of Sprawl," and "The Dream of Wearing Shorts Forever"—are not a sequence, but together they propose a distinctively Australian moral code.

"The Dream of Wearing Shorts Forever" is especially revealing of Murray's mind, and of his language, which delights in making the familiar strange: "If the cardinal points of costume / are Robes, Tat, Rig and Scunge, / where are shorts in this compass?" The words are Australian slang, but they may as well be invented; the poem's purpose is to define each one, to build concepts under them. "Robes," of course, are a formal garment, associated with official public roles:

> the toga, the kilt, the lava-lava
> the Mahatma's cotton dhoti;
>
> archbishops and field marshals
> at their ceremonies never wear shorts.

"Tat," on the other hand, is a kind of hypocritical, trendy casualness:

> Shorts can be Tat,
> Land-Rovering bush-environmental tat,
> socio-political ripped-and-metal-stapled tat,
> solidarity-with-the-Third World tat tvam asi.

It is noteworthy that Murray, so quick to attack cultural snobbery, here makes rather obscure use of the Sanskrit phrase *tat tvam asi*—"this art thou"—an expression of Vedic wisdom about the unity of all things. The poem disdains the fashionable embrace of such Indian mysticism, but it is clearly something Murray knows. Here is one sign, among many in his poetry, that the poet has a wider frame of reference than his "character" might suggest.

"Rig" is gear, shorts made for use:

> are farmers' rig leather with salt and bonemeal,
> are sailors' and branch bankers' rig,
> the crisp golfing style
> of our youngest male National Costume.

And finally there is "scunge," which sounds just like what it means:

> Scunge, which is real negligee
> housework in a swimsuit, pyjamas worn all day,
> is holiday, freedom from ambition.
> Scunge makes you invisible
> to the world and yourself.

This makes clear that Murray's dislike of pretension and fashion does not lead him to the opposite extreme, a Beat embrace of squalor and "dropping out." "Real negligee"—that, is real neglect—is another kind of sin.

If these four words have been defined as various distortions of shorts, then the ideal shorts must occupy the center of the sartorial "compass." Neither formal nor squalid, neither yuppie- nor hippie-fashionable, they are simple, comfortable, useful, unpretentious:

> Ideal for getting served last
> in shops of the temperate zone
> they are also ideal for going home, into space,
> into time, to farm the mind's Sabine acres
> for product or subsistence.

Delicately dropped into this slangy poem are the "Sabine acres" that take us back to Horace, and make clear that the quality Murray is praising—call it "equanimity," as he does in another poem, or self-sufficiency, or principled simplicity—is both Australian and Roman, both folk and literary. "Why exchange my Sabine valley for more wearisome wealth?" asks Horace; Murray asks, Why wear robes when you can wear shorts? At such a moment, the local escapes provincialism and becomes another habitation of the universal; and the poems in which Murray makes this flight are by far his best.

Such poems, however, are in the minority in *Learning Human*. More often, Murray approaches his native ground as a committed celebrant or chronicler, and these modes are less engaging. It is curious that even his mobile style leaves a description of "Water-Gardening in an Old Farm Dam" strangely inert:

Blueing the blackened water
that I'm widening with my spade
as I lever up water tussocks
and chuck them ashore like sopping comets
is a sun-point, dazzling heatless
acetylene, under tadpoles that swarm
wobbling, like a species of flies
and buzzing bubbles that speed
upward like many winged species.

There is no doubt that this is something Murray has closely seen, and his whimsical, ungainly, heavily worked language is an attempt to make the reader see it. (This is the style Derek Walcott called "a syntax that digests iron and spits out petals.") But it is weighed down by Murray's piety toward the land and working the land. Such piety—or, less pejoratively, such reverence—is antagonistic to eloquence; it grows out of silent work, and involves a surrender of the personal mind. This emotion is central to Murray's rural, working-class, and religious identity—it is the gift withheld from the "city storemen and accounts clerks" who, in another poem, go sightseeing in the wetlands, and are left, forlornly, "remembering things about themselves"—but, perhaps for that very reason, it drains the tension from his descriptive nature-poems.

Nature also provides less scope for Murray's fertile metaphorical imagination, which animates many delightful, darting poems. "The Chimes of Neverwhere" is a nearly Metaphysical series of counterfacts:

The neither state of Neverwhere
is hard to place as near or far

since all things that didn't take place are there
and things that have lost the place they took:

Herr Hitler's buildings, King James' cigar,
the happiness of Armenia,
the Abelard children, the Manchus' return
are there with the Pictish grammar book.

While Murray has written many poems about local legends
and what sound like family anecdotes, he seldom goes so far as
to tap that never-failing source of interest for most poets, himself. Yet when he does venture to explore his own personality
and history, the reader is surprised to find a vivid unhappiness
beneath the bluff persona. "Corniche" opens with a parody of
Philip Larkin, a poet with whom Murray has no surface similarities, and proceeds to outdo him in disgust and despair:

I work all day and hardly drink at all.
I can reach down and feel if I'm depressed.
I adore the Creator because I made myself
and a few times a week a wire jags in my chest. . . .

Laugh, who never shrank around wizened genitals there
or killed themselves to stop dying. The blow that never falls
batters you stupid. Only gradually do
you notice a slight scorn in you for what appals.

The specifically sexual disgust in "wizened genitals" is even
more prominent, and more personal, in "Burning Want":

But all my names were fat-names, at my new town school.
Between classes, kids did erocide: destruction of sexual
    morale.

> Mass refusal of unasked love: that works. Boys cheered as
>   seventeen-
> year-old girls came on to me, then ran back whinnying
>   ridicule.

In an earlier poem, "Quintets for Robert Morley," Murray (who is famously large) had praised "the fat" with comic hyperbole as "the earliest/civilized, and civilizing, humans,/the first to win the leisure,/sweet boredom, life-enhancing sprawl that require style." But here, being fat seems more like the wound that accompanies Murray's bow.

The pain of that wound can be gauged by the scale of *Fredy Neptune*, which might be seen as Murray's attempt to describe, explain, and cure it. A verse novel of some 1,250 eight-line stanzas, it is an *Odyssey* of erocide. Fredy Neptune's picaresque adventures are clearly inspired by Candide and Don Juan, and by the stunted hero of *The Tin Drum*. But where Juan's world travels are punctuated by fornication, Fredy is neutered: for most of the book, he is unable to feel anything. Clearly, such an affliction lends itself to metaphorical interpretation. But it is Murray's ability to balance symbol with realistic detail—to create objective correlatives for his feelings about sex, violence, class, and politics—that makes his long poem so successful. To a greater degree than might seem possible for a verse novel, *Fredy Neptune* is entertaining, challenging, and even beautiful for its whole length.

The title is the stage name of Fredy Boettcher, an Australian of German descent born in the late nineteenth century. The poem follows him from the outbreak of the First World War past the end of Second, as he travels everywhere—Istanbul, Berlin, Brisbane, Kentucky, Hollywood, Shanghai—and takes any job he can get—merchant sailor, lumberjack, movie extra, bounty hunter. He is driven from place to place by a strange disease, which he develops after witnessing a massacre of Armenian women by the Turks, and which deprives him of all bodily sensation. Each time Fredy begins to feel at home somewhere, his uncanny difference comes to light, and he is driven out in fear and loathing. At the same time, because he can no longer feel pain, he acquires superhuman strength.

The symbolism behind Fredy's disease is clear, but not simple; the poem escapes mere allegory by layering its meanings. Most obviously, Fredy's numbness is a defensive response to the evil of the world. Brought on by the Armenian genocide, it is fueled by all the large and small abominations he witnesses in his travels. Beyond this moral dimension, however, there is a psychological one. Like the Murray of "Burning Want," Fredy suffers sexual paralysis—one of the worst features of his curse is his inability to feel anything during sex, even with the wife he loves—and his combination of power and clumsiness can be read autobiographically, as Murray's fable of obesity. Then there is the political element: as an outsider, a freak, Fredy tests the tolerance of everyone he meets, and almost everyone is led to fear and hate him by the same instinct that leads to racism. ("The last, the very/last thing you allow ever: to be caught out both different and helpless./Humans kill you for less.") Finally, and above all, Fredy's disease is spiritual: he seeks everywhere for a way to reconcile soul and body, ghost and machine.

Yet *Fredy Neptune* is not weighed down by this cargo of meanings; it has the outsized simplicity and frantic pace of an action movie. The key to its success is Murray's decision to pair Fredy's weakness with his outlandish strength, turning him into a kind of Superman. He is forever lifting cars, or brawling with villains, or making narrow escapes, and thus avoids mere passive suffering. At the same time, the need to keep the extravagant story moving strips Murray's verse of its knottier excesses, while still allowing a witty, surprising use of language.

Language itself is one of the poem's themes. Fredy is bilingual in English and German, which is both an asset and a danger in time of war. During the First World War, he is asked why he was never wounded in combat: "I'd been sounded, politely, on how I kept out of the strafe. / (The punishment? Eh? Oh!) Torpedoed. Amidships. I was in the Navy." Murray leaves it to the reader to follow the bilingual slippage. In English, "strafe" is gunfire, combat; but Fredy hears it as the German word *Strafe*, "punishment." "Eh? Oh!" is the only clue that he has made and then corrected this mistake. Even less explicit, but still carefully intended, is the fact that he is led to this error by his intense fear of being found out: he is expecting the "punishment" for his strangeness at every moment.

Fredy's dual heritage also encourages a certain moral impartiality about the wars that surround him. Murray does not allow Fredy, or the reader, the consolation of seeing guilt and depravity only on the German side of the First, or even the Second, World War. ("There were no sides for me," Fredy says; "both were mine. I'd seen them both.") After the Armenian atrocity, Fredy goes on to witness a British massacre in Palestine:

> The Turks had been retreating from Nablus
> down to the Jordan. You can't take surrenders from the air,
> so the orders were: Destroy them. Day after bloody day,
>   packed thousands,
> anything standing, lay it out, anything still moving, nail it.
> The blood-splash of little bombs wet us, perking over the side
> at a hundred feet, two hundred.

Consistently, though never quite programmatically, Murray shows us a balance of evils. Fredy's widowed mother, born in Germany, takes up with a fanatical anti-Semite and moves back to Nazi Dresden; but she is driven to this step by the vicious Hun-baiting of her Australian neighbors. (Of course, she ends up being incinerated by Allied firebombs, another example, not of moral equivalence exactly, but of the awful consequences of the *lex talionis*.) Later on, Fredy manages to spirit out of Germany a retarded boy who would have been castrated under Nazi hygiene laws; but when he brings the boy to ostensibly free Australia, he is locked up in a barbaric mental hospital. One of the few appealing characters in the book is Sam Mundine, half Jewish and half Aborigine, a living example of the symmetry of persecutions.

This is not to say that *Fredy Neptune* reads like a catalogue of atrocities. Murray's vigorous language, curiosity, and love of detail keep it from ever becoming solemn or didactic. But he is intent on showing the many ways in which human beings pervert or blind themselves into doing evil. There is self-righteousness: "Everyone . . . /makes up a brief about themselves. Health's when they stop pleading it." There is patriotism: "*Our jail fought the German jail. No difference,*/was his slant on the Great War." There is the lust for control over others, symbolized for Murray by the police: "When the police revolution comes/you find you can't guess who are police." Most troubling of all, there is the possibility that evil is actually not abnormal but our truest, our primal condition. As an ex-Communist turned Nazi tells Fredy, "Nature's a Nazi./It's such relief, coming home to a bullshit-free State-principle./With Marx and old Jesus and the rest, you're always paddling/Against the natural flow of blood and shit."

Another name for that "flow," of course, is original sin. And

Fredy finds, after searching in vain for righteous men, that man alone is not powerful enough to overcome evil. Just after receiving his curse, Fredy visits the Holy Sepulchre in Jerusalem, where an anonymous priest prophesies: "If ever you can pray/with a single heart to be free of it, it will leave you that day." But it is not until the next to last page of the book that Fredy can bring himself to pray, and even then the prayer does not take the form he, or we, might expect. After all the evil he has seen, he finds he must ask not for God's forgiveness, but to forgive God:

> Forgive God, my self said.
> I shuddered at that one. Judging Him and sensing life eternal,
> said my self, are different hearts. You want a single heart, to
>   pray.
> Choose one and drop one. I looked inside them both
> and only one of them allowed prayer, so I chose it,
> and my prayer was prayed and sent, already as I chose it.

Coming at the end of such a long and difficult journey, the passage has a real spiritual integrity. It feels genuinely Christian in its call for a voluntary immolation of reason and judgment as a sacrifice to God. As in the Book of Job, God cannot be called to account, only submitted to; and only submission, for Murray as for Job, can bring the healing he so urgently and movingly seeks.

Czeslaw Milosz

"Undressing Justine," a poem from Czeslaw Milosz's 1995 collection *Facing the River*, meditates on the heroine of an 1888 novel by Eliza Orzeszkowa, *On the Banks of the Niemen*. In the novel, Justine is an idealistic young noblewoman who marries a peasant, and Milosz imagines her story's sequel in the next century:

> You rest your hands on a gnarly cane, the mother of a tribe,
> The last of your kin and your contemporaries.
> In floury snow you see sledges, convoys of sledges.
> You hear the shouts of soldiers, women's laments.
> And you know, feel, that this is how it looks, the end
> Of one earthly country. . . .
> The bars of cattle cars slam, by ancient trails, to a land of
>   shadows and murders.
> Though you never existed, let us light candles,
> Here, in our study, or in our church.

Milosz's expense of grief on a fictional character is movingly gratuitous. But it is only a small part of the poem, which sandwiches a page of verse between four of prose. Before the verse section, Milosz recounts the history and plot of the Orzeszkowa novel, as though he were laboriously teaching us what we need to know to appreciate his poem. After the verse section, however, "Undressing Justine" takes a genuinely strange turn. In conversational prose, the poet informs us that, after writing his poem, he happened to read an article about Orzeszkowa revealing that the character of Justine was based on a real woman. And just as he had imagined, the "real" Justine lived to see her peasant husband executed by the Soviets in 1939, along with their son.

Milosz presents this story without interpretation: "Probably a commentary is impossible, as, until now, no language has been invented comprehensible to both the living and the dead." But the tendency of "Undressing Justine" is clear, and absolutely characteristic of Milosz: it serves to undermine the distinction, not just between poetry and prose, but between life and art. The poem loses the status of artwork, and becomes a comment on, and an event in, the lives of real individuals—Orzeszkowa's models and their descendants, who are still alive to read it. In the strict sense, life prevents art—it comes before and after the poem, and the poet cannot escape it.

"Undressing Justine" is an elegant example of what deserves to be called Milosz's postmodernism. It might sound provocative to apply that label to this grave and humane poet if he had not already done so himself, in the essay "Against Incomprehensible Poetry": "It appears that we are witnesses to the disintegration of a complex of ideas which bears the name 'modernity,' and in this sense the word 'postmodernism' is applicable. Poetry has somehow become more humble, perhaps because faith in the timelessness and eternal endurance of the work of art has been weakened. . . ."

For nearly all of his career, Milosz set himself against modernism as he understood it. This is not a question of style—the polyvocal, the ironic, the obscure, were always important tones and tools of his art, and these are gifts of modernism. The mod-

ernism he opposes is, rather, the pampered child of the Belle
Époque—it is Symbolism, the ivory tower, the hermetic avant-
garde. It believes, or pretends to, that art is autonomous, and
deals contemptuously with the tame world of the bourgeois. In
"Against Incomprehensible Poetry," Milosz condemns "modern
poetry's chief tendencies . . . the floods of artistic metaphors
and a linguistic fabric liberated from colloquial meaning." The
same definition of modernist style is found in *A Treatise on
Poetry*, perhaps his greatest poem:

> A pure thing, against the sad affairs of earth.
> Pure, forbidden the use of certain words:
> Toilet, telephone, ticket, ass, money.
>
> A muse with long hair learns to read
> In the dark toilet of her parents' home
> And knows already what is not poetry,
> Which is only a mood and a breeze. It dwells
> In three dots, followed by a comma.

To read Milosz, then, is silently to redraw the poetic
chronology of the twentieth century. He convinces us that
modernism was not actually modern, but the necessary conclusion of four centuries of art and thought about art: it was the
desperate attempt to make art alone a sufficient source of
value. Modernism inflated poetry like a balloon with the vapors
of vanished meanings—religious, social, mythic—and produced monuments of fragile iridescence. Its zero hour was
1939–45, a time in which, as Milosz wrote of occupied Warsaw, Western civilization was unlearned. Only what came
afterward—the postmodern—is really new, the inauguration
of a different rule for the mind. The question for us, which we

have yet to answer and seldom even ask properly, is whether the postmodern will mean the dawning of nihilism or of a new, transformed humanism.

The great symbolic value of Milosz's life and work is as a defense of the second possibility, a humane postmodernism. Most manifestations of the postmodern in English poetry have been retreats and abdications. They have reacted to the failure of art for art's sake by making art against art—poetry that, because it is not self-sufficient, refuses to be even sufficient. Milosz is the most trustworthy guide to a different way forward: what might be called art for life's sake. The costs, no less than the rewards, of such an art can be seen with special vividness in his poetry.

Milosz's first steps on this path were taken in the midst of death, even before the Nazi occupation of Poland had ended. In 1943, Milosz wrote his first great poem, the cycle "The World." It is a child's primer, written in mock-naïve style, describing a world that has utterly ceased to exist: "The Porch," "The Dining Room," "Father in the Library." The effect can be overwhelmingly sad, especially in the sections on "Faith," "Hope," and "Love," and in "The Bird Kingdom":

What is the earth for them? A lake of darkness.
It has been swallowed by the night forever.
They, above the dark as above black waves,
Have their homes and islands, saved by the light.

If they groom their long feathers with their beaks
And drop one of them, it floats a long time
Before it reaches the bottom of the lake
And brushes someone's face, bringing news
From a world that is bright, beautiful, warm and free.

If modern poetry yearns for timeless validity, then "The World" is already postmodern, for it cannot be fully understood without its dateline, "Warsaw, 1943." It was written for those who were there, with the poet, in that time and place; and readers from elsewhere must travel there, imaginatively, to fully appreciate its devastating simplicity, its ironic refusal of irony. Milosz compels us to read historically. As he said, apropos of this poem, in *Conversations with Czeslaw Milosz*: "It would certainly be very nice to view a poem apart from its date and circumstances, but that can't be done. Besides, what do we want—marble, unshakable canons, beauty? I'm no Mallarmé. Dates are important."

Dates were especially important to Milosz in the first part of his career—roughly from 1943 to 1960, when he moved to America to take up teaching in California. Dates confess to man's historicality, which Milosz always saw as the truth behind the lie of Marxism, and the twentieth century's great metaphysical discovery. It is impossible to escape one's time and place, and ignoble to try. The poet, in particular, is charged with safeguarding the fact of history: "The words are written down, the deed, the date," Milosz warned Poland's Communist rulers. The temptation he had to fight against, in his work of this period, was to flee history for unchanging nature. Milosz gives this urge to his Prufrockian alter ego, Adrian Zielinski, in a sequence of poems written in 1943–44:

> What a wise man you are, Adrian.
> You could be a Chinese poet,
> You needn't care what century you're in.
> You look at a flower
> And smile at what you see.

How wise you are, how undeluded
By folly of history or passions of the race.
You walk serenely, the light, occluded,
Eternal, softening your face.

Peace to the house of the sage.
Peace to his prudent wonder.
O black treason, black treason—
Thunder.

To ignore history is treason. But to bow down before history is idolatry; this is the symmetrical danger Milosz recognized in Communism. At the beginning of World War II, he decided to leave the Soviet zone of occupied Poland for the German zone, a seemingly suicidal risk that he explained in *Native Realm*: "I had run from Stalin's state to be able to think things over for myself instead of succumbing to a world view imposed from without. There was complete freedom here, precisely because National Socialism was an intellectual zero."

Nazism was pure evil, which is an absence. Communism, on the other hand, was a seductive presence, which the lost souls Milosz wrote about in *The Captive Mind* could not resist, and it worked by claiming the power of history for its own. Milosz, who affirmed the importance of historical time and sought to make his poetry at home in it, had to find a way to resist this usurpation of history by the Soviet state. This was not so much a question of personal conduct—he defected from the service of People's Poland in 1950, and took on himself the bitter life of an émigré—as one of philosophical and artistic conscience. And it was fought—but only to a draw, not a victory—in *A Treatise on Poetry*.

This long poem, so important for understanding Milosz's whole work and development, was written in 1955–56, but remained untranslated until 2000. It is easy to see why translators, and the poet himself, hesitated to tackle it. It is saturated in the history of Poland between the wars; the whole second section, "The Capital," is a discussion of poets who are less than names to an English reader. Yet this section, obscure even when the reader is provided with explanatory notes, is a necessary part of the *Treatise* and serves its purpose well. In a poem about history, the poet must begin by acknowledging his own history.

The crux of the *Treatise* is the third section, "The Spirit of History." It is subtitled "Warsaw 1939–45," but it is concerned less with the Nazi occupation than with what came after. It describes the expiration of the old, romantic Polish patriotism in the Warsaw Uprising—a bloody massacre whose futility was evident even at the time. This was the "thunder" in which "the golden house of *is*/Collapses, and the word *becoming* ascends": eternal verities were discredited, and the world seemed to belong to those who were on the right side of history, the Communists. The survivors bowed down eagerly to the Spirit of History, figured as a monster who "wears/About his neck a chain of severed heads":

> "You have shown us the agony of this age
> So that we could ascend to those heights
> Where your hand commands the instruments.
> Spare us, do not punish us. Our offense
> Was grave: we forgot the power of your law.
> Save us from ignorance. Accept now our devotion."

But this sacrifice of the individual to the collective provokes the rebellion of something in man that is not historical:

So they forswore. But every one of them
Kept hidden a hope that the possessions of time
Were assigned a limit. That they would one day
Be able to look at a cherry tree in blossom,
For a moment, unique among the moments,
Put the ocean to sleep, close the hourglass,
And listen to how the clocks stop ticking.

This is the difficult dialectic that Milosz, in the *Treatise*, hopes to master. To be neither a drone of history nor a drone of nature: is this possible for a poet who feels the allure of both? *A Treatise on Poetry* does not find an artistically satisfactory answer. Milosz hopes to make history "serve again to rescue human beings," but he cannot say how this transformation might be wrought. Instead, the poem concludes on a note of bittersweet resignation:

And we, certainly, were happier than those
Who drank sadness from the books of Schopenhauer,
while they listened from their garrets to the din
Of music from the tavern below.
At least poetry, philosophy, action were not,
For us, separated, as they were for them,
But joined in one will: we needed to be of use.

To be of use: this is the honorable burden of the postmodern poet. Because he speaks from out of history, certain compensations are denied him—the belief in eternal fame, the creation of a permanent order through art. (The *Treatise* ends with a thwarted recollection of a poet who believed in both, Horace.) In their place is the possibility of being useful in a new way, not as a priest but as a fellow sufferer and a witness:

Whoever, in this century, forms letters
In ordered lines on a sheet of paper
Hears knockings, the voices of poor spirits
Imprisoned in a table, a wall, a vase
Of flowers. They seem to want to remind us
Whose hands brought all these objects into being.
Hours of labor, boredom, hopelessness
Live inside things and will not disappear.

This insight, already present in *A Treatise on Poetry*, was to move to the center of Milosz's mature poetry. Indeed, the last forty years of his career form a remarkably unitary "late period," in which the poet's calling is reimagined as one of remembrance and stewardship. This is Milosz's answer to the problem of how to serve history without emptily (and cruelly) endorsing whatever happens to happen. Instead of keeping a lookout for what comes next, the poet can turn back to what has already vanished. This means deepening the idea of history, which is secular and political, into that of time, which is spiritual and metaphysical. Equally, it means exchanging concepts for things, abstractions for concretions. One might say that Milosz places the poet in the role of Benjamin's Angel of History, a typically postmodern substitution for the Hegelian Spirit of the Age.

The outlines of Milosz's new understanding can be seen already in *King Popiel and Other Poems* (1962), his first collection after the *Treatise*. The subtle shift is marked in two lines of "Heraclitus": "Particular existence keeps us from the light / (That sentence can be read in reverse as well)." Increasingly, Milosz would read it in reverse, more interested in the particular than in the idea that purports to illuminate it. And this means that he would constantly press against the tendency of language to abstraction:

> I wanted to describe this, not that, basket of vegetables with a
>> redheaded doll of a leek laid across it. . . .
> I wanted to describe her, no one else, asleep on her belly,
>> made secure by the warmth of his leg. . . .
> In vain I tried because what remains is the ever-recurring
>> basket.

As these lines show, the abstract tends to defeat the particular in poetry, by forcing the poet to make abstraction itself his subject. Poetry is ill suited to grasping and presenting "particular existences." Painting does it much better; even fiction does it somewhat better, because it can afford to be lavish of description, to dote on differentia. But no poem could remain interesting at the length necessary to describe something—be it a leek or a woman—with even moderate specificity. What remains is the bare act of indication, which paradoxically diminishes the particularity it claims to affirm, through endless repetition of the gesture. Thus "City Without a Name," from 1969 ("Perhaps Anna and Dora Druzyno have called to me, three hundred miles inside Arizona, because except for me no one else knows that they ever lived"), is essentially the same poem as "Mister Hanusevich," from 1991 ("Once upon a time there was Hanusevich. And there was Nina./Once only, from the beginning till the end of the world").

If this is a flaw in Milosz's poetry, it is not a flaw of execution; it is the price paid for his conception of history. Marxist history is prodigal with individuals, because it recognizes no essential difference between Hanusevich and a million other people who are nearly Hanusevich. In his Norton lectures at Harvard in 1981–82, Milosz related a conversation he had with a Communist intellectual in occupied Warsaw, in which he expressed "reservations" about Soviet terror. "My interlocutor shrugged and replied: 'A million people more, a million people less, what's the difference?'" It is against this thinking that Milosz writes, patiently and even dully, about particular existences: "There is so much death, and that is why affection/for pigtails, bright-colored skirts in the wind,/for paper boats no more durable than we are. . . ."

There is still, however, one fatal objection to Milosz's poetics of observation. For the "we" who observe are "no more durable" than the things we love and remember. Even poetry is far from durable: the longest-lasting lasts no more than an eyeblink, measured in galactic time, and Milosz's historical sense will not allow him any smaller scale. Poetic memory is a pyramid scheme, an inefficient handing down, until finally there are no more hands.

Unless, of course, there is some One who remembers eternally, and who guarantees our memory. About this One, Milosz can be finely uncertain, as in "Annalena": "To whom do we tell what happened on the earth, for whom do we place everywhere huge mirrors in the hope that they will be filled up and will stay so?" The metaphor is wise, and we trust its implied pessimism: a mirror never stays filled. But more often Milosz pushes past doubt to affirmation, and it is here that his poetry is most persistently questionable. Milosz's idea of God is troubling in two complementary ways. At times, it is narrowly sectarian, the God of the Catholicism in which he was raised: thus the poems on Lourdes and Pope John Paul II, in which a nonbeliever cannot even artistically believe. But Milosz, of course, does not consistently believe in this God himself, as he acknowledges in the excellent "Six Lectures in Verse": "With almost good will but not quite,/We plod on with hope. And now let everyone/Confess to himself. 'Has he risen?' 'I don't know.'"

Milosz's other alternative is to cover this metaphysical deficit with ethical currency: to write and live *as if* he believes. According to his own carefully worked-out premises, some kind of God—not an actor or even a savior, but at least an observer—is necessary to ensure that human goodness is honored, that memory and poetry are valid. Goodness and poetry are desirable; therefore a God must exist, Q.E.D. The error in logic is compensated for by an earnestness of tone, as in "Elegy for Y.Z.": "I would like everyone to know they are the king's children/And to be sure of their immortal souls,/I.e. to believe that what is most their own is imperishable. . . ."

But when Milosz writes of a former lover, "You are entrusted to the eternal keeping/That preserves a butterfly's trace in the air," the echo of Tennyson's worm that is not cloven in vain is too powerful to ignore. At such a moment, Milosz's humane postmodernism seems to be sanctioned only by a brittle faith, and cries out for a course of Nietzschean intellectual hygiene. One dissents, finally, from the credo he advanced in "If Only This Could Be Said," a 1991 essay: "To put it very simply and brutally, I must ask if I believe that the four Gospels tell the truth. My answer to this is 'Yes' . . . and by that response I nullify death's omnipotence. If I am mistaken in my faith, I offer it as a challenge to the Spirit of the Earth."

One dissents not from the wager on faith, but from the covering bet, the "challenge" to the Spirit of the Earth. For if there is no God, there is no Devil, and no nullifying, and no challenge: there is only a gesture. Perhaps this is the logical conclusion of Milosz's humane postmodernism, the risky final step he often refuses to take. If we do live in history, and never reach beyond it, not even through art—if no person and no poet occupies a higher ground, but all are fellow sufferers, marking through language their common residence in one corner of history—then the man who continues to devote his life to art is taking a large unsecured risk. Perhaps in the West it is easier to accept a merely metaphorical Angel of History because that risk itself is metaphorical. For Milosz, it was an actual risk of his life—when he resisted Nazism and when he resisted Communism—and the support he sought was correspondingly actual.

Yet the dialectical fineness of Milosz's mind survives his commitments. Some of the last poems he published before his death in 2004 were among the most skeptical and darkest he ever wrote. He anticipates all of the reader's possible doubts in "Zone of Silence":

> It didn't happen that way.
> Yet no one dares to tell how it did happen.
> I am old enough to remember,
> and yet like others I repeat the socially acceptable words,
> for I do not feel authorized
> to reveal a truth too cruel for the human heart.

The poem manages to capture each moment of Milosz's internal argument: the doubt about proclaiming a specious good news, the desire to tell the cruel truth, and the compunction that stops him from doing so. Indeed, that argument, expressed in poetry and prose over seventy years, is Milosz's legacy to the English-speaking world, even more than any individual poem. The nobility, intelligence, and ultimate honesty of his encounter with history are what make Milosz one of the master spirits of the twentieth century.

Adam Zagajewski

CAN A MODERN POET write convincing mystical poetry? The work of Adam Zagajewski, the preeminent Polish poet of his generation, provides the beginning of an answer to this question. Zagajewski was born in Lvov, in eastern Poland, in 1945. Within the year his family was transplanted to the western city of Gliwice, victims of the postwar redrawing of Poland's borders. As a student he moved to Kraków, and after several clashes with the authorities emigrated to Paris in 1982. Today he divides his time between Poland, France, and the United States, where he is one of the rare foreign-language poets to be regularly translated into English.

Zagajewski emerged as a prominent poet and polemicist in 1974 with the publication of *The Unrepresented World*, a critical manifesto that, according to the Polish writer Stanisław Barańczak, "stirred up one of the greatest controversies in postwar Polish culture by attacking the noncommittal literature of the previous decades." As Zagajewski ruefully remembered years later, "I took my place among the Catos of this world for a while, among those who know what literature should be and ruthlessly exact these standards from others." Of this phase of his career, American readers know nothing firsthand. His first English publication, *Tremor*, did not appear until 1985, well into his Paris period. Yet Zagajewski's early career is crucial for understanding his later development, which has been a deliber-

ate flight from politically engaged poetry. Indeed, the antithesis between politics and poetry, the collective and the private,
is the main subject of his mature work.

Zagajewski's flight from history was itself a product of history. After the Solidarity movement rose to prominence in
1980, the poet could sense that Communism in Poland was in
retreat. Not defeated, of course—Solidarity was driven under-
ground by the proclamation of martial law in 1981—but
beginning its decline; within ten years it would be dead. And
Zagajewski's poems and essays of the 1980s look forward quite
consciously to a life after totalitarianism, in which antitotalitarianism will no longer be a sufficient worldview. He prepares
himself, and his readers, for a world beyond the old definitions
of good and evil, in which a truly private mental existence,
unfettered but also unenergized by the struggle with Communism, will have to find other sources of meaning.

These concerns are announced in the title of *Solidarity, Solitude*, the remarkable collection of essays Zagajewski published
in 1990. As he writes in the preface, "The word 'Solidarity' on
the jacket of this book stands mostly for the Solidarity, a
dynamic, robust, political and social movement in Poland. . . .
Solitude stands for literature, art, meditation, for immobility."
Zagajewski is not for solitude and against Solidarity, or solidarity; a concern for public justice is a given for men of goodwill.
But neither is he for solidarity at the expense of solitude, which
gives access to another realm, the world of art, beauty, and
mystical experience. Against the "piercing sense of community"
so intensely fostered by "that half-legendary country of Poland,"
Zagajewski insists, in the essay "Two Cities," that "not everything belong[s] to everybody. We are different and we also
experience things which social groups will never know."

The dilemma of solidarity and solitude is unfamiliar in

America, and it is difficult for an American reader to enter into it fully. Here poetry is such a minor, sidelined pursuit that its practitioners seldom even consider the possibility that their art has a duty to a larger cause. For some critics—George Steiner, most vocally—this amounts to a complacency that diminishes American art. On this view, the moral crisis of Eastern Europe under Communism gave poetry an urgency and stature it can never have in the United States, where it is largely a hobby confined to writing workshops.

Zagajewski's work is important for its rejection of this belief. He reminds us of the deformities of an art under too much public pressure. As a poet who feels poetry to be a calling in an older, more Romantic sense, Zagajewski knows that there is a zone of privacy and irresponsibility that is necessary for writing perfectly achieved poetry. Indeed, he mocks the Steiner view in his short prose sketch "Central Europe":

> He was an unremarkable, tiny man with dark greasy hair combed flat across his head who, without waiting for permission, joined my table. It was clear he was dying to talk. He would have exchanged half his life for a moment of conversation.
>
> "Where are you from?" he asked.
>
> "From Poland," I said.
>
> "Ah, how lucky, how lucky you are!" he exclaimed, overcome by genuine Mediterranean enthusiasm. "Mourning! Long live mourning! . . . You are a lucky man."
>
> "Why lucky?"

"Force. Force of conviction. Categorical feelings. Moral integrity. A literature that is not alienated from the polis. You have not experienced that alarming split. . . . I always felt in you the desire for unity, the Greek dream of combining emotion and courage. . . ."

This European is using Poland just as generations of modern Europeans have used Greece, or the Renaissance, or the Middle Ages: as an imagined ideal, an instrument of vicarious living, a name for a condition of spiritual wholeness. He values the "mourning" country for its solidarity; he even envies it.

For Zagajewski, however, solidarity is not a mode in which the poet—or, indeed, any reflective person—can come to rest. Rather, he sees solidarity as the antithesis that arises in opposition to the thesis of totalitarianism: "Totalitarians have their own primitive seal, which they stamp onto the wax of reality. Antitotalitarians have fashioned their own seal. And it, too, shapes the wax. . . . Poor wax, lashed by seals!" Solidarity is something with which Zagajewski would like to dispense, in the way that one puts away a tool that has served its purpose. Scorn, hatred, loathing for totalitarianism is everywhere in his work; but so is a distrust of antitotalitarianism, the other seal that disfigures the wax of reality.

Solidarity, Solitude, then, is a manifesto, but not of the kind Zagajewski produced in *The Unrepresented World*. It is a manifesto against manifestos, a warning against too much solidarity, written at a time when solidarity was both a necessary commitment and a moral intoxicant. Zagajewski reminds his countrymen that "we have to conquer totalitarianism in passing, on our way to greater things, in the direction of this or that reality, even though we may be unable to say exactly what reality is." When one considers how difficult and lonely a private definition of "reality" is, the nobility of such a statement begins to emerge. At a time when collective thought and collective identity came under the seductive sign of liberation, Zagajewski was self-possessed enough to remain wary of history.

But once Zagajewski has made his choice for privacy and the inner life, he is faced with a more difficult problem, and one that is less specific to Poland. To write against the public and historical, and in favor of the private and individual, is still to be conditioned by the public, even if one's response to it is negative. In *Solidarity, Solitude* Zagajewski turns his back on one definition of life and its purpose, but it is not yet clear what he has turned toward.

In fact, when Zagajewski begins to write about things not conditioned by history—and, in his books, this is clearly the role set aside for poetry, as opposed to prose—we find him strangely inexplicit. He is, in some sense, a mystical poet; he has written a book called *Mysticism for Beginners*, and throughout his work we find a longing toward the mystical as the consummation of the ahistorical. But Zagajewski is not a mystic in the sense that Yeats was a mystic. He doesn't possess a doctrine or a system or a single truth. Instead, he remains at the point of hoping that such a truth exists, while acknowledging that he will probably never comprehend it.

In this paradoxical way, Zagajewski transcends his post-Communist context and becomes a representative modern poet: he is a mystic of the liberal imagination. He cannot abide oppression of the spirit, even when it comes wearing the friendly face of the Solidarity movement. He insists on solitude, on the freedom to go where his thoughts lead him. But then he finds that they lead him no place in particular.

Already in *Tremor*, his first American book, it is evident that what matters most to Zagajewski is the feeling of completion and clarity that is the hallmark of mystical experience. He never allows the reader to forget, however, that such enlightenment is necessarily transitory: "Clear moments are so short./There is much more darkness. More/ocean than firm land. More/shadow than form."

Those "clear moments" become still more important in Zagajewski's later work. In *Canvas* (1991) and *Mysticism for Beginners* (1997), there is a growing sense that the instant of rapt attention to the world is the essence of life, and the only true subject for poetry. These poems are shot through with intimations of immortality:

> So what if Pharaoh's armies pursue you,
> when eternity is woven
> through the days of the week like moss
> in the chinks of a cabin?
> Turn off the glaring sun,
> listen to the tale of the seed of a poppy.
> A fence. Chestnut trees. Bindweed. God.

But for Zagajewski, such intimations can never become full-fledged revelations. And this leads to the central problem of his poetry, which is the problem of poetry in the face of the mystical: the mystical experience is not loquacious. The poet may seek "the still point of the turning world," but stillness writes no poetry. All he can express is the experience of waiting for the sudden illumination—waiting for it, or remembering it, or lacking it. Thus Zagajewski is condemned to a kind of eternal recurrence of the same poem. The conclusion of poem after poem in *Mysticism for Beginners* reveals his predicament:

I've taken long walks,
craving one thing only:
lightning,
transformation,
you.

   . . . take me to Tierra del Fuego,
take me where the rivers
flow straight up, horizontal rivers
flowing up and down.

This moment, mortal as you or I,
was full of boundless, senseless,
silly joy, as if it knew
something we didn't.

The inspiration for all these poems is the same: the moment of opening out to the insensible object of the soul's yearning, whether it is described as "silly joy" or allegorized as "Tierra del Fuego." The poem is always heading to this same destination, and whatever it describes along the way is a means to an end, not an end in itself. Zagajewski explains this phenomenon in his aphoristic essay "The Untold Cynicism of Poetry": "The inner world, which is the absolute kingdom of poetry, is characterized by its inexpressibility. . . . What then does this inner world accomplish if in spite of its inexpressibility it wants more than anything to express itself? It uses cunning. It pretends that it is interested, oh yes, very interested, in external reality."

A poet faced with this dilemma must choose between two strategies. One is to describe "external reality" as attentively as possible; the other is to honor the inexpressibility of the "inner world" by making poetry out of silences. Zagajewski, however, is in no danger of falling silent. He is not an otherworldly or ascetic mystic, who feels driven from this world by hints of another. In this way, too, he is a poet of the liberal imagination: his vision of the mystical does not present an overwhelming existential demand. Not for him wagers or leaps of faith. He is content to see the lineaments of something higher peeking through the things of this world, without demanding that it reveal itself completely.

The clearest sign of Zagajewski's attachment to the world is his wit. Mysticism and humor do not usually go together, but quick and memorable absurdities temper the melancholy of much of Zagajewski's poetry. "What are baroque churches? Deluxe/health clubs for athletic saints," he writes in "September." Sometimes he is simply comic, as in the title of another poem, "Franz Schubert: A Press Conference." ("No, I'm not familiar with Wagner's music.") But more often his wit is employed to intimate a darkness without stating it, as in this miniature theodicy:

> At the Orthodox
> church in Paris, the last White
> gray-haired Russians pray to God, who
> is centuries younger than they and equally
> helpless.

Or this, about Stalinism:

> One day apes made their grab for power.
> Gold seal-rings,
> starched shirts,
> aromatic Havanas,
> feet squashed into patent leather.

This side of Zagajewski's sensibility seems far removed from the yearning mystic, and it is what makes him attractive even to readers who have little patience with epiphanies. Wit gives evidence of an unconstrained, undogmatic intelligence; with its rapid and unlikely juxtapositions, it tends to undermine certainty. When you begin to see commissars as cigar-smoking apes, you have stolen their old authority; a doubleness of perspective has set in.

In this respect, wit is intimately bound up with the liberal imagination. In *Solidarity, Solitude*, Zagajewski writes that "one must think against oneself . . . otherwise one is not free." But this principle implies that thinking freely is more important than thinking rightly. The highest value is no longer correctness but nimbleness of mind: churches are not churches but health clubs, God is not God but an old Russian émigré. And the mystical is, perhaps, not the mystical at all, but merely a moment of contentment, a sensation, a shadow. This possibility haunts the title poem of *Mysticism for Beginners*, itself a fine example of Zagajewski's philosophical wit:

> The day was mild, the light was generous.
> The German on the cafe terrace
> held a small book on his lap.
> I caught sight of the title:
> Mysticism for Beginners.
> Suddenly I understood that the swallows
> patrolling the streets of Montepulciano
> with their shrill whistles . . .
> and the dusk, slow and systematic,
> erasing the outlines of medieval houses,
> and olive trees on little hills . . .
> and any journey, any kind of trip,

are only mysticism for beginners,
the elementary course, prelude
to a test that's been
postponed.

Zagajewski does not disavow mysticism in this poem, but he makes it the subject of a conceit, and thus puts it at an immense remove from belief. It is the same thing that happens when Donne begins a poem about the Judgment Day with "At the round earth's imagined corners, blow/Your trumpets, angels": since we know that there are no corners, we start to question whether there are angels. Similarly, in Zagajewski, the unlikeliness of mysticism "for beginners," as if it were a hobby like woodworking, makes us wonder about mysticism itself. The test has been postponed—or has it been canceled? Perhaps the test was never scheduled at all.

And so the mystical, for Zagajewski as for most of us, can never free itself from doubt. As he writes, in a perfect summary of his conscientiously unsettled and unsettling work:

Two contradictory elements meet in poetry: ecstasy and irony. The ecstatic element is tied to an unconditional acceptance of the world, including even what is cruel and absurd. Irony, in contrast, is the artistic representation of thought, criticism, doubt. Ecstasy is ready to accept the entire world; irony, following in the steps of thought, questions everything, asks tendentious questions, doubts the meaning of poetry and even of itself. Irony knows that the world is tragic and sad.

That two such vastly different elements shape poetry is astounding and even compromising. No wonder almost no one reads poems.

Joseph Brodsky

Joseph Brodsky, who died in 1996 at the age of fifty-five, now enjoys three posthumous lives. First, and by far most important, is the Russian poet who was frequently called the best of his generation, the heir to Akhmatova, Mandelstam, and Tsvetaeva. This body of work is totally inaccessible to most American readers, but Brodsky himself saw it as the heart of his achievement. In 1987, after he received the Nobel Prize, an interviewer asked him if he had won as an American poet of Russian origin, or a Russian poet living in America. He firmly replied, "A Russian poet, an English essayist, and, of course, an American citizen."

Brodsky's second legacy is his uniquely passionate and humanistic defense of poetry, made in the face of Soviet repression and American indifference. He was one of the few writers who could or would argue, without embarrassment, that "poetry occupies a higher position than prose, and the poet, in principle, is higher than the prose writer"; more, that "literature—and poetry in particular, being the highest form of locution—is, to put it bluntly, the goal of our species." He even claimed, contrary to his beloved Auden, that literature is of direct moral benefit to its readers: "I'll just say that I believe—not empirically, alas, but only theoretically—that for someone who has read a lot of Dickens, to shoot his like in the name of some idea is somewhat more problematic than for someone who has read no Dickens." And when Brodsky wrote such things, his audience could not easily dismiss them, knowing that his own life offered an example of poetry saving a soul from tyranny.

The story of that life has been told and retold, though seldom by Brodsky himself. ("For a writer to mention his penal experiences," he wrote, "is like dropping names for normal folk.") In his early twenties, Brodsky was savaged in the Soviet literary press and hauled before an official tribunal, which demanded, "Who included you among the ranks of the poets?" His reply—"Who included me among the ranks of human beings? I think . . . that it comes from God"—has since become legendary, but at the time he paid for it with a year and a half in an Arctic labor settlement. Prevented from publishing, he was eventually expelled from the USSR in 1972, never to see his parents or his country again. The courage with which Brodsky then remade his life and career in the United States is equally impressive. Avoiding the émigré's self-pity and parochialism, he resolved to participate in American literature, and taught himself to write in English—first critical prose, then translations of his own poetry, and finally original poems.

Which brings us to Brodsky's third, and most problematic, posthumous identity: the English poet. His *Collected Poems in English* contains three volumes of poetry that appeared in America between 1980 and 1996—*A Part of Speech*, *To Urania*, and *So Forth*—as well as a short section of uncollected poems. It is not a complete English edition: it does not include some of the poems written in Russia which appeared in Brodsky's first English volume, the Penguin *Selected Poems* of 1973, nor "translations by other hands of poems in Russian written after 1972 that Brodsky was unable to see through translation during his lifetime." And it is certainly not a translation of Brodsky's complete works, since, as editor Ann Kjellberg writes, "the author was able to render into English about a third of his mature work in Russian."

Nonetheless, the *Collected Poems in English* offers the best opportunity we have to consider Brodsky as an American poet. Kjellberg, following Brodsky's example in *So Forth*, identifies the translator of each poem only in the book's endnotes, thus issuing "an invitation to the reader to consider the poems as if they were original texts in English." It is hard to know whether the poet himself would have issued this invitation, at least so explicitly. He did write in English, and he did translate his Russian poems; but no one was more alive to the incommensurability of languages, especially languages as different as Russian and English. "What a poet actually listens to, what really does dictate to him the next line, is the language," he wrote. "Whatever language's gender happens to be, a poet's attachment to it is monogamous, for a poet, by trade at least, is a monoglot." Or, still more emphatically, in an essay on Mandelstam: "What translation has in common with censorship is that both operate on the basis of the 'what's possible' principle, and it must be noted that linguistic barriers can be as high as those erected by the state."

The author of those sentiments would not, it seems clear, want readers to pass lightly over the gulf dividing his Russian from his English verse. It is impossible to read Brodsky's *Collected Poems in English* as though they were the work of an American poet—they aren't, and they don't sound as if they were. They are, with a few exceptions, translations, although the author and the translator are sometimes the same person; and while Brodsky's own translations naturally have a unique status, they are not necessarily definitive.

By preserving the organization of Brodsky's three books, the *Collected Poems* does not present the poems chronologically in order of writing. But it reflects, at least roughly, the order of translation, and this is probably more important. Indeed, the three books represent three not completely distinct stages in Brodsky's American career. In the first, largely represented in *A Part of Speech* (1980), he relied on professional translators and other poets to render his work into English. In the second, the years of *To Urania* (1988), he began to make his own translations, with very mixed results. In the third, corresponding to *So Forth* (1996), the aims and methods of his translations changed for the better, and he began to include a number of original English poems.

To read the *Collected Poems* from beginning to end, then, is to hear Brodsky's own voice come to the fore, haltingly at first, then more confidently, but never as the voice of a native English writer. In fact, for clarity and poetic decorum, the earliest translations—by a variety of hands, including Anthony Hecht, Richard Wilbur, and Derek Walcott—are the best. When Brodsky began to take part in the translation, this decorum was broken by a more colloquial, humorous, at times chatty style, which may or may not be the tone of his Russian verse, but certainly seems to be the tone he wanted for his English poems. Yet Brodsky's wide-ranging diction, awkward or jokey rhymes, and rapid transitions often result in confusion and semantic obscurity. Often the poems that seem most ambitious in conception are the least successful in translation. Their power can be guessed at, even imagined, but not really felt.

What does come through in translation, at every stage in Brodsky's career, is his extremely fertile metaphorical imagination, his delight in significant and unlikely conceits. Brodsky, who read the English Metaphysical and modernist poets as a young man in Russia, had a gift for their sort of ironically suggestive metaphors. He recalled that reading Macneice,

Spender, and Auden "unshackled me," in particular, by "their common knack for taking a bewildered look at the familiar." When other elements of a translation fail, those "bewildered looks" remind us of the quality of Brodsky's mind: "death in its speckledness/looks like the vague outlines of Asia"; "This pull in one direction only has made/me something elongated, like a horse's head"; or, best of all, from "The Thames at Chelsea":

And when you sleep, the telephone numbers
of your past and present blend to produce a figure—
astronomical. And your finger turning the dial
of the winter moon finds the colorless, vile
chirp, "Engaged," and this steady noise
is clearer than God's own voice.

That translation, by David Rigbee, belongs to Brodsky's early American phase—lucid, the rhymes unobtrusive, sense coming before sound. But the same agility and unlikeliness that we admire here can become, when the poet himself takes over the translation, rapid and clotted to the point of confusion. This is perhaps the result of Brodsky's attempt to transfer into English the nuance and variety he saw as characteristic of Russian verse. "Russian poetry," he wrote, "on the whole is not very topical. Its basic technique is one of beating around the bush, approaching the theme from various angles. The clear-cut treatment of the subject matter, which is so characteristic of poetry in English, usually gets exercised within this or that line, and then a poet moves on to something else; it seldom makes for an entire poem."

This describes fairly well the rapid movement of ideas in "December in Florence," from 1976, one of the first poems Brodsky translated himself:

A man gets reduced to pen's rustle on paper, to
wedges, ringlets of letters, and also, due
to the slippery surface, to commas and full stops. True,
often, in some common word, the unwitting pen
strays into drawing—while tackling an
"M"—some eyebrows: ink is more honest than
blood. And a face, with moist words inside
out to dry what has just been said,
smirks like the crumpled paper absorbed by shade.

The number of different conceits packed into these lines makes
them almost incomprehensible. The sound, too, is unappealing,
in a phrase such as "wedges, ringlets of letters." Most obtrusive
of all is the rhyming, which requires unnatural and unrhythmic
line breaks: "to/wedges," "true,/often, "inside/out."

But Brodsky's insistence on retaining a poem's rhyme
scheme in translation, even to the detriment of its sense and
music, was not an idle choice. He wrote often about his principled, even moral, attachment to strict form, and believed that
a translator must carry over the form of the original: "It should
be remembered that verse meters in themselves are kinds of
spiritual magnitudes for which nothing can be substituted. They
cannot be replaced even by each other, let alone by free verse.
Differences in meters are differences in breath and in heart-
beat."

The irony is that, in a poem like "December in Florence,"
Brodsky sacrifices so much for the sake of the meter that the
poem loses the energy meter is supposed to provide. If one
compares Brodsky's own translations with those made by
accomplished American poets, such as Anthony Hecht's "Lullaby at Cape Cod," the difference is immediately clear:

> Like a carried-over number in addition,
> the sea comes up in the dark
> and on the beach it leaves its delible mark,
> and the unvarying, diastolic motion,
> the repetitious, drugged sway of the ocean,
> cradles a splinter adrift for a million years.

Perhaps this sounds more like Hecht than like Brodsky. But as Brodsky himself wrote, "Translation is a search for an equivalent, not for a substitute," and the poem is both clearer and more pleasing for being respoken in Hecht's poetic voice.

Other poets, whose energies are mainly devoted to metaphor, do not suffer as much as Brodsky does in translation. (Wisława Szymborska's darkly comic conceits, for instance, come across very clearly in English.) But Brodsky's verse seems to depend more on rhythm, sound, and rhetoric than on image and argument, and so it has more to lose. Even when the sense is clear, the urgency that comes from well-handled form usually decays in these English versions. "Twenty Sonnets to Mary Queen of Scots," translated by Brodsky with Peter France, proposes the queen as a symbol of romance and doomed passion, in opposition to the prosaic, politics-minded "Good Queen Bess." The sequence is witty and various, but it is too rhythmically halting to take flight:

> May God send you in others—not a chance!
> He, capable of many things at once,
> won't—citing Parmenides—reinspire
> the bloodstream fire, the bone-crushing creeps,
> which melt the lead in fillings with desire
> to touch—"your hips," I must delete—"your lips."

One perverse result of these defects in translation is that Brodsky's most striking English poems are those with a more limited compass: occasional and political poems, elegies and narratives. In these modes, Brodsky's ironic understatement and eye for significant detail—both reminiscent of Auden—come through with great immediacy, as in "Lines on the Winter Campaign, 1980," about Soviet soldiers in Afghanistan:

> The dreams are identical, as are the greatcoats.
> Plenty of cartridges, few recollections,
> and the tang in the mouth of too many "hurrahs."
> Glory to those who, their glances lowered,
> marched in the sixties to abortion tables,
> sparing the homeland its present stigma.

Those last three lines are incredibly audacious, in a way that no didactic protest-poet could manage without sounding shrill and offensive. (Imagine how an American poem about the Vietnam War might use the same conceit.) Brodsky is effective because of his restrained tone, his seeming objectivity. In the same way, in "Mexican Divertimento," translated by Brodsky and Alan Myers, he evokes a corrupt society in six lines:

> The constitution is beyond
> reproach. The text with traces of leapfrogging
> dictators lies enshrined within
> the National Library, secure beneath green bullet-
> proof glass—it should be noted, the very same
> as fitted in the President's Rolls-Royce.

And in "An Admonition," which might be read as an homage or response to Auden's "Atlantis," Brodsky conjures an Asia that is part historical, part sinister fable, through a series of instructions:

> If somebody yells "Hey stranger!" don't answer. Play deaf and
>   dumb.
> Even though you may know it, don't speak the tongue.
> Try not to stand out—either in profile or
> full face; simply don't wash your face at times. What's more,
> when they rip a cur's throat with a saw, don't cringe.
> Smoking, douse your butts with spittle. And besides, arrange
> to wear gray—the hue of the earth—especially underclothes,
> to reduce the temptation to blend your flesh with earth.

The concrete detail may not be Brodsky's most characteristic mode of expression, but it is the mode that comes across best in English, partially because, as we have seen, it shows the influence on Brodsky of English poetry. He often said that what he valued in English was precisely this specificity, in contrast to the rhetoric and emotion of Russian: "In Russian, what matters is the combination; the main question you ask yourself when you write is whether it sounds good. In English you ask yourself whether it makes sense. . . . It's a language of reason, whereas Russian is basically a language of texture."

Of course, English too has its textures, and it is quite possible to be imprecise in the language of Shelley and Hart Crane. But one can imagine that part of Brodsky's novelty, as a Russian poet, was to import this particular vision of English into his native language, much as Eliot made over the French of Laforgue and Corbière into English. Ironically, when Brodsky crosses the border back into English, his innovations sound more familiar than they would have been to his original audience.

It was not until *So Forth* that Brodsky attained his fullest ease as a translator and an English poet. The poems written originally in English tend to be modest, balladlike, and sentimental. But within this restricted compass, there is a purity of tone that can be very pleasing. "Tornfallet" is a muted, Hardyesque love poem:

> I took her in marriage
> in a granite parish.
> The snow lent her whiteness,
> a pine was a witness. . . .
>
> And at night the stubborn
> sun of her auburn
> hair shone from my pillow
> at post and pillar.

The influence of early Auden, too, is strongly felt in late Brodsky. A poem such as "Anthem" makes excellent use of the meter of "This lunar beauty," raising it from the lyric to the philosophic:

> What I have in common
> with the ancient Roman
> is not a Caesar,
> but the weather.
>
> Likewise, the main features
> I share with the future's
> mutants are those curious
> shapes of cumulus. . . .

then a rational anthem
sung by one atom
to the rest of matter
should please the latter.

In these stanzas we can see, comparatively clearly, the theme
that winds its way through all of Brodsky's work. This is the distinction between "Caesar" and "weather," history and nature,
determinism and freedom—or, as Brodsky often has it,
between Clio, the muse of history, and Urania, the muse of
astronomy. It seems inevitable that Brodsky, who was pressed
so closely by the dialectical-materialist view of history, would
rebel, praising instead the free and unbounded, whether in
nature or human nature. His statement of this opposition is
sometimes excessively obscure, as in "Lithuanian Nocturne":

. . . these words, with their fear of the morning,
scattered thinly at midnight by some slurring voice—
a sound more like houseflies
bravely clicking a tin,
and which won't satiate
the new Clio adorning
checkpoint gowns, but in which
ever-naked Urania is to rejoice!
Only she, our Muse
of the point lost in space, our Muse of forgotten
outlines can assess, and in full,
like a miser, the use
of small change, immobility's token
paid for flights of the soul.

Awkwardly, Brodsky opposes Clio, who is "gowned" in the uniform of a soldier at a checkpoint, to "ever-naked Urania," who shuns such political divisions, preferring instead to be "lost in space." "Cause" and "effect" are other names Brodsky uses for these antagonists. But unless the reader has this specific meaning in mind, Brodsky's use of the words often sounds vague and grandiose, as in "Portrait of Tragedy": "the aria of effect beats cause's wheezes." Only if the reader connects cause and effect with Clio and Urania can he perceive that, in this phrase, Brodsky is denigrating "cause"—everything that explains, limits, and determines human activity—in favor of "effect"—the individual human being allegedly inferior to the cause, but superior in being able to sing. Specifically, it is the poet who sings the "aria of effect," affirming his freedom and singularity. In Brodsky's late poems, this conception of the poet takes on a cosmic dimension, a kind of pantheistic belief that the universe itself delights in his arias—the "rational anthem / sung by one atom / to the rest of matter." As he puts it in "Via Funari":

> In any case, it's no less probable
> that the famous inanimateness
> of the cosmos, tired of its pretty vicious
> infinitude, seeks for itself an earthly
> abode; and we come in handy.

This poem, from 1995, was translated by Brodsky, and even this brief excerpt shows that he has moved a long way toward mastery. The greater clarity of idea, sense, and movement in his translations from the 1990s makes the reader regret, all the more, the lack of these qualities in many of the *To Urania* poems. Brodsky's fluency in English came very quickly, and it would be hard to find a native speaker more sensitive to the nuances of the language, as he demonstrates in his essays on Auden and Frost. But the ability to shape an English poem came later, and in the meantime many of his translations suffered.

Even if Brodsky knew this, he probably felt that the sacrifice was worthwhile, for his decision to write in English was not just an aesthetic one. In his lecture "The Conditions We Call Exile," delivered to a convention of émigré writers, he wrote movingly of the psychological dangers of that condition: "The reality of [exile] consists of an exiled writer constantly fighting and conspiring to restore his significance, his leading role, his authority." Turning himself at least partially into an American writer allowed Brodsky to escape this sense of inadequacy and to lead a literary life in his new country—which he did with astonishing success, even becoming the American Poet Laureate. His refusal to return to St. Petersburg after the fall of Communism was, perhaps, motivated by the feeling that going back would imply that his decades in America really were an exile, a hiatus in his life. By remaining in the United States, he confirmed that it was a second home, not just a place of refuge. And, of course, his love for America and the English language was deep and genuine. In the same lecture, he said that going from Russia to America is, "in many ways, like going home—because [the exile] gets closer to the seat of the ideals which inspired him all along."

The *Collected Poems in English* is a testament to that inspiration. If it does not fully communicate Brodsky's poetic stature, we should not be surprised. To accomplish in poetry what Nabokov or Conrad did in prose is probably impossible, and Brodsky's own translations are always interesting, even when they are not poetically successful. It would be a shame, however, if they were to preempt any future translator from trying to carry over his Russian music into English. Only when other intelligences, with other linguistic resources, are applied to Brodsky's work will we approach—though never, perhaps, attain—a full appreciation of its power.

Billy Collins

WHEN BILLY COLLINS was named Poet Laureate in 2001, the press reacted with man-bites-dog enthusiasm. Imagine, a poet who sells! A poet who earns six-figure advances! The AP report read like a royalty statement. Nor does Collins's publisher hesitate to beat the drum. The flap copy on *Sailing Alone Around the Room: New and Selected Poems* announces that "his last three collections of poems have broken sales records for poetry," and that his last book, *Picnic, Lightning*, "sold more than 25,000 copies in its first year." This is hardly the big money—indeed, all the astonishment condescends to poetry, where such small sums count as fortunes—but it helps to soothe the bad conscience of a minority art in a mass culture.

In the face of the Collins phenomenon, it is important to remember that popularity weighs not at all in the scale of merit. But that means it weighs neither for nor against—Rod McKuen was a bestseller, but so was Robert Frost. And if Billy Collins is a crowd-pleaser, it is for a fairly elevated crowd. His ideal reader is a well-educated, literate person, probably an English major, maybe even the holder of an M.F.A., who can recognize the surprisingly wide range of reference in his poems: Wordsworth and Stevens, Izaak Walton and Duns Scotus, Nick Adams and Emma Bovary. Though Collins often borrows the tones and strategies of stand-up comedy, making ingratiatingly clever observations on the trivia of life, his poetry is not all jokes.

In fact, the basis of Collins's appeal is a vision of life and the world, of ethics and art, that can be found everywhere in contemporary life, including contemporary poetry. He writes out, in a large, babyish hand, one of the major poetic scripts of our time: the one that finds transcendence in the ordinary, and holds attentiveness to be the last remaining form of prayer. His poetics are a debased form of the poetics we can also find in many more difficult writers, from Wallace Stevens to Czeslaw Milosz. The difference is that, in Collins, devotion to the ordinary is not a disciplined response to disenchantment. It is, rather, a peculiarly American form of mental laziness.

Collins's genuine poetic gift is his wit, which he often degrades into mere comedy, though it occasionally has the power to startle. In "Walking Across the Atlantic," he imagines "what/this must look like to the fish below,/the bottoms of my feet appearing, disappearing"—and this precise image does jolt us into seeing from the fish's perspective. Conversely, "The Dead" looks down from on high: "They watch the tops of our heads moving below on earth,/And when we lie down in a field or on a couch . . . /they think we are looking back at them." In a poem called "The Norton Anthology of English Literature," Collins seizes on the "parentheses that are used to embrace our lives,/as if we were afterthoughts dropped into a long sentence." These are moments of modest but genuine vitality, in which our normal mode of thought and vision is disrupted, and they are gratifyingly frequent in Collins's poetry.

The basis of such wit is taking words literally—seizing on tired phrases and familiar idioms and attending to what they really say. "Walking on water" is a cliché that becomes vivid when Collins adopts the fish-eye view and notices the feet, appearing and disappearing on the surface. At its most powerful, this kind of wit can be truly creative. If, as Emerson said, every word began life as a metaphor, wit resurrects the metaphor hiding in dead words.

But if true wit attends to the relations of words to things, it is closely related to mere punning, which is interested only in the relations of words to other words. The poets of the seventeenth century, masters of wit, were also adept at this form of low comedy, which is another way of taking words literally. The kind of joke we find in Donne's epigram—"I am unable, yonder beggar cries,/To stand or move; if he say true, he lies"—can seem the fine excess of an alert linguistic intelligence. But it is finally of limited interest, because it calls attention, not to the world, but to the way we speak about the world; it points to the foolish defects of language, which uses the one word "lies" for two different things. To deal only in punning wit may even indicate an essential falsehood in the poet's view of his art, as though language were only interesting when it is defective, never when it is a tool of discovery. Relentless joking can be a way of discouraging curiosity, ambition, and endeavor, without which there is no greatness in art.

This may be too grave a charge to bring against Collins, who seems interested mainly in ingratiating himself with the reader. But there is no doubt that his fondness for a certain kind of joke is of a piece with his work's deliberate praise of triviality, homeliness, and laziness. Collins seldom makes actual puns, but his wit is of the punning kind: he makes idioms ridiculous through inflation, hyperbole, and repetition. A good example is "Schoolsville," from his 1988 book *The Apple That Astonished Paris*. The poem begins with a cliché: "I realize the number of students I have taught/is enough to populate a small town." But then, taking the phrase literally, he goes on to imagine that town:

> The population ages but never graduates . . .
>
> Their grades are sewn into their clothes
> like references to Hawthorne.
> The A's stroll along with other A's.
> The D's honk whenever they pass another D.

The ingenuity of the poem lies in extrapolating each feature of school life to the life of the town. There is no theoretical limit to the number of features that could be seized upon—one can imagine a poem like this going on for pages. Of course, the joke would wear thin eventually, and part of Collins's talent is knowing when to stop—his poems are generally a page long, seldom more than two. But the very easiness of the joke suggests its limitation: it is funny only because of that initial phrase, "enough to populate a small town." Once we remind ourselves that, in fact, the students Collins has taught do not all live in a small town—once we understand that the target of the joke is merely an expression—the piling up of new details begins to seem a poor use of his cleverness.

Most of Collins's poems have this same additive logic: they are riffs on an initial category-mistake. What if you described the human heart in the language of a museum catalogue? Then you would get "My Heart":

> It has a bronze covering inlaid with silver,
> originally gilt;
> the sides are decorated with openwork zoomorphic
> panels depicting events in the history

of an unknown religion.
The convoluted top-piece shows a high
level of relief articulation. . . .

What if you applied the pop-culture nostalgia for recent decades to the distant past? That is the joke—repeated four times—of "Nostalgia":

Remember the 1340s? We were doing a dance called the
    Catapult.
You always wore brown, the color craze of the decade,
and I was draped in one of those capes that were popular. . . .

And what if you pretended that the musicians you listen to on a CD were actually playing for you, as in "Man Listening to Disc":

all I can say is watch your step

because the five of us, instruments and all,
are about to angle over
to the south side of the street
and then, in our own tightly knit way,
turn the corner of Sixth Avenue. . . .

The mistakes in each of these poems are not mistakes anyone ever makes, of course; their implausibility is what makes them funny. There is a similar technique at work in a different kind of Collins poem, of which "Victoria's Secret" is a good example. Here, the humor lies in a more subtle kind of mistake—taking the nonlanguage of advertising as though it were real communication.

The one on the facing page, however,
who looks at me over her bare shoulder,
cannot hide the shadow of annoyance in her brow.
You have interrupted me,
she seems to be saying,
with your coughing and your loud music.
Now please leave me alone;
let me finish whatever it was I was doing
in my organza-trimmed
whisperweight camisole with
keyhole closure and a point d'esprit mesh back.

Most obviously, the joke is on the foolish, artificial language of the catalogue, which Collins quotes (or parodies) plentifully in the poem. But more than the language is treated ironically here. The very idea that the model "seems to be saying" anything is a similar irony, because it pretends to take the model seriously as an actual human being, when we know that she is merely a simulacrum. Perhaps writing a poem about the Victoria's Secret catalogue is itself ironic in just the same way: it means paying attention, a traditionally serious and complex form of attention, to something stupid and evanescent.

Collins appears in such poems as a very contemporary kind of clown, a man who blunders by taking silly things seriously. Such clowning is designed to amuse the reader by flattering him, for he knows that he would never be so inattentive, or so gullible. And, of course, we know that Collins is not either, not really; the poet and the reader exchange winks over the head of the poem.

This kind of irony serves a necessary function when it comes to warding off the encroachments of mass culture. It is a way to protect genuine human relations from imbecile commodification. Irony allows us to acknowledge that we live among texts and images—like the Victoria's Secret catalogue—with a palpable design upon us, and to announce that we have not succumbed to that design. (The snobbish implication of this irony, of course, is that there are other people, less sophisticated, who have succumbed.)

All of this is a familiar, though problematic, part of contemporary culture. What makes it objectionable in Collins's poetry is that the target of his belittling, deadpan, superior humor is not only mass culture but genuine culture. His poetry is aimed at that small segment of Americans who are familiar enough with literature to have grown jaded about it. But it is impossible really to grow jaded about literature, or culture, or history, or spiritual aspiration, all of which are slated for drowning in the cold bath of Collins's humor. One can only fail to be equal to them, and disguise one's failure as condescension.

To see how Collins's small, inoffensive jokes imperceptibly grow into large and offensive ones, take "Earthling":

You have probably come across
those scales in planetariums
that tell you how much you
would weigh on other planets.

You have noticed the fat ones
lingering on the Mars scale
and the emaciated slowing up
the line for Neptune.

As a creature of average weight,
I fail to see the attraction. . . .

How much better to step onto
the simple bathroom scale,
a happy earthling feeling
the familiar ropes of gravity.

157 pounds standing soaking wet
a respectful distance from the sun.

The initial joke—fat and thin people reach a normal weight by going to other planets—turns into a philosophical statement in defense of earthliness, of literal mundanity. Life on earth is "better" because it is "happy" and "familiar": these are minimal, animal terms, suggesting that human desires are simple and easily sated. More, they sound like a wise resignation, as though Collins has refused to follow Icarus into the stratosphere.

There is nothing inherently wrong with this idea, and in other contexts it can have a definite integrity. But in Collins it sounds rather too much like "there's no place like home," which is the motto, not of those who return, but of those who never leave. Very many of his poems are in praise of effortlessness, in the sense of declining to make an effort. Take "Osso Buco":

I am swaying now in the hour after dinner,
a citizen tilted back on his chair,
a creature with a full stomach—
something you don't hear much about in poetry,
that sanctuary of hunger and deprivation.
You know: the driving rain, the boots by the door,
small birds searching for berries in winter.

But tonight, the lion of contentment
has placed a warm, heavy paw on my chest. . . .

Collins's praise for the civilian pleasures of being lazy, tired, and well-fed is natural enough; everyone enjoys these things. What is strange is to suggest that these pleasures are virtues, as though there were something especially meritorious about having eaten a good dinner. But the note of self-congratulation here is unmistakable—the sly use of "citizen" sounds it—and Collins points to its source: it is that such simple, sensual pleasures are "something you don't hear much about in poetry." Rhetorically, then, Collins ranges himself on the side of the reader against "poetry," which doesn't want him to enjoy his dinner. This way, poet and reader can have both sensual pleasure and self-esteem; they can have their osso buco and eat it too.

Not taking poetry too seriously is a point of pride for Collins, as in "Lines Composed Over Three Thousand Miles from Tintern Abbey":

I was here before, a long time ago,
and now I am here again
is an observation that occurs in poetry
as frequently as rain occurs in life.

The fellow may be gazing
over an English landscape,
hillsides dotted with sheep,
a row of tall trees topping the downs. . . .

But the feeling is always the same.
It was better the first time.
This time is not nearly as good.
I'm not feeling as chipper as I did back then.

Here we see pop-culture irony returning with a vengeance, except this time its target is one of the greatest English poems. Collins's joke is now at the expense of Wordsworth, who wrote at Tintern Abbey about the loss of his early feeling for nature:

> The sounding cataract
> Haunted me like a passion: the tall rock,
> The mountain, and the deep and gloomy wood,
> Their colors and their forms, were then to me
> An appetite; a feeling and a love
> That had no need of a remoter charm,
> By thought supplied, nor any interest
> Unborrowed from the eye.——That time is past,
> And all its aching joys are now no more,
> And all its dizzy raptures.

These are some of the most famous lines in English poetry because they express the absolute tragedy of time passing—not sententiously and abstractly, but as a dignified personal confession. Just the phrase "a remoter charm by thought supplied" contains a whole psychology of childhood and adulthood. Yet this is the poet Collins addresses as a mere whiner, a "fellow" who complains of not feeling "chipper."

This is the same type of irony Collins has previously used to belittle the Victoria's Secret catalogue: the deadpan repetition of Wordsworth's ideas, with the clear implication that neither the reader nor the poet could possibly take such things seriously. Yet it is clearly not the case that Collins is an illiterate, a Babbitt, for whom poetry is just a bunch of nonsense. He is, in fact, a poet, an English professor, an educated man. And what he is really expressing is a discomfort peculiar to the educated: a guilty impatience with the demands of culture. They have read

Wordsworth, probably in college; they have an ingrained sense that literature is worthy; but they do not have the time and patience for a genuine encounter with a work of art. Poems like "Tintern Abbey" exert a pressure and make a demand which we are often unable to meet; they expose our distractedness and triviality. The guilt of such a failure can be dealt with in two ways. It can be acknowledged as legitimate, and spur us to more serious reading in the future; or it can be illegitimately turned back on the work of art that provoked it. Collins's irony at Wordsworth's expense is such an act of self-defense.

That irony finds an even bigger target in "The Death of Allegory":

> I am wondering what became of all those tall abstractions
> that used to pose, robed and statuesque, in paintings
> and parade about on the pages of the Renaissance
> displaying their capital letters like license plates. . . .
>
> They are all retired now, consigned to a Florida for tropes.
> Justice is there standing by an open refrigerator.
> Valor lies in bed listening to the rain. . . .
>
> Here on the table near the window is a vase of peonies
> and next to it black binoculars and a money clip,
> exactly the kind of thing we now prefer,
> objects that sit quietly on a line in lower case. . . .

The problem Collins approaches here is one of the central concerns of modern poetry: "what to make of a diminished thing," as Frost put it, or in Stevens's words, the effort to see "nothing that is not there." Allegory, which was merely antique in the nineteenth century, became a vital problem for the modernist poets because it is a system that guarantees meanings, and therefore a standing challenge in a time when meanings are relativized or simply absent. Eliot, in particular, tried to make modern readers understand that Dante's Christian allegory is not a primitive rebus, but a style of thought now beyond our power.

In Collins's poem, this history and this challenge are drained of tension and reduced to another piece of irony. Allegorical figures like Justice and Valor are just "capital letters" like those found on license plates, mere typographical conventions. Once they "paraded about" in an unforgivable display of arrogance, but now they are safely ridiculous, "standing by an open refrigerator" in an old-age home. Our littleness is assuaged by "objects that sit quietly on a line in lower case," which mean nothing larger than themselves: we can pride ourselves on our realism, our coolheadedness. Again, Collins is out to assure us that we need not take the past and its ambitions too seriously.

Collins can get a respectful hearing for this idea because, for the last fifty years or more, poets have been saying something similar. For a number of serious poets, the best response to the death of religion has been to donate its dignity to the secular world. Passionate observation of the ordinary is a way to endow it with the significance it otherwise lacks. Thus Czeslaw Milosz in "One More Day":

> The voices of birds outside the window when they greet the
>   morning
> And iridescent stripes of light blazing on the floor,
> Or the horizon with a wavy line where the peach-colored sky
>   and the dark-blue mountains meet.
> Or the architecture of a tree, the slimness of a column
>   crowned with green.

All that, hasn't it been invoked for centuries
As a mystery which, in one instant, will be suddenly revealed?

The merely natural, those "objects that sit quietly on a line in lower case," are transformed through intent meditation into a mystery. Such a conception of holiness is not necessarily new— it is what Auden called the "Vision of Dame Kind," and found to be characteristic of Protestant mysticism—but it has a particular use in our time. Against the failure of religion, it asserts the holiness of nature; against the failure of allegory, it asserts the intelligibility of the world; against the failure of totalizing ideology, it asserts the dignity of the particular.

But there is nothing dialectical about Collins's simplicity, which is really just simplification. This is nowhere clearer than in the humorously titled "Reading an Anthology of Chinese Poems of the Sung Dynasty, I Pause to Admire the Length and Clarity of Their Titles." Here Collins contrasts poems like "Viewing Peonies at the Temple of Good Fortune on a Cloudy Afternoon" and "On a Boat, Awake at Night" with other titles, whose time and place we know all too well:

There is no iron turnstile to push against here
as with headings like "Vortex on a String,"
"The Horn of Neurosis," or whatever.
No confusingly inscribed welcome mat to puzzle over. . . .

How easy he has made it for me to enter here,
to sit down in a corner;
cross my legs like his, and listen.

Modern poetry, Collins's imaginary titles suggest, is pretentious and needlessly obscure; it wards off the common reader out of self-infatuated snobbery. Collins, and by implication his reader, naturally prefers the lucid and limpid poems of the Chinese. But this is a false choice, because nothing in Collins's work suggests he even knows there is a place for difficulty in poetry. His amused indifference resembles wisdom only, to borrow a phrase from *Four Quartets*, "as death resembles life."

Sharon Olds

To OVERTURN a repressive regime—philosophical or political—usually means just that: to turn it over, so that what was the most base becomes the most lofty. Society teaches that sexuality is sinful, so Blake, or Shelley, or Lawrence, declares that it is holy; and the attraction of these poets resides largely in the passion of their revolt, the sincerity and conviction with which they attempt to right a wrong. Yet, for this very reason, such poets remain trapped within the old categories. They are an antithesis, not a new synthesis, and are condemned to the ultimate dispensability of all merely partial and polemical views.

Whenever we find sexual radicalism—the kind that declares sex the highest human activity and the seat of enlightenment—we are certain to find someone still thrashing in repression's grip. There is no better example of this rule in contemporary American poetry than Sharon Olds. She writes in *Blood, Tin, Straw*, her sixth book, of her "Calvinist lips," and the major—almost the only—subject of her poetry is her fierce and unrelenting fight against a childhood Calvinism, emotional if not theological. She has said that "I grew up in what I now call a hellfire Episcopalian religion—I think that communicates the atmosphere," and the burns are everywhere evident in her poetry. Does religion say that sex is evil, that the body will return to ash, that the soul is our only noble part? Then Olds will insist that sex is glorious, that the body is the only reality, that the soul can be endlessly defiled. Her poems are engagements in the war of biology against theology, hymns to the "central meanings" of her poem "Prayer" (from her first book, *Satan Says*):

> Let me be faithful to the central meanings:
>
> the waters breaking in the birth-room which suddenly
> smelled like the sea;
>   that first time
> he took his body like a saw to me and
> cut through to my inner sex,
> the blood on his penis and balls and thighs
> sticky as fruit juice;
>   the terrible fear
> as the child's head moves down into the vagina . . .

No one who really believed in the sheer corporeality of sex and birth, out of a pre-Christian paganism or a post-Christian materialism, would write about them with such pointed prurience. Olds's aim is not clarity but blasphemy, as she makes clear in the childish title poem of *Satan Says*:

>   Satan
> comes to me in the locked box
> and says, *I'll get you out. Say*
> *My father is a shit.* I say
> my father is a shit and Satan
> laughs and says, *It's opening.*
> *Say your mother is a pimp . . .*
> *Say shit, say death, say fuck the father,*
> Satan says, down my ear.

Olds warms to this role, the naughty child, and tries by increase of naughtiness to bring on some cataclysm in which either she or the godlike enemy would be destroyed. That enemy is a whole complex of political, social, and religious attitudes that devalue sexuality and oppress women, often represented by her own alcoholic father, the demon of her unhappy childhood. The most naughty thing, of course, is sex; and the only thing naughtier than sex is sex with one's parents or children. In Olds's work, every permutation of this sin is played out. She imagines her parents having sex, imagines having sex with her parents, imagines her children sexually. Thus "Saturn," in which Olds's drunken, stuporous father is imagined eating her little brother:

> as he crunched the torso of his child between his jaws,
> crushed the bones like the soft shells of crabs
> and the delicacies of the genitals
> rolled back along his tongue . . .
> > he could not
> stop himself, like orgasm. . . .

Again, in "The Source," performing fellatio ("to grasp that band of muscle on the male/haunch and help guide the massed/heavy nerve down my throat . . . ") quickly transforms into a fantasy about the father:

> myself the glass of sourmash
> my father lifted to his mouth. Ah, I am in him,
> I slide all the way down to the beginning, the
> curved chamber of the balls. . . .

Everything bodily, everything sexual, is hurled at the Father-God, with the fury of a tongue-tied infant's insult. But the tragedy of such Satanic rebellion is only a step away from comedy, once we realize that the all-powerful patriarch is a Wizard of Oz, that the rebellion is as unnecessary as the tyranny is imaginary. The comedy can be seen in the very title of the poem "A Woman in Heat Wiping Herself," from *The Gold Cell*. Such a poem ("the gold grease of the floss/flows through the follicle, beading and rippling back and/curving forward in solemn spillage") suggests that even the most trivial bodily fact can be enlisted in the struggle, which itself trivializes the struggle.

The most significant problem with Olds's single-minded revolt, however, is that it breeds a disfiguring narcissism in the rebel. Her foe seems to her so all-powerful that she does not need to consider whether her aggression is logical or becoming. Her personal struggle is as important a struggle as the world can show. And this all-out attack implicitly confirms her enemy in the power which she would deny it. It is as though the father, or the patriarchy, or religion, is so strong that no weapon can really harm it, so that all weapons can be fairly used. Olds's rhetoric is pitched at the highest possible level:

> It had happened to others.
> There was a word for us. I was: a Jew.
> It had happened to six million.
> And there was another word that was not
> for the six million, but was a word for me
> and for many others. I was:
> a survivor.

Only a world-class narcissist could so casually annex the Holocaust as a symbol for her antipathy to her father. In her later work, Olds's narcissism shows itself in other ways, most signally in the unembarrassed use of trivial autobiographical facts, as though anything that happens to the poet should automatically be interesting to other people:

> I knew, all day, that when night came,
> at the sleepover, at Dinny Craviotto's,
> I would challenge Shelly Ashby to a fight
> for picking on Betty Jean Hadden.

Olds has no interest in abstracting from the contingent details of her life to a larger, more universally valid idea or symbol. And she does not see this as a deficiency; it is rather a kind of principle, as she has said: "just being an ordinary observer and liver and feeler and letting the experience get through you onto the notebook with the pen, through the arm, out of the body, onto the page, without distortion. And there are so many ways I could distort. If I wrote in a sonnet form, I would be distorting. . . . It's kind of like ego in a way, egotism or narcissism."

This lamentably common attitude toward poetic form simply means that the poet is exempting herself from the difficult dialectic of all art, and indeed all thought—the dialectic that places every mind always already in the midst of assumptions and distortions, and requires that we exchange one set of distortions, not for total clarity or honesty, but for another, better set. The belief that one need not engage in this process is the greatest and most limiting egotism; and of course Olds, so far from being free from distortion, has such a fixed vision that everything she sees looks the same. The remarkable uniformity of her poems throughout her career is not due to uninterrupted contact with "reality," but to a narrow and unchanging set of assumptions. Everything hinges on sex, and so we find, in *Blood, Tin, Straw*, "The Promise":

we are also in our
bed, fitted, naked, closely
along each other, half passed out,
after love, drifting back
and forth across the border of consciousness, our
bodies buoyant, clasped.

And "Animal Music":

I love resting on him,
dark rest, on the staff line, then I
love to feel it mount, again,
as if from the base of matter. My eyes
were closed, I was in the flesh. . . .

And "The Factors":

One could not call it
patience, the hour you kneel, turn,
rise, drawing the, pressing the, made
love out; inside each blossom
a half-god, calling to the other
half-one, in the other blossom,
come, come, yes, my darling, my
sweetheart, come.

And "Dear Heart":

I was
floating out there, splayed, facing
away, fucked, fucked, my face,
glistening and distorted, pressed against the inner

caul of the world. I was almost beyond
pleasure, in a region of icy, absolute
sensing. . . .

There is a reason why there have been so many poems about
love and so few about the act of sex, and these examples
demonstrate it. It is only when sex is made to serve as a focus,
an objective correlative, for complex feelings that it becomes
poetically alive. And since Olds has one simple and finally
unsurprising feeling about sex—that its bodily goodness
refutes its social or religious badness—the varied descriptions
of sex in her poetry are monotonous. They are also curiously
self-infatuated, as though having good sex is proof of the poet's
intimacy with the highest things.

As these hymns to sex suggest, in *Blood, Tin, Straw* Olds pur-
sues her old themes in a new emotional climate. The turning
point in her career came with *The Father*, which appeared in
1992. It is a gruesome account of her father's slow death from
cancer, offering many opportunities for the disturbing por-
trayal of corporeal facts:

> The tumor
> is growing fast in his throat these days,
> and as it grows it sends out pus
> like the sun sending out flares, those pouring
> tongues. So my father has to gargle, cough,
> spit a mouthful of thick stuff
> into the glass every ten minutes or so. . . .

But at the same time this illness is a kind of liberation. The
father figure, always associated in her poems with stifling guilt
and drunken cruelty, is finally killed: he is revealed to be vul-

nerable after all, not a demon but a human being. And with his disappearance, the motive for Olds's rebellion also largely disappears. In her later work, she insists less on the blasphemy of sex than on its holiness, as the ultimate rebuke to those who call it unholy. The result is a sentimentality that might seem at odds with the anger of her earlier poetry, but is in fact its inevitable complement:

> an embryo
> in the belly of a woman whom recent loving has made
> musical, the body's harmony
> audible, as if matter itself were merciful.

> we see the blood pour slowly from our sex,
> as if the earth sighed, slightly,
> and we felt it, and saw it,
> as if life moaned a little, in joy. . . .

> His eyelid lifts—
> justice, mercy.

An eyelid, menstrual blood, an embryo—also semen, sweat, the genitals—become signs of the justice, harmony, and joy that pervade all matter. Instead of a Calvinist-hellfire world where Satan tempts you to say that your mother is a pimp, there is a sex-paradise, "the world as heaven, your body at the edge of it." Yet these worlds are equally monotonous, the heroes and villains too clearly marked. Beneath all the surface agitation of Olds's poetry—the vulgar language, the programmatically unfeminine sexual bravado—there is a deadening certainty that makes each poem unsurprising, and therefore ultimately consoling. She has a devoted following for just this reason. A reader of Olds is never made to question himself, only to congratulate himself on his fine sensitivity, his openness to the holy in the profane.

There are always readers who want and need the kind of consolation Olds provides, which is why she is one of the most beloved of contemporary poets. Her poems are written directly out of the trivia of her life and can be directly assimilated by the reader; there is no abstraction and no surprise, only the videotape of life played back at full volume. Randall Jarrell once wrote that the poems he received from strangers in the mail were like torn-off limbs with the words "this is a poem" scrawled on them: testimony, not art. Olds's poems are everything that testimony should be: sincere, resounding, unambiguous, consolatory. But art has other demands, and these, most of the time, she does not even want to meet.

Individual Talents:
David Yezzi, Joe Osterhaus,
Joshua Mehigan, A. E. Stallings

No poetic injunction was ever so eagerly obeyed as Ezra Pound's "Make it new." In twentieth- and now twenty-first-century American poetry, the new has been like the Ypres salient, constantly claimed and fought over to no one's lasting profit. More than ninety years after Pound's Imagism became the first product to roll off the modernist assembly line, it remains standard practice for young poets to claim attention and reward for what is most advertisably "new and improved" in their work—if at all possible, as part of a school with a critic-friendly label.

But to ask, before anything else, what is new about a young poet's work is a mistake, for at least two reasons. First, there is the obvious fact that every genuine poet is a new beginning for poetry: the new is each writer's inalienable birthright, regardless of style or school. The real measure of originality is not up-to-dateness but artistic invention and courage. Does the poet write poems no one else could have written, or does he or she simply rearrange stale conventions? This leads to the second objection to newness: that, after a hundred years of modern poetry, techniques and ideas that were once new can now seem as venerable and unthreatening as rhyme royal. Verbal collage was new for Pound, typographical whimsy was new for Cummings; but the beasts the modernists trapped in the wild come to today's poets in zoo cages. In fact, the intelligent, fruitful use of premodernist techniques, like rhyme and iambic pentameter, is today considerably more surprising than the most estranging experimentation.

Young poets, however, are seldom judged by that deeper and truer standard of originality which T. S. Eliot laid out long ago, in "Tradition and the Individual Talent":

> In a peculiar sense [the new poet] will be aware also that he must inevitably be judged by the standards of the past. I say judged, not amputated, by them; not judged to be as good as, or worse or better than, the dead; and certainly not judged by the canons of dead critics. It is a judgment, a comparison, in which two things are measured by each other. . . . [W]e do not quite say that the new is more valuable because it fits in; but its fitting in is a test of its value.

Happily, however, there are young poets now at work who have demanded and earned, in their first book or books, the right to be "judged by the standards of the past." These poets, none of whom has published more than two collections, are doing some of the most moving and vital writing in their poetic generation. Reading them offers the same species of pleasure we get from reading the good poets of the past—the same species, but not a mere clone, for as Eliot also said, "to conform merely [to the standards of the past] would be for the new work not really to conform at all." I do not know much about their relations with one another, and I have no intention of grouping them together in a school. They are poets I have read with pleasure and admiration, and whose development will be of interest to anyone who cares about American poetry.

THE POWER of David Yezzi's *The Hidden Model* is generated by a fusion of two kinds of poetic energy that usually pull in opposite directions. First, there is ambiguity, that vanished discipline of the New Critics, so long disparaged as an obstacle to sincerity and self-expression. It is worth remembering, however, that the poets who did most to demolish the New Critical regime were themselves its most accomplished products: poets like Robert Lowell and Randall Jarrell, who studied at the feet of John Crowe Ransom and Allen Tate. (*The Hidden Model* carries an epigraph from Tate, a subterranean influence on so many intelligent poets from Lowell to Geoffrey Hill.) In fact, the kind of ambiguity practiced by Eliot and Pound, and systematized by Empson, Brooks, and Wimsatt, was never merely formal and dogmatic. It was deeply expressive, and remains the ideal vehicle for certain kinds of poetic feeling. Ambiguity stops the flow of language, charging each word with tension and scruple. It forces words to play double and triple roles in the line and the sentence, demanding that the reader pay close attention to what is ordinarily obvious. It is, in short, the music of doubt and self-doubt.

Yezzi's verse is full of this kind of ambiguity, in which the pun is raised to the level of aporia. "Aporia," in fact, is the title of a sonnet sequence in which Yezzi offers five emblems of doubt or frustration, each studded with double meanings. Looking at a foggy New York cityscape, he remembers that "the grains a solvent will not hold we call/*precipitate*, and buildings are the forms/these crystals take." This is a Donnean kind of punning—by returning the weatherman's word for rain to its chemical origins, Yezzi can then use that scientific etymology to construct a new, beautifully suggestive metaphor. Another kind of ambiguity opens the next sonnet: "Ivory beneath a wind-whipped swell of bays,/a peony has flowered overnight." Following immediately on the vision of fog, that first line seems to return us to the sight of the Hudson River in a storm. But the bays, we realize, are actually bay-leaves, and the "ivory" is not whitecaps but white petals.

This kind of alienation, in which the meaning of a sentence changes as it unfolds, is one of Yezzi's favorite effects. In "Nostalgia for a New City," he delights in pushing it to an extreme. Sentences unspool first as a kind of riddle, an almost random string of words, until with a click their actual meaning comes clear: "Carp trawl on tanbark mirrors/clearer than oolong we drain for its cut leaves, you insist." Next to the childish fracturing that passes for linguistic energy in so much contemporary poetry, Yezzi's carefully deceptive syntax seems like the work of an adult, one who knows the language so thoroughly he is able to transform it at will.

The feeling of mastery that suffuses *The Hidden Model* is owed in large part to the second type of poetic energy Yezzi draws on: the elegant fluency whose most obvious sponsor is Auden. If Tate's ambiguity tends to choke off speech, Auden's facility urges speech onward; it makes possible Yezzi's ample periods, his gracefully ironic tone, his delight in rare words. If his sure control allows him to wreathe language into knots, it also, and more often, allows him to send it cascading through ornate stanza forms, like a river through cataracts:

> Confetti in the streets
> coagulates like spoors of dragon's blood,
> running gold and purple underfoot,
> as the horse-year stumbles beneath the ram-year
> and fire spills from children's hands.
> We've come too late to see

the pageant go. This codicil
of scraps, of gaping faces glowing past,
points away from celebration, back
toward street-ruin and spiking temperatures,
as the old year slackens and rasps.

Yezzi's ability to translate visual into verbal splendor is very
rare, and stems from his instinctive understanding of the difference between the genres: while a painting exists in a luminous
instant, a poem must cunningly prepare its effects. So in these
stanzas from "Chinese New Year"—as in poems like "Chekhovian Landscape" and "Casco Passage"—Yezzi seduces with lavish-
ness, before surprising with seriousness. For this richly
rendered carnival scene gives way to a Chinese emigrant's recollection of what seems to be the Cultural Revolution: "I'm
glad you lived,/that you scraped through when thousands
died/and war rooted in frozen earth." And the tourist exoti-
cism of the Chinese dragons ("I buy a dragon/for my daughter,
just turned one") inevitably reminds the poet that history has
real dragons, not so easily dispelled ("She understands nothing
of dragonkind"). In "Chinese New Year," as in all the best poems
in *The Hidden Model*, Yezzi brings together beauty and skepti-
cism, eloquence and doubt, the visual and the verbal. Reading
him reminds us that poetry is capable of the most subtle perception and the most civilized thought, if only a poet takes himself and the art seriously enough to achieve them.

THE COVER of *The Hidden Model* displays a Morandi painting of
bottles, in beautiful and slightly eerie stillness. Joe Osterhaus's
Radiance, on the other hand, greets the reader with the buzzing
diagonals of a Lichtenstein painting of the Statue of Liberty. The

image is perfectly chosen, in the way it unsettles patriotic iconography with Pop-inflected vibrancy. For Osterhaus is fascinated by the difficulty of telling the whole truth about America and its history, especially the history of the present. His best poems want to capture the feel of living in a particular time and place, one of the most valuable things any poet can do, and one of the most difficult. To render the Kennedy years in verse, for instance, or just the few scandalous months of the Lewinsky affair, means reminding the reader of what he already knows— the facts, the official reference points—while giving them a new arrangement and coloration. It means condensing a whole historical period into a verbal icon, and making the poet's own impression of the times so powerful that the reader will accept it, at least provisionally, as the truth. Take, for instance, Osterhaus's "1998," which races through the scandals of that year and culminates in an image of tabloid culture as a giant incinerator:

> no center, no regard, no honor left
> as oil-stoked furnaces burn through our trash;
> last week's charges go up like bits of foil
> that leave an oily stain; a sheath, collapsed.

A poet who complains about "no honor left" risks sounding merely censorious, but Osterhaus's daring final image—the used condom, ironically euphemized with the archaic word "sheath"—shows that he too is at home in the profane culture he regrets.

One of the most appealing things about *Radiance*, in fact, is the sense that Osterhaus must force himself to overcome his natural delicacy in order to write about the indignities of sex, which play so large a part in both national and personal destinies. In his address to the muse, "To One of the Dugout

Nine"—a title that characteristically merges Helicon and Fenway Park—Osterhaus gives a sense of the range of places the poet must be willing to haunt:

> where are you hiding now; where do you comb
> leather shops for ridged pleasure toys, or steam
> mosaics till their gold leaf flakes the tomb;
>
> which alleys do you piss in; on which grates
> or hotel featherbeds do you awake . . . ?

If transgressive sexuality seems like a major ingredient in this recipe, that is because Osterhaus, unusually among contemporary poets, really feels the transgression in sex, and allows the reader to feel it. Graphic anatomical descriptions of sex inevitably come across as polemical and self-conscious, which is why the sex poems of Sharon Olds, for instance, feel so unerotic. To understand what a spirit genuinely embarrassed by lust sounds like, we can turn instead to the opening poem of *Radiance*, "The Tree Rings in the Surface of the Butcher's Block," with its impacted music and densely suggestive imagery:

> A virus riveting the skin and mind
>
> connects the close-watched second-hands to the drops
> beaded on the panes of butcher shops,
> that swell, edge, burst, and run in a thin crest
>
> whose warp distorts the sweetbreads as they're dressed.

For Osterhaus, the god of desire is not Venus but a shambling Satan, "goat-footed, bent, and shawled," as he writes in

"Shadow, Hawk, and Dove." The insult of sex is not so much to Puritan morality—which troubles Osterhaus, like most of us, not at all—but to the illusion of self-control, the way it forces the mind to serve the body. This is the humiliating experience encoded in Osterhaus's coolly ruthless description of pleasure: "And though his love/was mixed up with his pain,/the pin-prick, needling shards of it/were angels on a pin."

For a poet compelled by history and sexuality, John F. Kennedy, with his lurid heroism, seems like an inevitable subject. Osterhaus's eight-sonnet sequence "The Depth of Things" approaches this familiar terrain with exactly the right combination of cynicism and susceptibility; he is suspicious about the sources of Kennedy's charisma, but never dismisses the fact of it. As the title suggests, Osterhaus approaches Camelot through its things, its vanished properties: "their thin lapels,/manual typewriters, and tripod cameras," which still keep the glamour of the modern even now that they are obsolete. No poet who didn't live through them has evoked America's early 1960s so confidently:

> Rough stands of chokecherry, bronzed by thick heat;
> gray aircraft carriers and Berlin wall;
> Bull Conner's German Shepherds in the street;
> moon craters lapped with dust; and the lyrical
>
> blue earth, seen from a pear-shaped craft.

Best of all is the fifth sonnet in the sequence, which summons the true but nightmarish vision of Jackie Kennedy's aides prowling the Library of Congress at night, looking for precedents for her husband's state funeral. In the "incisions" of their roaming flashlights, Osterhaus finds an indelible metaphor for the chaos and enchantment of history: "What made that random lightstorm beautiful?"

This is not to say that every poem in *Radiance* is dedicated to a familiar or celebrated figure—though Fred Astaire, Sam Cooke, and Buster Keaton all make appearances. The book's tour de force is a long narrative poem, "The Villa Basque," about the habitués of a forlorn restaurant in the California desert— the crooked owner John, the drug-dealing cook Tony, the veteran waitresses Sally, Annette, and Ruth. "The Villa Basque" combines the plot and characters of a good tale with a good poem's intensity of language and deliberate pacing. All by itself, it constitutes a powerful argument for the continued viability of the narrative poem in an age of lyric. Here, as throughout *Radiance,* Osterhaus uses established forms to express a daring, cunning, and completely new sensibility.

To GET A SENSE of the bleak and illusionless intelligence that animates Joshua Mehigan's poetry, the best place to start is the title poem of his first collection, *The Optimist*. Optimism, of the quiet, bourgeois, cheerfully resigned variety, is something contemporary poetry hardly needs more of. Reassurance, minor epiphanies, the solace of everyday things—these are some of our most popular poets' most popular subjects.

But Mehigan's optimist, we soon discover, is a woman dying of cancer: "Touch burned out first, then vision." And where another poet would play this death for bathos, Mehigan makes it yield a genuinely astringent recognition. This is not simply that we are all destined to die, but rather that death exposes the hollowness of our desires. The dying woman's last request, to pick out the dress she will be buried in, is presented not as a brave assertion of personality in the face of oblivion, but as a reflexive operation of will, as helpless as the jerks and twitches of the hanged man:

> She wasn't making light. It seemed to her
> that cancer just rehearsed life's attitude
> that one's desires must taper to a point
> which has position, but no magnitude.

A poet who can wrest such an insight from such a subject is in no danger of "making light," in any sense of the phrase. Indeed, the more cheerful a poem's title in "The Optimist," the more certain it is to betray its promise of happiness. "Progress" turns out to be about nothingness, both cosmic and existential: "in truth nothing was in him, around him, / substantial, pervasive, and all of that—/ even atomic." "Merrily" seems to invoke "merrily we roll along," but its epigraph from Donne ("from the womb to the grave we are never thoroughly awake") suggests a very different kind of journey. In Mehigan's parable of life as a river voyage, he insists that we are not pilots of our destinies, merely their cargo: "As if to steer, / I drop a hand in. Oh well. Anyhow, / the scenery is mesmerizing here."

If Mehigan's understanding of life is consistently dark, however, it is not insistently so. He does not complain, argue, or preach about the state of affairs his poems reveal; in fleeing from optimism, he does not end up a pessimist. Rather, the terse eloquence of his formal verse seems to constrain him to direct, accurate observation. (Or, rather, his instinct for directness and accuracy leads him to use formal verse, whose artifice is, paradoxically, the best way to avoid mere rhetoric.) The quietness of Mehigan's poetry is made possible by a genuine formal mastery, rare for any poet today, and doubly impressive in a first collection.

For an example of how rhythm can express a poem's meaning even more effectively than words, look at "A Questionable Mother," about a woman who has murdered her child. This ripped-from-the-tabloids subject might seem too garish for poetry, or at least to demand an equivalent garishness in its treatment, such as Frank Bidart brings to his tales of serial killers and madmen. Mehigan, on the other hand, enforces an extraordinary atmosphere of hopelessness simply through a series of pentameter lines, each dragging to a halt on a weak syllable:

> Here thoughts of murder weren't that uncommon.
> Nakedness was uncovered by the hour.
> Within, the suspect cried they must believe her.
> The female officer behind a window
> of thick green glass typed slowly without stopping.

It is typical of Mehigan to show the crime not in the overwhelming instant of its commission, but in the bleary, routine aftermath. Life, too, goes on "slowly without stopping": that is the truth he always returns to, and which makes his sadness convincingly unmelodramatic.

This complex of formal, tonal, and philosophical gifts makes Mehigan akin to Robert Frost, and at least one poem in *The Optimist* seems a deliberate response to a famous Frost poem. Just as Frost, in "Out, Out—," sternly elides the moment of a boy's death in an accident—"Little, less, nothing!—and that ended it"—so Mehigan, in "The Spectacle," relegates a couple's death by fire to a line break:

> They slept a moment more but didn't wake
> until the gas was on them like a tongue,
> and then they were asleep again.

The chilling kindness of the euphemism is also Frostian, as is the concluding turn away from the victim to the survivors: "the firemen said, 'Stand back, please . . . please stand back . . . '" Yet despite the similarities, "The Spectacle" does not read like a pastiche of Frost. Rather, it is Mehigan's expression, in his own idiom, of a similar experience of the world.

Nor does that experience only take the extreme forms of the poems discussed here—murder, disease, accidental death. It is equally present in Mehigan's wrenching poems about family life, whether he writes from the point of view of the child, as in "After a Nightmare," or the father, as in "Runaway Daughter," or the husband, as in "The Tyrant." There is more insight into domestic grief in these and other poems in *The Optimist* than in a dozen louder, more overtly confessional poets. This sense of insight born from experience is what makes Mehigan's work so moving and impressive. Few American poets, old or young, seem to know so much.

THE FIRST POEM in A. E. Stallings's second collection, *Hapax*, suggests that Elizabeth Bishop plays the same tutelary role in her witty, intelligent poems that Frost does in Mehigan's. "After-shocks" employs a famous rhyme from "One Art"—master, vaster, disaster—and invokes "cartography," the favorite subject of the author of "The Map" and *Geography III*. At the very least, the situation of the lovers in "Aftershocks"—who find to their surprise that "We are not in the same place after all," who ask "have we always stood on shaky ground?"—suggests that Stallings, like Bishop, is a poet who approaches the world warily. She has a coolly ironic sense of the way things fall, not dramatically apart, but unsettlingly askew—the way, as she puts it in "The Doll-house," "lives accrue, / With interest, the smallest things we do."

The most appealing of Stallings's gifts is her sense of play, though she is not a ludic poet, if that word suggests the linguistic somersaults of a Paul Muldoon. Rather, her delight in the artificiality of language—the way it can be coaxed into rhymes and patterns—is decorous, even slightly aloof. The pun in those lines from "The Dollhouse," drawing out the double meaning of "interest," is highly characteristic. It bespeaks a poet who pays as strict attention to her words as to her thoughts, and who finds both kinds of attention a source of pleasure. That is why verbal conceits abound in *Hapax*. At a funeral, "silence sounds its deafening report"; a poem titled "Thyme" is also, inevitably, about time. "Minutes" compares the passing moments, with their easily refused demands on our attention, to beggars, and then works out the metaphor with Metaphysical thoroughness:

> Who's to say which one of them finally snags you,
> One you will remember from all that pass you,
> One that makes you fish through your cluttered pockets,
>   Costing you something. . . .

Stallings's ideal reader would be able to recognize the Sapphic stanza she employs here, since the Greek classics are her favorite subject and resource. (The book's title is the Greek word for "once.") She comes by this interest honestly—she is an American expatriate in Athens—but drawing on Greek myth for emotional resonance is a perilous tactic, and she does not always avoid its pitfalls. Temperamentally, in fact, she seems drawn to a certain classicist's donnishness, as in her long series of limericks about gods and heroes ("Arachne, Athena beside her,/Let her ego grow wider and wider"), which would not sound out of place in a senior common room.

But Stallings deserves praise for mostly avoiding the misuse of the classics that is much more usual today, in poets from Ted Hughes to Louise Glück: treating them as a ready-made storehouse of tremulous, Gothic intensity. Stallings's scrupulous intelligence never serves her better than in her understated approach to myth, as in "Asphodel," a poem about the flowers of hell: "I noticed a strange fragrance. It was sweet,/Like honey—but with hints of rotting meat." Such precise imagination allows her to do justice to the real foreignness of ancient Greece, and provides some of the most memorable images in *Hapax*: a dead dog "touching noses/Once, twice, three times, with unleashed Cerberus"; the "needling milk teeth" of Actaeon's hounds, who will grow up to devour him; Persephone who "weeps kerosene/And wipes it on her sleeve." Stallings describes this technique—the poet guiding herself through the unknown by holding fast to the concrete—in "Explaining an Affinity for Bats": "Who find their way by calling into darkness/To hear their voice bounce off the shape of things."

But the most intriguing direction that *Hapax* opens up for the future of Stallings's poetry lies in more personal subjects. Her poems about love, sex, and heartbreak have that rare combination of emotion and reason, sweetness and sourness, that used to be called worldly-wise. If few poets sound this way anymore, it is because few recognize, as Stallings does, that feeling is most poetically effective when it is mastered by form and irony. When Stallings writes about shattering emotion, as in "Fragment," she does not use "I" even once, preferring to give herself wholly over to the metaphor of a dropped glass:

> It breaks because it falls
> Into the arms of the earth—that grave attraction.
> It breaks because it meets the floor's surface,
> Which is solid and does not give. It breaks because

It is dropped, and falls hard, because it hits
Bottom, and nobody catches it.

In the matter-of-factness of that last line, we seem to hear Stallings's true note—as we do in the miniature drama of disconnection in "Failure," and the compressed history of a love affair in "Flying Colors: Flags of Convenience." It is a note that already makes Stallings one of the best younger poets, and that promises to grow even stronger in the work that lies ahead.

Two Modern Classics

The Waste Land

According to the calendar, *The Waste Land* is more distant from us today than *In Memoriam* and *Leaves of Grass* were from T. S. Eliot when he completed his masterpiece in 1922. Yet as Eliot himself proved, poetic time, like Einsteinian time, is relative. Dante and Donne, he argued in his essays, were closer to the twentieth-century poet than Tennyson and Whitman. By the same token, even though *The Waste Land* has been making Aprils cruel for more than eighty years, it remains more modern than any poem written since.

In fact, the poem may be stranger today than it has ever been. On the one hand, *The Waste Land* now appears unmistakably a product of its time, full of dated references, falsified prophecies, and obsolete novelties. Parts of it are as redolent of the 1920s as the silent-movie and vaudeville effects it so brilliantly incorporates. Yet it also remains genuinely surprising, creating before our eyes the very atmosphere and vocabulary of modern poetry. Next to *The Waste Land*, the best works of later generations—*Life Studies*, *Questions of Travel*, *The Whitsun Weddings*, right down to the most distinguished books of the last few years, like *The Bounty*—seem positively traditional in their formal and lyric assumptions.

All of these paradoxes are implied in the oxymoron that no discussion of *The Waste Land* can avoid: "modern classic." Indeed, the best way to approach the poem today may be through a dissection of the concept of the modern, which Eliot did so much to create. For the essays Eliot wrote in the late 1910s and early 1920s, around the time he was writing *The Waste Land*, suggest that his understanding of modernism was actually a compound of two very different ideas. Each of those ideas had a revolutionary power, and helped to inaugurate the poetic era in which we are still living. But while one of them is sound and still valuable, the other was flawed from the beginning, and has become increasingly burdensome. And they can both be seen in action, with all their good and ill effects, in the laboratory of modernism that is *The Waste Land*.

The seldom disguised purpose of Eliot's early criticism was to commit literary parricide. His constant theme was the debility of the nineteenth-century English poetic tradition, the tradition of Shelley, Tennyson, and Swinburne. It was only by deposing this etiolated dynasty that Eliot and his peers could ascend their throne. The Victorians are always Eliot's polemical target, whether he is writing about Marvell ("The effort to construct a dream-world, which alters English poetry so greatly in the nineteenth century . . . makes a poet of the nineteenth century, of the same size as Marvell, a more trivial and less serious figure"), or Dryden ("Where Dryden fails to satisfy, the nineteenth century does not satisfy us either; and where that century has condemned him, it is itself condemned"), or the Metaphysical poets ("Tennyson and Browning are poets, and they think; but they do not feel their thought as immediately as the odour of a rose").

The ambiguity in Eliot's revolutionary poetics arises when he must explain the reason for his dissatisfaction with his immediate predecessors. The superficial explanation, and therefore the one that was easiest for later poets and critics to assimilate, is that the Victorians failed because they were not up-to-date enough. They did not accurately reflect the times they lived in, but retreated into fairy tales and verbal opiates. To be successfully modern, poets must courageously confront the modern world, as Eliot declares in the famous peroration to "The Metaphysical Poets": "We can only say that poets in our civilization, as it exists at present, must be *difficult*. Our civilization comprehends great variety and complexity, and this variety and complexity, playing upon a refined sensibility, must produce various and complex results."

In other words, a civilization different in kind from any that has come before demands a new kind of poetry. This idea appears again and again in Eliot's prose. "Art," he declares in his July 1921 "London Letter" for *The Dial*, "has to create a new world, and a new world must have a new structure." In the September 1921 "Letter," he praises Stravinsky for having succeeded in this absorption of the new: *The Rite of Spring*, he writes, "did seem to transform the rhythm of the steppes into the scream of the motor horn, the rattle of machinery, the grind of wheels, the beating of iron and steel, the roar of the underground-railway, and the other barbaric cries of modern life." In this quasi-Futurist vision, the best poet is the one with the toughest alimentary tract, able to suck nutrition from the hard rind of the twentieth century.

This is the principle at the heart of modernism, for which the modern is no longer a premise but an ideology. It was especially tempting in a century when technological change was constantly accelerating. After all, if poetry must assimilate "the scream of the motor horn," why not every subsequent development in technology—the roar of the airplane, the static of the television, the whine of the modem? Doesn't it follow that poetry must remake its own technologies just as often? It was by this logic that the twentieth century produced an endless series of avant-gardes, which, like Fibonacci numbers, had to summarize and transcend all their predecessors.

But Eliot's charge that the nineteenth century was not modern enough is only superficially an argument about up-to-dateness. After all, the lodestars of his criticism are poets of the fourteenth and seventeenth centuries. In his Clark lectures, published as *The Varieties of Metaphysical Poetry*, he drew a plumbline from Dante through Donne to Laforgue and, by implication, himself. What all these poets had in common was not modernity but a certain kind of daring—the quality Eliot describes in "Prose and Verse" as "courage and adventurousness in tackling anything that had to be expressed." "Great poetry," he writes still more explicitly, "capture[s] and put[s] into literature an emotion." And the poets Eliot admires are those who captured experiences, sensations, and states of being that had never before been brought into poetry. Such poetic pioneers were, in another phrase from "The Metaphysical Poets," "engaged in the task of trying to find the verbal equivalent for states of mind and feeling."

Poetry of this kind, what might be called the poetry of discovery, is only superficially related to modernist poetry. Both are in pursuit of some sort of novelty. But the poet of discovery wants to create something new in literature, something that has never been adequately expressed before, while the modernist poet believes he must respond to something new in "civilization." When Eliot castigates the Victorians, it is really their failure of discovery, not their failure of contemporaneity, that infuriates him. Thus he objects to Milton and Tennyson on the grounds that they wrote "language dissociated from things"—language that was not a "verbal equivalent for states of mind and feeling" but merely "a style quite remote from life."

For Eliot, then, stylistic innovation is not something that must be undertaken self-consciously, in order to produce a novel effect. It should be the natural result of a poet's attentiveness to new subjects, new feelings, new complexions of consciousness. And this kind of discovery continues to be what we value highest, both in the poetry of our own time and in the poetry of the past. Eliot remains our most important critic, even in these days of his seeming eclipse, because we instinctively assent to his demand that each poet offer us a sense of reality—or, to use Matthew Arnold's phrase, a criticism of life—which we cannot find in any other poet. For the age of Johnson, a poet's merit lay in his mastery of conventions; for the age of Eliot, the poet is a master only if he puts those conventions to new uses.

Is it possible to disentangle the two principles that are conflated in Eliot's criticism? The best way to answer that question is to return to *The Waste Land,* and to its strange double existence in the past and future of poetry. For the poem now appears, after several generations of reading and interpretation, to combine two kinds of novelty—the period modernism of the 1920s, with its swagger and pose, its urban nihilism and fashionable despair; and the enduring newness of Eliot's own spiritual and musical discoveries.

Take, for instance, the most famous of literary clairvoyantes, Madame Sosostris. Her pack of Tarot cards is one of the necessary binding elements in Eliot's fragmentary poem. "The drowned Phoenician sailor" prepares the way for Phlebas, whose appearance in Part IV creates one of the poem's most effective shifts of tone—an eerie submarine interlude between the "burning" of "The Fire Sermon" and the "stony places" of

"What the Thunder Said." (Ezra Pound's sure editorial touch, so surprising in so erratic a poet, prevented Eliot from cutting the whole of Part IV: Phlebas, Pound advised, "is needed ABSoloootly where he is.")

Similarly, Madame Sosostris's "one-eyed merchant" looks forward to Mr. Eugenides, in Part III; and her "Those are pearls that were his eyes. Look!" returns to terrible effect in the neurotic dialogue of Part II. The whole Sosostris episode helps to create that illusion of hidden coherence that gives *The Waste Land* its mythic power—even though, as Eliot himself acknowledged in 1956, it is finally no more than an illusion: "I regret having sent so many enquirers off on a wild goose chase after Tarot Cards and the Holy Grail."

Yet Madame Sosostris is also a manifestation or a casualty of one of the most dated impulses in *The Waste Land*, Eliot's attack on twentieth-century decadence. Her fashionable spiritualism, we are meant to see, usurps the traditional prestige of religion, and preys on the insecurities of a rootless bourgeoisie. Mrs. Equitone, the fortune-teller's client, announces her lack of conviction in her very name. Later, in *Four Quartets*, Eliot would again name those who "haruspicate or scry" as agents of spiritual confusion.

From this point of view, Madame Sosostris belongs with the poem's other emblems of modern depravity: the predatory Mr. Eugenides, who tries to arrange an assignation at the Cannon Street Hotel, and the "young man carbuncular," "one of the low" whom a leveling capitalism has allowed to get above himself. Together, these characters vividly evoke Eliot's sense of a world in which traditional boundaries—of nation and religion, sex and class—have collapsed, leaving sterility and anxiety in their wake. This is, of course, one of the most sinister tropes of the interwar period, and sheds a great deal of light on Eliot's attraction to anti-Semitic stereotypes (in "Bleistein with a Baedeker, Burbank with a Cigar" and "Gerontion") and his sympathy for a protofascist figure like Charles Maurras. Possibly it was only Eliot's turn to Christianity, in the late 1920s, that prevented these tendencies from developing into the fanatical rage for order that was Pound's downfall.

Madame Sosostris, then, is a Tiresias-figure in a way Eliot never intended, at once a Joycean myth and a Spenglerian demon. And a similar ambiguity runs through the whole of *The Waste Land*. At certain moments, Eliot seems to be staging his despair, in order to call attention to the moral strenuousness that allegedly distinguishes the moderns from the Victorians— their determination, as he puts it in the brief essay "The Lesson of Baudelaire," "to arrive at a point of view toward good and evil." The passage beginning "What are the roots that clutch" has something of this histrionic quality, as does the evocation of "hooded hordes swarming" in Part V. Then, too, Eliot's allusiveness can sometimes seem programmatic, as though written to fulfill the prescription of "Tradition and the Individual Talent": "the feeling that the whole of the literature of Europe from Homer and within it the whole literature of his own country has a simultaneous existence and composes a simultaneous order." Many of Eliot's allusions are magically effective, seeming to spring without premeditation from his auditory imagination; but others are showily eclectic, including the flourished "shantihs" that conclude the poem.

Where *The Waste Land* is still unquestionably vital, however, is in that element of poetry which can never be forced or forged: its music, and especially its rhythm. It was Eliot who established, by precept and example, that the rhythm of a poem is just as important a tool of discovery as its diction and argument. Nothing is more eloquent of a poet's individuality, or more essential to his conquest of experience for art, than the patterns of nerve and thought recorded in his voice. "A poem," Eliot avows in "The Music of Poetry," "may tend to realize itself first as a particular rhythm before it reaches expression in words." That may be why some of the best and most convincing passages in *The Waste Land* approach as nearly as possible to pure rhythm:

> If there were water
> And no rock
> If there were rock
> And also water
> And water
> A spring
> A pool among the rock . . .

Or, again, from the song of the Thames-daughters in Part III:

> The river sweats
> Oil and tar
> The barges drift
> With the turning tide
> Wide
> To leeward, swing on the heavy spar.

In fact, it might be possible to discern the essence of Eliot's artistic and spiritual biography strictly from a study of his evolving rhythms. Such a study would also show how Eliot captured for poetry the sound and movement of whole areas of human experience. Even today, almost a century later, adolescence is still the plangent hesitation of "Prufrock"; sexual disgust is the stern bite of "Sweeney Among the Nightingales"; spiritual quest, with its necessary doubt and self-suspicion, is the spiraling repetition of *Four Quartets*. And *The Waste Land* is all of these and more, including something that cannot be precisely named—except as the signature in verse of Eliot's unrepeatable genius.

Howl

ALLEN GINSBERG surely would not want a reader to approach *Howl* by way of Lionel Trilling. But Trilling's role in Ginsberg's intellectual life was so significant, and his reaction to the poem seems so perverse, that his part in the creation myth of *Howl* is worth considering. As a student at Columbia in the 1940s, Ginsberg was close to Trilling, one of the greatest twentieth-century critics and an especially potent influence on a young man with literary ambitions. But when Ginsberg sent *Howl* to his teacher in 1956, just before it was published, Trilling dismissed the poem in seemingly impossible terms: it had "no real voice," it was "all prose . . . without any music," and worst of all, it was "dull."

Howl, of all poems, dull? Maybe today, fifty years after it first appeared in that iconic, squared-off, black-and-white paperback from City Lights Books, Ginsberg's provocations have been staled by custom. As David Gates remarks in *The Poem That Changed America*, a collection of essays on *Howl* and its influence by a variety of novelists, poets, academics, and Beat veterans, the poem "is on somebody's syllabus in almost every American college except Bob Jones University, and nobody says boo."

But it is useful to remember, now that *Howl* has its very own *Festschrift* like some white-haired emeritus professor, that when Ginsberg mailed out the first copies of the book, Gary Snyder referred to them as "bombs." And for a few delightful months, it looked as if the Establishment agreed, calling in the legal equivalent of the bomb squad. Customs stopped a shipment of books at the border, and Lawrence Ferlinghetti, Ginsberg's publisher and the owner of San Francisco's City Lights Bookstore, the Beat headquarters, was prosecuted for obscenity. By the late 1950s, however, such censorship could only be half-hearted, just enough to give *Howl* a banned-in-Boston allure. Customs reversed its blockade, and Ferlinghetti was quickly acquitted.

Instead, America found an infinitely more effective way to smother whatever mental explosive Ginsberg had packed into *Howl*: the commodification of dissent. The famous reading at the Six Gallery, when Ginsberg, Snyder, and four other poets unofficially launched the San Francisco Poetry Renaissance, was on October 13, 1955; by 1959, millions of squares were enjoying the antics of Maynard G. Krebs, the work-shy beatnik on *The Many Loves of Dobie Gillis*. Ginsberg himself became one of the licensed jesters of the 1960s, chanting mantras in college auditoriums, going on tour with Bob Dylan. Before he died in 1997, writes Jonah Raskin in *American Scream: Allen Ginsberg's Howl and the Making of the Beat Generation,* Ginsberg "called the White House to ask if President Bill Clinton might grant him a literary award." This from the poet who wrote, in "Death to Van Gogh's Ear!":

> fortunately all the governments will fall
> the only ones which won't fall are the good ones
> and the good ones don't yet exist
> But they have to begin existing they exist in my poems
> they exist in the death of the Russian and American
>   governments

What accounts for the warm embrace between the poet of *Howl*—chieftain of the "angel-headed hipsters," "who burned cigarette holes in their arms protesting the narcotic tobacco haze of Capitalism"—and the society he denounced as "Moloch whose poverty is the specter of genius"? *The Poem That Changed America* offers a clear explanation, repeated by virtually every contributor who first encountered *Howl* as a teenager between 1955 and 1980: the poem functions as a perfect lifestyle advertisement. Especially for bookish young men, it seems, *Howl* is less intriguing for its mystical invocations of "Plotinus Poe St. John of the Cross telepathy and bop kabbalah" than for its rapturous knowingness about sex and drugs: "who copulated ecstatic and insatiate with a bottle of beer a sweetheart a package of cigarettes a candle and fell off the bed, and continued along the floor and down the hall and ended fainting on the wall with a vision of ultimate cunt and come eluding the last gyzym of consciousness."

For Sven Birkerts, Ginsberg's "'negro streets' pull[ed] the white boy like rap pulls other white boys now, coding a whole panorama of the 'real' before which nothing in my life could hold a plea." For Luc Sante, "the poem was a travel brochure for the colorful world I would settle in as soon as I could get away from my parents." For Robert Pinsky, it "felt like the party I was desperate to discover." And to Billy Collins, *Howl* appeared no more or less transgressive than "the outcries of 'Rock Around the Clock' and *Rebel Without a Cause*."

The best way of responding to such serene misappropriations of Ginsberg's poem is to ask whether they are really misappropriations after all. To be sure, Ginsberg intended *Howl* as much more than a commercial for the counterculture. It was a visionary lament, suffused with the spirits of Blake and Whitman, and the poet always recognized it as his masterpiece. In

1982, when it was already clear that Ginsberg would never write a poem better than *Howl* (though he rivaled it in *Kaddish*), he insisted on the rarity and difficulty of the achievement: "You have to be inspired to write something like that. It's not something you can very easily do just by pressing a button. You have to have the right historical situation, the right physical combination, the right mental formation, the right courage, the right sense of prophecy, and the right information."

The most important thing that *Howl* got right, however, was a form. Like most poets, Ginsberg knew his true subject long before he was able to treat it appropriately and originally in verse. That subject was a genuine longing for transcendence, a conviction that space and time are the disguises reality wears and might, in supreme moments, put off. For most of his life, Ginsberg claimed to have experienced just such an epiphany in the summer of 1948, when he had a hallucination of a deep voice reading Blake's poem "Ah! Sun-flower," heralding a moment of mystical union with the cosmos. It may be doubted whether the episode took place in just this way, or was rather an aspiration so intensely cherished that it could pass for fulfillment. (John Berryman had a similar vision, at a similar age, involving W. B. Yeats, which he clearly considered a metaphor rather than a haunting.) Raskin quotes Ginsberg's acknowledgment, late in life, that "I cooked it up, somehow."

Whether Ginsberg ever enjoyed a true vision or not, it was the longing for ecstasy, not the experience of it, that motivated his early poetry. "Am I to spend/My life in praise of the idea of God?" he asked in 1949's "Psalm II," and for the next six years he was constantly yearning to move from the idea to the reality. In "Hymn" he wrote about "this clock of meat bleakly pining for its sweet immaterial paradise"; in "Siesta in Xbalba," recording a trip to Mexico in 1954, he insisted "there is an

inner/interior image/of divinity/beckoning me out/to pilgrimage." In his most moving pre-*Howl* poem, "The Green
Automobile," he cast this pilgrimage in what would become
typically erotic terms. Imagining a reunion with Neal Cassady,
Ginsberg writes:

> childhood youthtime age & eternity
> would open like sweet trees
> in the nights of another spring
> and dumbfound us with love

> for we can see together
> the beauty of souls
> hidden like diamonds
> in the clock of the world

The problem with mystical longing as a subject for poetry is
that, since it necessarily treats of consummation deferred, it
always threatens to become a contentless form, with each new
poem reiterating the same desire and the same disappointment.
What made *Howl* a revolution in Ginsberg's poetry was his discovery of a form that makes longing genuinely dramatic. That
form involves three simultaneous innovations. First is incantation: each of the poem's three sections uses a repeated word or
phrase ("who," "Moloch," "I'm with you in Rockland") as an
anchor, establishing a rhythmic and syntactical frame for its
wild flights of rhetoric.

Second is the verbal recklessness within each strophe (Ginsberg's first title for the draft poem was "Strophes"), the magically felicitous combination of seemingly unrelated words. In
lesser hands—including Ginsberg's own, in some of his more
tedious poems—the magic fails, and the result is what the

poem itself calls "lofty incantations which in the yellow morning were stanzas of gibberish." (Take, for instance, a line from
"Television Was a Baby Crawling Toward That Deathchamber":
"I myself saw the sunflower-monkeys of the Moon—spending
their dear play-money electricity in a homemade tape-record
minute of cartoony high Sound.")

But in *Howl*, Ginsberg achieves a telescoping of ideas and
images of which Donne would be proud. "Hydrogen jukebox"
captures the pop energy and nuclear anxiety of the 1950s;
"hotrod-Golgotha," their James Dean–inspired teenage alienation; "Moloch the stunned governments," the Cold War and its
mutually assured paranoia. *Howl* itself describes the technique
perfectly: "who dreamt and made incarnate gaps in Time &
Space through images juxtaposed, and trapped the archangel of
the soul between 2 visual images and joined the elemental
verbs and set the noun and dash of consciousness together. . . ."
Last, the poem brilliantly uses its long lines to outpace the natural rhythm of breath. As with Shelley's "Adonais" (an acknowledged model for Ginsberg), reading it aloud results in a kind of
oxygen-deprived elation.

Howl was the consummation of Ginsberg's ecstatic longing,
the ideal expression of his yearning for the "ancient heavenly
connection to the starry dynamo in the machinery of night."
How, then, did this genuinely mystical poem fit so neatly, as
Philip Lopate writes, "into our bag of anarchic provocations,
along with *Mad* magazine, the raunchier lyrics of rhythm and
blues, and, a bit later, Lenny Bruce"? The answer lies in the all-
too-perfect fit between Ginsberg's mysticism and the American
materialism he set out to oppose. The second section of *Howl* is
a formal curse against that materialism, considered as
"Moloch," the child-eating God to whom the young casualties
of the poem's first part were sacrificed. Ginsberg's Moloch is a

vision of America as Blake's Urizen—repressively rational, intent on domination and accumulation, its crimes summed up in a single, ominous phrase: "Moloch whose name is the Mind!"

By identifying mind as the enemy, however, Ginsberg necessarily allies himself with all that is not-mind: both that which is higher, the spirit, and that which is lower, the appetites. The antinomian premise of *Howl* is that these two avenues to ecstasy are essentially the same: that the hipsters and petty criminals who burned out on sex and drugs were really spiritual seekers, who "broke their backs lifting Moloch to Heaven." For Ginsberg himself, a man with a genuine calling and talent for mysticism, it seems fair to say that these really were avenues to transcendence. LSD and peyote, mantras and meditation all formed part of his quest.

But most of his audience, especially the 1960s teenagers riding the crest of American affluence, read *Howl*'s equation of sense and spirit backwards. Instead of pleasure offering a route to transcendence, transcendence was demoted to a species of pleasure. *Howl*, in truth, does everything possible to encourage this deeply American fallacy, which amounts to the apotheosis of consumerism. Doesn't the catalogue of victims in Part I seem like exactly that, a catalogue, laying out various kinds of pleasure for purchase? Music ("floating across the tops of cities contemplating jazz"), crime ("went out whoring in Colorado in myriad stolen night-cars"), drugs ("the endless ride from Battery to Holy Bronx on benzedrine"), sex ("sweetened the snatches of a million girls"), all are offered up for the reader's voyeuristic enjoyment. Read this way, the suffering the poem describes looks like a proof of purchase: how much pleasure would one have to experience before coming out, exhausted, on the other side?

This is the point at which Trilling's verdict on the poem, that it was "dull," starts to look especially peculiar. Many sins might be laid at the door of *Howl*, though it is impossible to separate the influence of the text from that of the period it inspired and came to symbolize, the beat fifties and hippie sixties. The glorification of violence, the sentimentality about mental illness, the contempt for reason, the political self-righteousness, the waste of reformist energy in theatrical gestures, the confusion of narcissism with moral superiority: all that is worst about the counterculture is foreshadowed in *Howl* and Ginsberg's subsequent poems. But it would take a pretty jaded palate to find *Howl* dull.

What Trilling really meant to communicate to Ginsberg, however, was not that *Howl* would fail to excite its readers. Rather, Trilling foresaw that it would excite them in a way which he himself, and many other imaginative people, had already judged disastrous. For while Ginsberg's belief in radical innocence and radical excess was new to the baby boomers, it was not at all new to Trilling, or to modernists like Yvor Winters and Allen Tate, each of whom had experienced the suicide of Hart Crane as a parable of the personal cost of imaginative chaos. The antinomianism of *Howl*, Trilling would have recognized better than anyone, is one of the fundamental impulses of modern literature, and readers who were in their fifties when Ginsberg was in his twenties had wrestled with it long before. "It seems to me that the characteristic element of modern literature," Trilling wrote in an essay that was not about *Howl,* but could have been, "is the bitter line of hostility to civilization which runs through it. . . . It asks us if we are saved or damned—more than with anything else, our literature is concerned with salvation."

The moral and intellectual sophistication of Trilling's work comes from his recognition that this Manicheanism is the fuel of some of the greatest modern writing, but is also profoundly at odds with the liberal virtues of reason, tolerance, and decency. Trilling acknowledges that the liberal imagination "inclines to constrict and make mechanical its conception of the nature of mind"—in other words, that it inclines toward Molochdom. Yet his response to this inherent weakness of the liberal mind is to look to literature to deepen and complicate it—to teach it the values of "variousness, possibility, complexity, and difficulty."

Trilling's tragic vision, in other words, is the exact opposite of Ginsberg's comic one, which yearns for unity, simplicity, and childlike ease: "Everything is holy! everybody's holy! everywhere is holy!" The dullness that Trilling found in *Howl* is the dullness of an error he himself had long since seen through and overcome. This does not mean that *Howl* is vitiated as a poem: on the contrary, the energetic expression of an error can be wonderfully good poetry. But it does mean that *Howl* is a poem to read early, before you outgrow what Ginsberg himself called, with shrewd and saving humor, "Dreams! adorations! illuminations! religions! the whole boatload of sensitive bullshit!"

Yvor Winters

"A CRITIC may even be specifically wrong yet theoretically right. Paul Elmer More, for instance, damns all modern literature with one irritated and uncomprehending gesture; he is academic and insensitive. The tragedy of it is, that most modern writers could learn a great deal from him if they did not find his irritation so irritating."

When he wrote these lines, in 1930, Yvor Winters was a young instructor at Stanford University, and a poet well regarded in avant-garde circles; his first book of criticism was still seven years in the future. Yet in describing More, a sage of the neo-Humanist movement, Winters gave an oddly precise verdict on his own career as a critic of poetry. Of all the eminent poet-critics of his generation—John Crowe Ransom, Allen Tate, R. P. Blackmur—none is more often "irritating," "insensitive," and "specifically wrong" than Winters. These qualities made him a figure first of controversy, then of ridicule. But it is also true that poets and readers of poetry still have important things to learn from Winters—as long as we are prepared to be irritated.

For to read Winters with profit means reading him with suspicion, even resistance. His personality on the page is unpleasant—arrogant, sarcastic, brutal in controversy—and his views are not argued but promulgated, like papal bulls. Indeed, Winters presents himself as poetry's anti-Pope, relentless in his heresies about the nature and history of the art. Any poet conventionally regarded as a master, Winters treats as a buffoon or worse. Wordsworth, for instance, is "notable mainly for a handful of fine lines and short passages and for his infinitely tedious pomposity and foolishness." On the other hand, poets the educated reader has never heard of are precariously elevated: Jones Very and F. G. Tuckerman replace Emerson and Whitman as the nineteenth-century American masters. Whole centuries are put under interdict: "If I were to say that there was little or no English poetry of real distinction between Chaucer and Wyatt, few people would be surprised: the textbooks tell us the same thing. I am telling my reader now that the eighteenth and nineteenth centuries were low periods in the history of English poetry; the text-books will convey this message to my reader's grandchildren."

Winters wrote as if he were separating the saved from the damned, and he demanded total adherence to his creed. Over his long teaching career, he assembled a coterie of true believers, for whom he propagandized vigorously. Of these, Edgar Bowers, J. V. Cunningham, and Thom Gunn went on to win wider acclaim, but most of the others are remembered, if at all, only for their association with Winters. Sometimes—as in the pages of *Quest for Reality*, the anthology he coedited—this makes his canon seem like a toy kingdom, a Monaco of poetry existing in placid unrelation to the empire all around it.

Rather than submit so completely to Winters, any sensible reader would choose to join the distinguished ranks of his opponents, including Stanley Edgar Hyman ("We find Yvor Winters . . . an excessively irritating and bad critic") and Delmore Schwartz ("Mr. Winters . . . displays prejudices which are wholly arbitrary"). But in the history of criticism there has not been so much intelligence that we can afford to ignore any of it, even when it is buried as deeply as Winters sometimes buried it. He deserves to be read sympathetically, with attention not just to his outrageous conclusions but to his serious and still compelling motives.

To understand how Winters ended up at his peculiar critical terminus, it is necessary to see where he started out. Born in 1900, the son of a stockbroker, he was raised in Los Angeles, Seattle, and Chicago, where he enrolled at the University of Chicago in 1917. But his studies were immediately derailed by tuberculosis, which sent him to a New Mexico sanatorium for nearly three years. The result was that Winters was largely an autodidact; though he made literary friends (including the young Glenway Wescott) and had an extensive correspondence, his sensibility was formed in nearly complete isolation. This was unfortunate, not so much for his knowledge—he read furiously and widely—as for his temperament. As early as 1921, he admitted to Marianne Moore that he had "a rather dogmatic nature," and dogmatism quickly hardened into arrogance. At the age of twenty-four, for example, he told Harriet Monroe that "I have, in the past few years, conducted investigations into the nature of poetic method farther than anyone else, past or present, has ever done."

Much of what is objectionable in Winters, then, can be chalked up to simple provincialism. Even after he left the sanatorium, he stayed far away from big cities. He taught school in a mining camp, studied at the University of Idaho in Moscow, and finally earned a doctorate at Stanford, where he spent the next forty years. At the age of thirty-two, he wrote to Lincoln Kirstein, "I have never been east of Wolf Lake, Indiana, and have lived mostly in obscure and remote villages." One result was that, as he acknowledged, "there may be much in modern urban life that I do not understand." (This may explain his entire failure to grasp the power of *The Waste Land*, which he called, on its publication, "by all odds the worst thing Eliot has done.") More profoundly, his isolation meant that Winters was always his own greatest authority. He redrew the map of American literary culture, so that Palo Alto became the capital and New York the boondocks. As he wrote to Malcolm Cowley in 1957, "I know that you all regard me as an eccentric. But you are the eccentrics, or rather the provincials."

While isolation bred eccentricity and resentment, however, it also gave Winters the confidence to dissent completely from the standard literary opinions of his day—which have become the standard literary history of our own. And this dissent was founded, not on bad temper, but on a principled objection to the basic assumptions of modern poetry.

Winters's mature view of poetry grew out of his encounter with Hart Crane. The two men were already friends when, in 1927, Winters wrote a review praising *White Buildings* as a masterpiece. Specifically, he valued Crane for being representative of the age, essentially modern: "a poet who accepts his age in its entirety, accepts it with passion, and who has the sensitive equipment to explore it." Three years later, however, the friendship collapsed when Winters published a profoundly negative review of *The Bridge* in *Poetry*. It was not that Winters had lost respect for Crane's abilities. The difference was that, while Crane had previously been significant for his virtues, he now seemed still more significant for his vices. Winters called *The Bridge* a "public catastrophe," a document of intellectual chaos, which showed that Crane was "headed precisely nowhere." He even predicted, accurately as it turned out, that Crane would "develop a sentimental leniency toward his vices and become wholly their victim." (The signal difference between Winters's age and our own, of course, is that he considered Crane's homosexuality one of his "vices.") In other words, Crane still "accept[ed] his age in its entirety," but now it seemed to Winters that the age itself was killing him.

All of Winters's later criticism can be seen as a response to Crane's downfall. Indeed, the matter was even more urgent than that, for Winters himself felt the allure of disintegration. As he wrote to Blackmur in 1936, "I had a capacity for going under and might have done it." His later writing about Crane and about modernism in general had the character of an exorcism, as he explained in his most moving essay, "The Significance of 'The Bridge' by Hart Crane; or What Are We to Think of Professor X?" "If we enter the mind of a Crane, a Whitman, or an Emerson with our emotional faculties activated and our reason in abeyance," Winters warned, "these writers may possess us as surely as demons were once supposed to possess the unwary."

In linking Crane to Whitman and Emerson, Winters suggests the basis of his new critique of modern poetry. All three writers were ruined, in his view, by what he defines as the Romantic theory of literature, which "assumes that literature is mainly or even purely an emotional experience." Because the Romantics believe that human nature is essentially good, they see poetry as a matter of letting the emotions speak for themselves, freed from the interference of rational thought. "Literature thus becomes a form of what is popularly known as self-expression. It is not the business of man to understand and improve himself, for such an effort is superfluous: he is good as he is, if he will only let himself alone, or, as we might say, let himself go."

Winters's best criticism—it is collected in the volume *In Defense of Reason*—traces the effects of this Romantic error on modern American literature. Crane represents the extreme case, a man who deliberately deranged his own intellect in order to make contact with the irrational sources of poetry. As he implores the Indian medicine man in a famous passage from "The Bridge": "Lie to us,—dance us back the tribal morn!" But Winters sees more subtle transgressions in virtually every major modern poet. In a brilliant essay on T. S. Eliot, he shows, through sustained attention to Eliot's criticism, that this self-proclaimed classicist is in fact a Romantic fatalist, who believes that "our individual natures are determined for us, and our actual way of feeling cannot be changed." To Winters, this represents a dangerous abdication of reason: "If we are bound to express our emotions without understanding them, we obviously have no way of judging or controlling them."

Control, in fact, is the key word in Winters's aesthetics. "The spiritual control in a poem," he writes, "is simply a manifestation of the spiritual control within the poet." With an intensity that approaches the neurotic, he fears losing control, and fears the poets who seem to approve or abet such a loss. In *The Anatomy of Nonsense* (1943), Eliot, Stevens, and Ransom are all prosecuted for their encouragement of emotional irresponsibility. In *Maule's Curse* (1938), Winters traces the same vice through the nineteenth-century American classics. Mostly free from the personal abuse and polemic of his essays on living writers, it is his most appealing book of criticism; the studies of Poe, Melville, and James are especially fascinating.

Fear of loss of control sharpened Winters's critical senses. But it also led him to an exceedingly narrow understanding of what poetic control means and looks like. He proposes that, for a poem to be respectably rational, it must explicitly repudiate anything irrational, overly emotional, vague, or obscure. *Primitivism and Decadence* (1937) is largely a catalogue of such prohibitions, with illustrations from contemporary poets. Finally, the only acceptable poems seem to be those which demonstrate "a feeling of dignity and of self-control in the face of a situation of major difficulty": that is, what Winters called in a letter "the good bitter stoicism of Hardy and Emily Dickinson." It is in obedience to this criterion that Winters prefers Tuckerman's "The Cricket" to "Song of Myself"; and purely on his own terms, he is right to do so.

But faced with such a preference, we cannot avoid the conclusion that somewhere along the line there has been a mistake. Winters makes an a priori judgment, based on sound moral arguments, about what poetry ought to do, and then judges individual poems by that standard. But real critical judgment is dialectical; it proceeds not just from rule to example, but also from example to rule. The reader's response to a poem may be refined in the course of critical judgment, but it cannot be simply negated or ignored. In other words, if it comes down to a theory or two centuries' worth of the most beloved poems in English, it is the theory that must yield.

This does not mean, however, that Winters's reasoning must be entirely abandoned. What is needed is a more sophisticated and supple concept of poetic control, which can yield more accurate and fruitful judgments of individual poems. In writing about Allen Tate's sonnet "The Subway," Winters suggests that the poet's "feeling of dignity and self-control" is "inseparable from what we call poetic form," since "the creation of a form is nothing more nor less than the act of evaluating or shaping (that is, controlling) a given experience." But this suggests that only the feeling of self-control is compatible with poetic expression, which is patently untrue. Poetry can also give form to embarrassment ("The Love Song of J. Alfred Prufrock"), despair (Hopkins's "terrible" sonnets), nervous exaltation (Shelley's "Hymn to Intellectual Beauty"), or still more questionable emotions.

In fact, the only tenable criterion of a poem's merit is fidelity to experience, including the most ambiguous and troubling phases of experience. Winters faults poets like Laforgue and Eliot for expressing "a state of moral insecurity which the poet sees no way to improve." But often, perhaps most of the time, we do not see a way to improve our weaknesses, and to say otherwise would be artistically dishonest. This is why, as writers from Plato to Thomas Mann have agreed, there is something essentially immoral about poetry. The only possible compromise between the standards of art and the standards of ethics is a version of Aristotle's: that the experience of pity and terror benefits the reader as a purgation or, what is more likely, as a consolation. If a reader is so far gone in moral invalidism that poetry is an immediate danger to him—as Winters thought it was to Crane, and feared it would be to himself—then the only solution is for him to avoid poetry altogether. What makes Winters seem perverse is that he will neither avoid art for the sake of morality, nor broaden his narrow morality for the sake of art; instead he tries to make art conform to the demands of morality. It is a Procrustean solution, and it leads him to amputate much of the corpus of English poetry.

If Winters is wrong to demand that the poem "control" the experience it treats, however, he is right to ask that the poem "shape" that experience. Some of Winters's sharpest criticism was directed at poets who took the opposite approach, believing that a poem's subject matter should dictate its form—so that, for instance, mental confusion should be expressed in a confused and disjointed poem. This error, which he named "the fallacy of imitative form," is still more prevalent in our own time than in Winters's. Many of today's most ambitious poets take as their subject consciousness itself, with the goal of mimicking in verse the precise motions of intellection. In different ways, the metaphor of the transcript guides the poetry of John Ashbery and Jorie Graham.

But neither of these poets, not to mention their many epigones, succeeds in capturing "the way it feels to think," since this kind of mimesis is foreign to the very nature of poetry. They do succeed, however, in destroying the subtle music of verse, which can only exist within a highly organized form. Still worse, they destroy their devotees' ability and desire to hear that music. The best argument for formal poetry remains Winters's pragmatic one: "the absence of a metrical frame accounting for the agreement or variation of every syllable . . . makes exact and subtle variation and suggestion impossible."

In making this defense of form, at a time when form was increasingly seen as outmoded, Winters set another important example for today's poets and critics. He refused to engage in the extreme historicism that made a god of the modern and demanded that poets worship it. This is simply another version of the fallacy of expressive form—the belief, as Winters summarized it, "that [the] age must give [the poet] not merely his subject matter but his entire spiritual shape, as it were, so that the form of his art will be determined by the quality of his age." As we have seen in the generations since modernism, competition for the favors of the Zeitgeist leads to a self-annihilating series of schools and styles, each claiming to be "what comes next." This itch for novelty reduces the reader to the status of a consumer, keeping up with the latest makes and models. Worse, it leads the poet to neglect the mastery of traditional form, which alone allows meaningful departures from tradition.

At the same time, Winters's career also serves as a warning about the cost of battling the idols of the age. Bitterly aware that his views were considered outmoded—that he was "not a recipient of the grace of the Zeitgeist"—he responded by retreating into a ghetto of his own making. We find in Winters the first example of what might be called, echoing his own coinage, the problem of defensive form. Increasingly over the last hundred years, poets have been haunted by the knowledge that to write in traditional meters is to take a position, however unwillingly, in the sterile combat of "conservative" (or "formalist") and "avant-garde." And since this contest was defined, waged, and to most appearances won by the avant-garde, the conservative position is a thankless one. To drown out the accompanying self-doubt, Winters turned his criticism into a roar. Indeed, his last book, *Forms of Discovery*, published just before his death, ends with something very like a curse on the age, looking forward to the day when "my distinguished reader, his favorite poets, his favorite subjects, and all the members of his elite group will have turned to dust."

But this proud isolation is, finally, just as much a victory for the Zeitgeist as the most slavish submission. Winters allowed the thesis of modernism to turn him into a mere antithesis, where what was needed was the nimble transcendence of the old opposites. That remains the challenge for poets and critics today, and it is no easier now than it was for Winters. Serious poets still seek to master the traditional forms and subjects, without becoming reactionary or antiquarian; to be of their moment naturally, not self-consciously; to shape experience without tyrannically controlling it. In all of these tasks, we should not miss the opportunity to learn from Winters's insights, from his example—and from his mistakes.

The Modern Element in Criticism

THE TWENTIETH CENTURY, besides its more serious crimes, must be held responsible for poetry's neurotic obsession with the modern. Ezra Pound was the first victim of this sickness, declaring in 1917 that "no good poetry is ever written in a manner twenty years old." This principle condemned poetry, like a decrepit mansion, to constant renovation. Each generation had to find its own way of being up-to-date, from William Carlos Williams ("A new *Zeitgeist* has possessed the world") to Charles Olson ("Verse now, 1950, if it is to get ahead . . . must, I take it, catch up"), all the way down to Alice Fulton ("Synthesis and unity are fundamentally premodern concepts. . . . [A] truly engaged and contemporary poetry must reflect this knowledge").

But just as the Puritan could never be sure he was one of the elect, so the twentieth-century poet could never be certain he was writing in the way that "the age demanded" (as Pound put it in *Hugh Selwyn Mauberley*). His only hope was to recognize the state of grace from outward signs, which meant brandishing his modernness like a placard. So in style, too, the stakes of newness were constantly being raised. Pound demanded "direct treatment of the 'thing,'" and Williams announced "we are *through* with the iambic pentameter"; Olson looked to "possibilities of the breath, of the breathing of the man who writes," while Fulton plumps for "asymmetrical or turbulent composition."

As a result, the poetry criticism of the last century often sounds like a madhouse, with each patient floridly expounding his delusion. To understand how we got to this point, it is necessary to go back to the beginning of modern thought about poetry, which lay in the Renaissance's return to Plato—a return which was also an overturning. For Plato, poetry was suspect on both ethical and ontological grounds. The charge that it "feeds and waters the passions," however, is no longer likely to dismay any reader of poetry. More challenging is the Platonic accusation that poetry is deficient in its very being.

In the *Republic*, Socrates argues that poetry should be held in contempt because it is "third in the descent from nature." Only the Ideas, what Yeats called the "ghostly paradigms of things," are essentially real. Actual, concrete objects—a bed, a tree, a ship—merely copy that ideal reality; and fictions, poetic or painterly, only copy the copies. Even though *poiesis* means "making," Plato denies that the poet is "a creator and maker." At best "the tragic poet is an imitator, and therefore, like all other imitators, he is thrice removed . . . from the truth."

There are two ways of braving this Platonic contempt for poetry. The first is Aristotle's, and might be called pragmatic. In his *Poetics*, Aristotle denies that there is a suprasensible realm of Ideas, insisting that our ordinary world is the only reality. And he honors poetry as an artful imitation of that reality. There is no disgrace in such imitation, because, as he points out, "imitation is one instinct of our nature." Moreover, because poetic imitation is deliberate and not slavish, poetry actually improves on reality, "making a likeness which is true to life and yet more beautiful."

Such a poetics honors the poet for accurate and subtle knowledge of the world and human life, and it values style as the means by which the poet communicates that knowledge. It follows that when the Aristotelian mind turns to criticism, as in the neoclassical essays in verse and prose of Dryden, Pope, and Johnson, it will attend mainly to practical rules and concrete observations, confident that—as Pope wrote in his *Essay on Criticism*—"Those RULES of old discover'd, not devis'd, / Are Nature still, but Nature Methodiz'd."

The other way of looking at poetry, which became dominant in the early nineteenth century and remains deeply influential, is the Romantic. The Romantic critic agrees with Plato that there is a divine realm, of which our world is a flawed reflection. But instead of scorning poetry as an imitation of the lower world, the Romantic worships it as a means of direct access to the higher. Not philosophy but poetry becomes the ladder on which we ascend to the heavens. If this is a contradiction of Plato, it is no less alien to Aristotle, since it removes poetry from the realm of worldly understanding and secular skill. Instead of an art, poetry becomes a magic.

Sir Philip Sidney made the first approach toward this idea, significantly tying his "Defense of Poetry" to a subversive reading of Plato as "of all philosophers . . . the most poetical." Sidney praises poetry exactly insofar as it is not an imitation of life: "to borrow nothing of what is, has been, or shall be; but range, only reined with learned discretion, into the divine consideration of what may be and should be." The poet is not only not "third in descent from nature," but, "lifted up with the vigor of his own invention, doth grow, in effect, into another nature." And like every subsequent Romantic critic, Sidney sees meter as, at best, a mere garment of poetry's spiritual body: "Verse being but an ornament and no cause to poetry, since there have been many most excellent poets that never versified."

The Romantics of the early nineteenth century continued to disparage verse in theory, though they never abandoned it in practice. In the preface to *Lyrical Ballads*, Wordsworth lamented that "confusion has been introduced into criticism by this contradistinction of Poetry and Prose, instead of the more philosophical one of Poetry and Matter of Fact, or Science." Poetry, on this view, is not metrical language, but a form of superior wisdom: "Poetry is the first and last of all knowledge—it is as immortal as the heart of man." It follows that one earns the title of poet, not by writing verse, but by spiritual excellence, "a more comprehensive soul than [is] supposed to be common among mankind." No wonder that, as Coleridge recalled in *Biographia Literaria*, "Mr. Wordsworth's admirers . . . were found too not in the lower classes of the reading public, but chiefly among young men of strong ability and meditative minds, and their admiration . . . was distinguished by its intensity, I might almost say, by its *religious* fervor."

This religious conception of poetry shifts its focus from the poem, an object with certain formal qualities, to the poet, who writes to express his extraordinary soul. Only in this light can we understand the strange pronouncements of Coleridge, that "a poem of any length neither can be, or ought to be, all poetry"; of Shelley, that "a man cannot say, 'I will compose poetry' . . . when composition begins, inspiration is already on the decline"; or of Emerson, that "when we adhere to the ideal of the poet, we have our difficulties even with Milton and Homer." Poetry, it seems, is not poems; it is not a skill practiced by the poet; and it cannot be found in even the greatest poets of the past. It has become a name for a mystic experience that can never be more than approximately described, as in Shelley's Platonic rhapsody: "A poet participates in the eternal, the infinite, and the one; as far as relates to his conceptions, time and place and number are not."

Probably no poet today would repeat Shelley's creed word

for word. But the modern understanding of poetry is still profoundly influenced by Romanticism, if only because modernism and postmodernism were dialectical responses to it.
Modernism, under the (more modest and useful) name of Symbolism, came to French poetry before English. But the French
Symbolists were themselves influenced by an American, the
much-misunderstood Edgar Allan Poe. And Poe's essay "The
Philosophy of Composition" was a torpedo aimed directly at
Romanticism and its religious pretensions.

Far from being "the first and last of all knowledge," Poe claims,
a poem is simply a technology for producing aesthetic sensations.
When we think we are being elevated by a poem, we are really
just being stimulated by "some amount of suggestiveness—some
undercurrent, however indefinite, of meaning. It is this latter, in
especial, which imparts to a work of art so much of that richness
. . . which we are too fond of confounding with the ideal." By
divorcing poetic pleasure from all ethical and metaphysical concerns, Poe returns our focus to the poem itself, which now
becomes only a pattern of stimuli—as he demonstrates in his
cold-blooded account of writing "The Raven."

Filtered through Symbolism, this became the dominant
understanding of poetry among the American modernists. It
had a profound influence on Pound, Eliot ("The effect of a work
of art upon the person who enjoys it is an experience different
in kind from any experience not of art"), and Stevens ("A poet's
words are things that do not exist without the words"). In the
New Criticism of the 1930s and 1940s, the idea was reduced to
an academic doctrine. "The meaning of poetry," Allen Tate
declared, is "its 'tension,' the full organized body of all the
extension and intension that we can find in it." Or, as the young
Yvor Winters put it, the poem "is not a means to any end, but
is in itself an end."

The poetry criticism of the mid-twentieth century was largely an attack on this modernist principle, which had begun to seem like the arid formalism of what Kenneth Rexroth called a "Reactionary Generation." "No avant-garde American poet," Rexroth declared in 1957, "accepts the . . . thesis that a poem is an end in itself, an anonymous machine for providing aesthetic experiences." Instead, the influential poets of the 1950s and 1960s advanced a new ideal of the poem as a faithful record of experience. This ideal received different inflections at the hands of different poets. For Charles Olson it is the outer world that must be recorded ("Objectism is the getting rid of the lyrical interference of the individual as ego, of the 'subject' and his soul"), while for Denise Levertov it is the inner sensation ("The sounds, acting together with the measure, are a kind of *extended onomatopoeia*—i.e., they imitate, not the sounds of an experience . . . but the feeling of an experience, its emotional tone, its texture").

In their hatred of artifice and their loyalty to individual perception, the experimental poets of the mid-century often sound like Romantics. But in fact, they resemble the Romantics only as a double-negative resembles a positive. For they were not in search of transcendence, only of authenticity. Indeed, the American generation that came after the modernists could most accurately be called the Authentic poets. Not to falsify one's personal experience, even or especially in the name of art, is their great principle. The poem, it follows, is only a means of synchronizing the reader's experience with the writer's. "The poem," Frank O'Hara wrote, "is at last between two persons instead of two pages."

It is in the pursuit of such authenticity that these poets made the great refusal about which the Romantics only speculated: the immolation of meter, rhyme, and form. They took Emerson's notion of a "meter-making argument" more seriously than Emerson himself, turning "the metric movement," in Levertov's words, into "the direct expression of the movement of perception." For just the same reason, Olson praises the typewriter, which allows the poet to "indicate exactly the breath, the pauses, the suspensions even of syllables." Here is the aggressive egotism of authenticity, which does not simply hand the poem over to the reader, but compels the reader to follow the writer's most detailed instructions. And here too is its puritanism, its hostility to pleasure. For meter, like all artifice, finds pleasure in the gratuitous, and the gratuitous is the enemy of authenticity.

Today, the poetics of authenticity is securely established. There have been isolated dissents from it, but no comprehensive rejection. Yet it should be clear by now that this poetics has thoroughly failed. It has made it more difficult for poets to produce major work, and its critical legacy is remarkable only for intellectual crudity and rhetorical violence. The sound of the critical madhouse is a thousand utterly authentic voices, all talking at once.

In the last twenty years, however, poets and critics have done little to challenge the ideal of authenticity. Instead, the most influential of them have turned from literary questions to sociological ones, focusing on the shortcomings of the institutional poetry world. In this category belong Robert Pinsky's thoughts on "poetry gloom," Donald Hall's on the "McPoem," and Dana Gioia's famous question, "Can Poetry Matter?" But the success or failure of American poetry is not determined by institutions—M.F.A. programs, publishers, magazines. Like any poetry at any time, it will compel recognition only by becoming great.

If criticism can make any contribution to this goal, it is to help us break free from the post-Romantic dialectic that obsessed American poetry in the twentieth century. For there is a saner, more sophisticated, more humane tradition in criticism: the pragmatic tradition of Aristotle and Horace, Johnson and Arnold. If we embrace it, we will not need to look to poetry for transcendence, or to flee into aestheticism when transcendence fails, or to flee into authenticity when aestheticism fails. We will be able to see how the twentieth century gave us poets of humane insight—Hardy, Frost, Moore, Larkin, Lowell—as well as poets of otherworldly magniloquence and hectic experimentalism. And if we are fortunate, our poetry will come to understand the full implications—ethical, intellectual, and aesthetic—of Horace's seemingly simple formula:

Of writing well, be sure, the secret lies
In wisdom: therefore study to be wise.

Acknowledgments

Grateful acknowledgment is made to the publications where these essays first appeared, often in a somewhat different form:

Contemporary Poetry Review: Individual Talents
Metre: Dennis O'Driscoll
The New Criterion: Two Modern Classics: *The Waste Land,* Yvor Winters
The New Republic: Derek Walcott, Jorie Graham, John Ashbery, Geoffrey Hill, Frederick Seidel, Louise Glück, C. D. Wright, James Merrill, Donald Justice, Anthony Hecht, Les Murray, Adam Zagajewski, Joseph Brodsky, Billy Collins, Sharon Olds
The New Yorker: Richard Wilbur, Theodore Roethke and James Wright
Poetry: Two Modern Classics: *Howl,* The Modern Element in Criticism
Times Literary Supplement: Derek Walcott, Charles Simic, Kenneth Koch, Czeslaw Milosz
The Walrus: Philip Larkin

IN WRITING the essays in this book, I had the good fortune to work with gifted and generous editors. I am glad to have the opportunity to thank Henry Finder and Leo Carey at *The New*

Yorker, Ruth Franklin and James Wood at *The New Republic,* Mick Imlah at the *Times Literary Supplement,* David Yezzi and Roger Kimball at *The New Criterion,* Christian Wiman at *Poetry,* and Ernest Hilbert at *Contemporary Poetry Review,* all of whom gave me the chance to write on subjects I care about, and helped to make my writing better.

Writing about books as a critic for the *New York Sun* has been an invaluable experience for me, both personally and professionally. I am grateful to Seth Lipsky, editor of the *Sun,* for his generosity and encouragement, and to the arts editors I have worked with, past and present: Robert Messenger, David Propson, Kolby Yarnell, Pia Catton, Robert Asahina, and Thomas Meaney.

I am also grateful to Anne Fadiman, who published one of my very first essays in *The American Scholar* and brought me into the fold, all too briefly, as literary editor; and to John Rosenberg, Craig Lambert, and Jean Martin, my editors at *Harvard Magazine.*

I am happily indebted to Princeton University's Council for the Humanities, whose award of a Hodder Fellowship helped me to complete *The Modern Element.* Jill Bialosky, my editor at W. W. Norton, guided the book (and its predecessor) to publication with an expert hand.

Finally, above all, I am grateful to Leon Wieseltier, the literary editor of *The New Republic.* Leon gave me my first job and my first opportunity to write about poetry. For ten years he has helped me to learn and grow as a critic, and more than half of the essays in this book first appeared in his pages—it literally would not exist were it not for him. Above all, he has been a friend and teacher, and a constant example of what it means to write and think passionately and responsibly.

Index

Abraham, 168
abstraction, 173
    in Ashbery's work, 43
    in Hill's work, 53
    Milosz and, 228–29
    in Walcott's work, 22
academic poetry, Koch's rant against, 187
"Adamant, The" (Roethke), 174
adjectives, Latinate, 56
"Admonition, An" (Brodsky), 250–51
"Adonais" (Shelley), 308
Adorno, Theodor W., 60
adventurousness, 298
aestheticism, 329
    of Hill, 61–62
    of Merrill, 130–31
Afghanistan, Soviet soldiers in, 250
afterlife, Justice's view of, 149
    see also Hell; Paradise
"After-school Practice" (Justice), 157
"Aftershocks" (Stallings), 291
"After the Last Bulletins" (Wilbur), 146
"Against Incomprehensible Poetry" (Milosz), 221, 222
"Against Sincerity" (Glück), 96, 98
"Ah! Sun-flower" (Blake), 306
"AIDS Days" (Seidel), 85–86
Akhmatova, Anna, 243
algebra:
    allegory compared with, 26
    reading Graham and, 26–33, 35, 36
allegory, 269
    in Collins, 267–68
    in Dante, 25, 26, 268
    in Eliot, 25
allusion, 19
    for courteous poet, 113, 123
    for discourteous poet, 114, 123

    in Eliot's work, 301
    in Hecht's work, 161, 162, 168
ambiguity, 282–83, 318–19
    in Eliot's poetics, 282, 296–97, 301
    of Tate, 56, 283
    in Yezzi's work, 282
ambivalence, of Walcott, 19–20
American Scream (Raskin), 304
"American Sublime, The" (Stevens), 50–51
Amichai, Yehuda, 61
Amis, Martin, 192
Anathemata (Jones), 34
Anatomy of Nonsense, The (Winters), 317
"Anaximander Fragment, The" (Heidegger), 32
Anderson, Sherwood, 151
"And He Answered Them Nothing" (Crashaw), 54
Angel of History, 228, 232
anger:
    in Hecht's work, 162
    in Hill's work, 69–71
"Animal Music" (Olds), 276
"Annalena" (Milosz), 230
"Anniversaries" (Justice), 152
"Another Life" (Walcott), 20, 21
"Anthem" (Brodsky), 252–53
"Antilles, The" (Walcott), 19
anti-Semitism, 301
anxiety, 184, 300, 308
    of Roethke and J. Wright, 173
"Apology for the Revival of Christian Architecture in England, An" (Hill), 61–62, 69
"Aporia" (Yezzi), 282
Apple That Astonished Paris, The (Collins), 259–60
Ararat (Glück), 98, 100, 102
arbitrariness, of Hill's work, 55
Area Code 212 (Seidel), 80–81, 84, 87–88, 91–93
Aristotle, 319, 323–24, 329
Arkansas Testament, The (Walcott), 23

Armenian genocide, 216
Arnold, Matthew, 9–13, 299, 329
art:
    for art's sake, 130–31, 173, 223
    Glück's dedication to, 96
    Hill's reverence for, 70, 71
    joy in, 140–41
    Justice's views on, 149
    life's prevention of, 221
    life turned into, 125–26
    preservation and caretaking of, 108
    as source of value, 222
artistic invention, 280
artistic talent, as responsibility, 133
Art of Love, The (Koch), 185, 189–90
"Art of Poetry, The" (Koch), 189–90
"Arundel Tomb, An" (Larkin), 198
Ashbery, John, 41–52, 80
    authenticity of, 47
    avant-garde playfulness of, 41–44
    consciousness as subject of, 319–20
    Eliot compared with, 41, 45, 46, 49
    Koch compared with, 184–85, 188, 189
    mannerism of, 52
    as Romantic, 41, 45–52
    self-indulgence of, 44
    Stevens compared with, 41, 45, 50–51
    verbiage of, 43–44
    Wordsworth compared with, 48
"Ash-Wednesday" (Eliot), 25
"As John to Patmos" (Walcott), 21
"Asphodel" (Stallings), 293
Associated Press (AP), 257
assonance, in Merrill's work, 128
Astaire, Fred, 288
"At Gracie Mansion" (Seidel), 82
"Atlantis" (Auden), 250
"At New York Hospital" (Seidel), 90–91
"At the Executed Murderer's Grave" (J. Wright), 179
"Aubade" (Larkin), 192
Auden, W. H., 23, 170, 177, 193, 209
    Brodsky compared with, 243, 250
    Brodsky influenced by, 247, 250, 252–53
    Brodsky's essay on, 255
    Hill compared with, 58–59
    Koch compared with, 190
    Merrill compared with, 129
    Roethke compared with, 178
    on "Vision of Dame Kind," 269
    Yezzi compared with, 283
Augustan Age, 136
Augustine, Saint, 37

Auschwitz, 60, 144
authenticity, 327–28, 329
    of Ashbery, 47
    of Glück, 95, 96
Authentic poets, 327
authority:
    authenticity and, 95
    of Eliot, 97
"Autographs" (C. D. Wright), 123–24
avant-garde, 321, 327
    Ashbery's playfulness and, 41–44
Averno (Glück), 95, 96, 100, 104–5

Bach, Johann Sebastian, 163–64
"Back Roads" (O'Driscoll), 202
"Bali" (Seidel), 89
Balzac, Honoré de, 74–75
Barańczak, Stanisław, 233
barbarism vs. culture, 159–60, 169
"Baroque Wall-Fountain in the Villa Sciarra, A" (Wilbur), 145
"Bathroom Door, The" (Seidel), 91–92
Baudelaire, Charles, 130
"Beacon, The" (Wilbur), 146
Beats, beatniks, 172, 304, 310
Beautiful Changes, The (Wilbur), 138, 139
beauty, 44
    Merrill's views on, 131–32
"Beauty and the Bag" (O'Driscoll), 202, 204
"Begotten of the Spleen" (Simic), 107–8
Being, 89
    Heidegger's view of, 32–33
    Simic's view of, 109, 110
Bell, George, 71
Bell Jar, The (Plath), 137
Benjamin, Walter, 228
Bernard of Clairvaux, 110
Berryman, John, 11, 169, 306
    confessional poetry of, 154, 172
    Seidel compared with, 80, 85
    Wilbur compared with, 138, 141
Betjeman, John, 196
"Beyond the Alps" (Lowell), 184
"Beyond the Hunting Woods" (Justice), 151
Bible, 25, 26, 162, 176
Bidart, Frank, 290
Biographia Literaria (Coleridge), 325
bird-poems, 27–33
Biretta, The (Heaney), 199
Birkerts, Sven, 305
Bishop, Elizabeth, 291
Blackmur, R. P., 312, 316

"Black November Turkey, A" (Wilbur), 146
Blake, William, 271, 305, 306, 309
blasphemy, 107
    of Olds, 272, 278
"Bleisten with a Baedeker, Burbank with a Cigar"
        (Eliot), 301
Blood, Tin, Straw (Olds), 271, 275–76
Bloom, Harold, 45
Bly, Robert, 172, 180–81, 182
body:
    in C. D. Wright's work, 117–18
    Olds's view of, 271, 277
Boehme, Jakob, 110
Bogan, Louise, 174
bogs, 203
Bonnard, Pierre, 157
Book of Ephraim, The (Merrill), 129–30, 133–34
Boole, George, 84
Bosch, Hieronymus, 107
Bounty, The (Walcott), 23, 295
bourgeoisie, *see* middle class
Bowers, Edgar, 313
Bowman, Ruth, 195
boxing, 170–71
Brahms, Johannes, 151
Branch Will Not Break, The (J. Wright), 181
Brennan, Maeve, 192, 196
Bridge, The (Crane), 315, 317
"Brief Account of Our City, A" (Hecht), 167
"Brief and Blameless Outline of the Ontogeny of
        Crow, A" (C. D. Wright), 121–22
British Empire, 62
Brixton race riots, 23
Brodsky, Joseph, 207, 243–56
    Auden's influence on, 247, 250, 252–53
    "cause" vs. "effect" in, 254
    courage of, 244
    as English poet, 244–56
    Nobel Prize of, 243
    penal experience of, 244
    poetry defended by, 243–44
    rhyme scheme retained by, 248
    as Russian poet, 243, 245, 251
    translation of, 244–50, 255–56
"Broken Home, The" (Merrill), 134–35
"Brooding Likeness" (Glück), 95
Brooks, Cleanth, 282
Browning, Robert, 296
"Buladelah-Taree Holiday Song Cycle, The" (Mur-
        ray), 208–9
Bunyah, 207
Burke, Kenneth, 171, 174

"Burning Truck, The" (Murray), 209–10
"Burning Want" (Murray), 214–15, 216
Byron, George Gordon, Lord, 128

Cain, 77–78
calling, poetry as, 96, 235
Calvinism, 271
Canaan (Hill), 66–69
Candide, 215
candor, Glück's views on, 96–97
canons:
    eccentricity of, 55
    of modernness, 12
Cantos (Pound), 72
Canvas (Zagajewski), 238
capitalism, 300, 305
Captive Mind, The (Milosz), 225
Capuzzi, Frank, 32
Caribbean, 17–24
    as Aegean, 20
    as habitation for English poetry, 24
    naïveté of, 19
Caribbean Voices (BBC program), 18
Carlyle Hotel, 83–84
Carson, Anne, 34
"Casco Passage" (Yezzi), 284
"Caserta Garden" (Wilbur), 147
Cassady, Neal, 307
Catholicism, Catholics, 61, 230
Catullus, 185
Celan, Paul, 160
"Celtic Tiger, The" (O'Driscoll), 204
censorship, 193
    Howl and, 304
    translation compared with, 245
"Central Europe" (Zagajewski), 235–36
Ceremony (Wilbur), 138, 140–41
Changing Light at Sandover, The (Merrill), 130, 133,
        136
"Charles on Fire" (Merrill), 132
Chatterton, Thomas, 141
Chaucer, Geoffrey, 313
"Chekhovian Landscape" (Yezzi), 284
"Childe Stauffenberg" (Hill), 68
"Childhood" (Justice), 157
children, childhood:
    in Hill's work, 65
    poetic approach and, 178
    in Seidel's work, 89
    in Wordsworth's poetry, 266
"Chimes of Neverwhere, The" (Murray), 213–14
"Chinese New Year" (Yezzi), 284

Chopin, Frédéric, 151
"Chorus for One Voice" (Simic), 107
Christianity, 301
    allegory and, 25, 26, 268
    in Graham's work, 37–40
    in Hill's work, 53–55, 68–72
    see also Catholicism, Catholics
"Church Going" (Larkin), 192
"Churchyard View" (O'Driscoll), 201
Circe, 100
"Circling the Square" (O'Driscoll), 203
City Lights Books, 303, 304
"City Without a Name" (Milosz), 229
Cixous, Hélène, 34
Clark Lectures, 298
"Clearing the Title" (Merrill), 134–35
Clinton, Bill, 73, 304
Clio, 253–54
Cobbett, William, 67
"Code, The" (Frost), 209
Cold War, 185, 308
Coleridge, Samuel Taylor, 325
Collected Poems, 1943–2004 (Wilbur), 138, 146–47
Collected Poems (Justice), 148, 154
Collected Poems (Koch), 185–91
Collected Poems (Larkin), 193–94, 197
Collected Poems (Merrill), 134–35
Collected Poems in English (Brodsky), 244–56
Collins, Billy, 257–70, 305
    devotion to the ordinary of, 258, 259, 263–65
    effortlessness praised by, 264–65
    irony of, 262–63, 266–67, 268
    popularity of, 257–58
    wit of, 258–59
communication:
    beyond words, 50, 52
    limits of, 26
    of meaning, 44
Communism, 229–30, 232, 235
    fall of, 255
    in Poland, 224, 225, 226, 234
compassion:
    of J. Wright, 178
    of Larkin, 197
complexity:
    Arnold's view of, 9–10, 11
    Eliot's view of, 11
    in Hill's work, 53
    obscurity vs., 40
conceits:
    of Brodsky, 246–48, 250
    Justice's use of, 152–53

"Conditions We Call Exile, The" (Brodsky), 255
confessional poetry, 95–96, 101, 172
    Justice's attack on, 154–55
Conrad, Joseph, 255
consciousness, 319–20
    Ashbery's views on, 47, 48–49
    Eliot's views on, 299
    of Glück, 104
    Heidegger's views on, 32–33
    Merrill's views on, 134
    poetry as transcript of, 35
    as wave, 48–49
"Contents Under Pressure" (Seidel), 87
"continent," Merrill's use of word, 127
control, Winters's concern with, 317–18, 319
Conversations with Czeslaw Milosz, 224
Cooke, Sam, 288
Corbière, Édouard Joachim, 251
"Corniche" (Murray), 214
cosmologies, 88–89
cosmopolitanism:
    of Trinidad, 18
    of Walcott, 24
Cosmos Poems, The (Seidel), 80, 87–89
Cosmos Trilogy, The (Seidel), 88
"Cottage Street, 1953" (Wilbur), 137–38
Coulette, Henri, 149
courage, 244, 280, 298
    confessional, 95
    of Larkin, 197
courteous poetry, discourteous poetry compared
    with, 113–14, 120
Cowley, Malcolm, 315
Crane, Hart, 141, 149, 251, 310
    Winters's views on, 315–17, 319
Crashaw, Richard, 54
"Cricket, The" (Tuckerman), 218
crime, 309
criticism, modern element in, 322–29
Cultural Revolution, 284
culture:
    barbarism vs., 159–60, 169
    as target of Collins's humor, 263, 265–67
Cunningham, J. V., 313

Dada, 41, 188
"Daffy Duck in Hollywood" (Ashbery), 41–42
"Dance, The" (Roethke), 177
Dante, 17, 76, 88, 149
    allegory in, 25, 26, 268
    Eliot's views on, 295, 298
    light for, 165

Darkness and the Light, The (Hecht), 161, 167

Daumier, Honoré, 74–75

Davie, Donald, 122

"Days of 1935" (Merrill), 126

"Days of 1941 and '44" (Merrill), 130–31

"Days of . . ." poems (Merrill), 134–35

"Dead, The" (Collins), 258

"Dear Heart" (Olds), 276–77

death:
    of fathers, 100, 277–78
    fear of, 195
    in Glück's work, 100, 104
    Hill's reflection on, 75
    in Justice's work, 150, 156
    in Larkin's work, 197, 201
    in Mehigan's work, 288–89, 291
    Metaphysical poets and, 201
    in O'Driscoll's work, 201–2

"Death of Allegory, The" (Collins), 267–68

"Death of the Ball Turret, The" (Wilbur), 140

"Death to Van Gogh's Ear" (Ginsberg), 304

"December" (Seidel), 93

"December in Florence" (Brodsky), 247–48

"Deceptions" (Larkin), 118

"deep image" poetry, 172, 181–82

Deepstep Come Shining (C. D. Wright), 115

"Defense of Poetry" (Sidney), 324

"De Jure Belli ac Pacis" (Hill), 68

Demeter myth, 94–95

Dennis, John, 128

Departures (Justice), 154, 156

"Depth of Things, The" (Osterhaus), 287

"Devotions of a Painter" (Hecht), 164–65

Dial, The, Eliot's London letter for, 297

Diana, Princess, death of, 73–74

Dickens, Charles, 243

Dickey, James, 171, 179–80

Dickinson, Emily, 34, 318

dictatorship, transformation compared with, 109

Different Person, A (Merrill), 131

difficulty:
    of obscurity vs. complexity, 40
    system of conventions and, 43

discourteous poetry:
    of C. D. Wright, 114–24
    courteous poetry compared with, 113–14, 120

discovery, poetry of, 298

disease, in Mehigan's work, 288–89, 291

"disintegration," Trilling's use of term, 143

Divine Comedy (Dante), 88, 149

divorce, 100, 104

"Dockery and Son" (Larkin), 196

"Doctor Love" (Seidel), 90

"Dollhouse, The" (Stallings), 291–92

Dolphin, The (Lowell), 23

Donald Justice Reader, A (Justice), 151

Don Juan, 215

Don Juan (Byron), 128

Donne, John, 23, 259, 289, 308
    Eliot's views on, 295, 298
    Zagajewski compared with, 242

Double Dream of Spring, The (Ashbery), 45

"Downtown" (Seidel), 92

"Dream of Wearing Shorts Forever, The" (Murray), 210–12

Dream Song #22 (Berryman), 80

Dream Songs, The (Berryman), 11

"Driftwood" (Wilbur), 138–39

drugs:
    antidepressants, 72
    Howl and, 305, 309

Dryden, John, 296, 324

Dublin, 203

Duffy, William, 181

"Dune Road, Southampton" (Seidel), 86–87

Duns Scotus, John, 257

Dylan, Bob, 304

Early Greek Thinking (Heidegger), 32

"Earthling" (Collins), 263–64

Eastern European poetry, 106

"Education of the Poet, The" (Glück), 101–2

effortlessness, Collins's praise of, 264–65

"Either" (O'Driscoll), 201

Ekelöf, Gunnar, 34

"Elders" (Hecht), 161

"Elegy for Y.Z." (Milosz), 231

"Elegy Is Preparing Itself, An" (Justice), 156

Eliot, T. S., 12, 23, 141, 172, 193, 200, 326
    allegory in, 25
    ambiguity of, 282, 296–97, 301
    Arnold compared with, 10, 11
    Ashbery compared with, 41, 45, 46, 49
    authority of, 282
    Clark Lectures of, 298
    French influence on, 251
    Glück influenced by, 97
    Hill compared with, 53
    myth used by, 101
    originality as viewed by, 281
    Roethke influenced by, 176, 177
    Seidel compared with, 84–85
    Winters's views on, 317, 319
    see also Four Quartets; Waste Land, The

Emerson, Ralph Waldo, 45, 259, 325, 327–28
    Wilbur compared with, 145, 146
    Winters's views on, 313, 316
Empson, William, 282
End of Beauty, The (Graham), 35
England, in Hill's work, 61–62, 65
English Augustans, 185
English language, Russian compared with, 245, 247,
    251
English Metaphysical poets, 246, 259
English poetry, English poets:
    Brodsky influenced by, 251
    Caribbean as habitation for, 24
    see also specific poets
enjoyment, Merrill's ethic of, 140–41
Ephraim (spirit), 133
epic poetry, 20
"Equanimity" (Murray), 210, 212
Erosion (Graham), 35
erotics, *see* sex
errancy:
    freedom and, 32, 33
    use of term, 31–32
Errancy, The (Graham), 27–33, 35, 36
Essay on Criticism (Pope), 324
"Europe" (Ashbery), 42
"Eve of Saint Agnes, The" (Keats), 183
evil, 301
    in Hecht's work, 159–60, 163, 167–68
    in Hill's work, 53
    in Murray's work, 216–19
    Nazism as, 225
    sex as, 271
exile, psychological dangers of, 255
"Explaining the Affinity for Bats" (Stallings), 293
extreme experiences, 96
"Ezra's Lament" (Wheeler), 80

Facing the River (Milosz), 220–21
"Factors, The" (Olds), 276
"Failure" (Stallings), 294
"Faith Healing" (Larkin), 192, 197
"Fall, A" (Hecht), 167
"Fall of Rome, The" (Auden), 58–59
Falstaff, 140
family, as destiny, 102
"Family Week at Oracle Ranch" (Merrill), 135
"Farewell, A" (Arnold), 10
Far Field, The (Roethke), 177
fascism, opposition to, 68
Father, The (Olds), 277–78

fathers, 100, 171
    of Olds, 273–74, 277–78
Ferlinghetti, Lawrence, 304
fiction, poetry compared with, 229
Fifties, The, 180–81
Final Solutions (Seidel), 87
Fincke, Reginald, 84
Firstborn (Glück), 99
"First Essay on Interest" (Murray), 210
Fitts, Dudley, 178–79
Flemish-painting spirituality, 165
Flow Chart (Ashbery), 43–44
"Flying Colors" (Stallings), 294
"Flying from Byzantium" (Merrill), 128
Fly in the Soup, A (Simic), 106, 108
"Folly of Being Comforted, The" (Yeats), 196
"Foreign Relations" (O'Driscoll), 203
"Forever" (Seidel), 88–89
form, 327
    Brodsky's attachment to, 248
    candor and, 96
    fallacy of expressive, 320
    fallacy of imitative, 319
    of Hecht, 160, 161, 163
    heuristic poetry and, 131
    of *Howl,* 306, 307
    Justice's attention to, 152, 153
    in Mehigan's work, 289
    Merrill's mastery of, 144–45
    Merrill's view of, 130
    as natural bound of poetry, 44
    Olds's attitude toward, 275
    problem of defensive, 321
    in Stallings's work, 293–94
    Winters's views on, 318–21
Forms of Discovery (Winters), 321
"For Proust" (Merrill), 125–26
For the Unfallen (Hill), 55–56
"For the Union Dead" (Lowell), 60
fountains, in Wilbur's work, 145, 147
Fourier, François Marie Charles, 110
Four Quartets (Eliot), 177, 270, 300, 303
    Ashbery influenced by, 45, 46, 49
"Fragment" (Stallings), 293–94
France, 233
    literature and painting of, 106
    Péguy's dream of, 63–64
France, Peter, 249
"Franz Schubert" (Zagajewski), 240
"Frederick Seidel" (Seidel), 91
Fredy Neptune (Murray), 208, 215–19

freedom, 20
    errancy and, 32, 33
    of Hill, 64–65
    of Keats, 17
French Symbolists, 326
"Fresh Air" (Koch), 187
Freud, Sigmund, 102
Freudian images, 174
friendship:
    in Catullus's work, 185
    in Koch's work, 185, 190, 191
    in O'Hara's work, 185
"*from* The Reformation Journal" (Graham), 37–38
Frost, Robert, 28, 145, 255, 257, 267, 329
    Mehigan compared with, 290–91
    Murray compared with, 208–9
Fulton, Alice, 322
"Funeral Music" (Hill), 56–57, 62, 65
Further Adventures with You (C. D. Wright), 115–18

Gates, David, 303, 305
generosity, 132, 198
Geography III (Bishop), 291
George, Stefan, 67
Géricault, Jean Louis André Théodore, 143–44
Germany:
    Kreisau conspirators in, 68
    myth of, 62
    in World War I, 217
    in World War II, 217, 218, 223, 225, 226
"Gerontion" (Eliot), 84–85, 301
"Getaway" (Seidel), 92
G.I. Bill, 187
Ginsberg, Allen, 172, 303–11
Gioia, Dana, 328
Girl in Winter, A (Larkin), 195
"global-regionalist" perspective, 203
Glück, Louise, 94–105
    authority of, 95
    egotism of, 99–100
    Eliot's influence on, 97
    irony lacking in, 103
    Lowell compared with, 99, 100
    myth used by, 94–97, 100–102, 293
    psychoanalysis of, 101–3
    religious poetry of, 103–4
God:
    Brodsky's views on, 244
    Glück's encounter with, 103–4
    in Hill's vs. Crashaw's work, 54
    Milosz's idea of, 230–31

    in Murray's work, 219
    in O'Driscoll's work, 202
    praising of, 165
    in *Swarm*, 37–38
Goethe, Johann Wolfgang von, 160
Going Fast (Seidel), 87
Gold Cell, The (Olds), 274
Goldengrove, 76–77
"Goliardic Song" (Hecht), 160–61
Gonne, Maud, 196
goodness, 231, 301, 316
    in Hecht's work, 163
    sex as, 277
"Goodness" (Seidel), 90
Graham, Jorie, 25–40
    algebraic logic of, 26–33, 35, 36
    consciousness as subject of, 319–20
    explanations for obscurity of, 34–35
    Heidegger's influence on, 32–33, 34, 108
    see also "Guardian Angel of Point-of-View, The"
"Grand Galop" (Ashbery), 45–46
Greece, classical, 9, 20, 292–93
Greek mythology:
    in Glück's work, 94–95, 97, 100–102
    in Graham's work, 38–39
    lack of cultic power of, 100
    Orpheus in, 164
    Persephone in, 39, 94–95, 100
    in Stallings's work, 292–93
"Green Automobile, The" (Ginsberg), 307
"greenhouse poems," of Roethke, 174–75
Green Wall, The (J. Wright), 170, 172–73,
    178–79
"Guardian Angel of Point-of-View, The" (Graham),
    27–33
Gunn, Thom, 182, 313

Haeften, Hans-Bernd von, 68
Hall, Donald, 179–80, 182, 328
Hapax (Stallings), 291–94
"happily ever after," 142–43
happiness, 72
Hard Hours, The (Hecht), 162
Hardy, Thomas, 318, 329
Harvard University, 187
    Norton lectures at, 229–30
Heaney, Seamus, 61, 193, 200, 203, 207
    O'Driscoll's essay on, 199
"Heart" (Justice), 154
Hecht, Anthony, 159–69, 179
    Brodsky translated by, 246, 248–49

Hecht, Anthony (*continued*)
    decorum of, 160–61
    strengths of, 169
Hegel, Georg Wilhelm Friedrich, 228
Heidegger, Martin, 32–33, 34, 108–9
Hell:
    of Dante, 25, 76, 88, 149
    of New York City, 88, 91
    in Orphic myth, 164
    Persephone's descent into, 95, 100
Henry IV (Shakespeare), 168
Herbert, George, 53, 97
heroism, of modern poets, 11, 131
Hersey, John, 122–23
"Her Song" (Seidel), 86
heuristic poetry, 131, 133
Hidden Model, The (Yezzi), 282–84
High Windows (Larkin), 193
Hill, Geoffrey, 53–78, 179
    aestheticism of, 61–62
    antidepressants used by, 72
    Auden compared with, 58–59
    childhood of, 65
    Crashaw compared with, 54
    freedom of, 64–65
    free verse of, 66, 69
    history in works of, 53, 55–58, 61–64, 68,
        69
    ingrown eroticism of, 64
    Pound compared with, 72, 73
    prose poems of, 65
    religious poetry of, 53–55, 64, 68–71
    solemnity of, 59
    Tate's influence on, 56, 282
Hiroshima (Hersey), 122–23
history, 177
    allusion and, 19
    Clio as muse of, 253–54
    dialectical-materialist view of, 253
    in Hill's work, 53, 55–58, 61–64, 68, 69
    Milosz's views on, 224–32
    as myth, 62
    Osterhaus's views on, 285, 287–88
    Walcott's views on, 17, 19–22, 24
    Zagajewski's view of, 237
History (Lowell), 23
Hitler, Adolf, 68
Ho Chi Minh, 92
Holocaust, 60, 159–60
    as Olds's symbol, 274
home, poetry as, 24

homelessness, Walcott's curing of, 21–22
Homer, 17, 20, 301, 325
homosexuality, of Crane, 316
honesty:
    appearance of, 97
    confessional, 95
Hopkins, Gerard Manley, 53, 73, 76, 90, 121,
    318
Horace, 212, 227, 329
House on Marshland, The (Glück), 94–95
Howe, Susan, 34
Howl (Ginsberg), 303–11
    commodification of dissent and, 304
    form of, 306, 307
    materialism criticized in, 308–9
    mysticism in, 307, 308–9
    obscenity of, 304
    sex and drugs and, 305, 309
    Trilling's views on, 303, 309–11
    verbal recklessness of, 307–8
Hughes, Ted, 193, 293
"Hugh Jeremy Chisholm" (Seidel), 84
Hugh Selwyn Mauberley (Pound), 322
Hull University Library, 192
humanism, 130, 160, 190–91, 223
human nature, Romantic view of, 316
humor, of Collins, 257–64
Hybrids of Plants and of Ghosts (Graham), 35
Hyman, Stanley Edgar, 313
"Hymn" (Ginsberg), 306
"Hymn to Intellectual Beauty" (Shelley), 50, 318

"I, I, I" poems, 80–81
iambic pentameter, 281, 322
Ideas, 323
identity, 79, 80–81
"I Do" (Seidel), 80–81, 92
"If, My Darling" (Larkin), 196
"If Only This Could Be Said" (Milosz), 231
Iliad (Homer), 20
imagination:
    in high Romantic period, 49–50
    of Justice, 157
    liberal, 311
    powers and limits of, 41
    Wordsworth's views on, 49
Imagism, 280
In a Green Night (Walcott), 23
In Defense of Reason (Winters), 316–17
India, British in, 62
Indians, disappearance of, 186

Inferno (Dante), 25
information, consuming of, 82
"In Love with You" (Koch), 189
"In Memoriam" (Seidel), 84
In Memoriam (Tennyson), 295
inner experience, as subject for poetry, 35, 69,
    99–100, 177
In Parenthesis (Jones), 34
intellectual deliverance, 9–10
"In the Field" (Wilbur), 141
"Invitation and Exclusion" (Glück), 99
Irishness, literary glamours of, 203
Irish poets, O'Driscoll's views on, 200
    see also Heaney, Seamus; O'Driscoll, Dennis;
        Yeats, William Butler
irony, 54, 55, 69, 103, 246
    of Brodsky, 250
    of Collins, 262–63, 266–67, 268
    of Justice, 152, 157
    of Merrill, 135
    of Milosz, 221, 224
    of O'Driscoll, 204–5
Isaac, sacrifice of, 168
Isaiah, Prophet, 71
island artists, problem of, 18
Italy, Walcott in, 24

Jackson, David, 126, 133
James, Henry, 142, 317
Japan, bombing of, 122–23
Jarrell, Randall, 138, 140, 279, 282
Jaurès, Jean, 63
Jesus Christ, 38
    in Hill's work, 55, 57, 58
Jill (Larkin), 195
Job, 103, 205, 219
"Job" (O'Driscoll), 205–6
John Paul II, Pope, 230
Johnson, Samuel, 299, 324, 329
Jones, David, 34
joy, Merrill's praise of, 140–41, 144
Jungian images, 174
Justice, Donald, 148–58
    aging in poems of, 155–56
    Lowell compared with, 148–49, 154
    poetic dedication of, 149
    as poet of sadness, 158
    Ransom compared with, 150
    Roethke compared with, 148–49
    romance of oblivion in, 149–50
    Southern childhood of, 150–51, 157

Stevens's influence on, 150
    as vocational poet, 148
Just Whistle (C. D. Wright), 120–23

Kaddish (Ginsberg), 306
Kaufman, Elaine, 83
Keaton, Buster, 288
Keats, John, 17, 28, 49, 141
Kees, Weldon, 149, 152, 157
Kennedy, Jackie, 287
Kennedy, John F., 184, 285, 287
King Log (Hill), 56–57, 59–60
King Popiel and Other Poems (Milosz), 228–29
"King's Daughters, Home for Unwed Mothers,
    1948" (C. D. Wright), 118
Kirstein, Lincoln, 314
Kjellberg, Ann, 244–45
knowledge, of Glück, 95, 104
Koch, Kenneth, 184–91
    Ashbery compared with, 184–85, 188, 189
    Dadaist poems of, 188
    humanism of, 190–91
    love poems of, 185, 188, 189
    wit of, 189, 191
Kreisau conspirators, 68
Krell, David Farrell, 32

"Lachrimae" (Hill), 54, 76
"Ladies by Their Windows" (Justice), 150
La Fontaine, Jean de, 140–41
Laforgue, Jules, 157, 251, 298, 319
landscape, in Caribbean, 19, 20–21
language:
    of courteous poet, 113
    failure of, 26
    incommensurability of, 245
    of Milton and Tennyson, 298–99
    as Murray theme, 217
    private, 44
Larkin, Philip, 192–201, 295, 329
    as favorite British poet, 193
    Hill compared with, 55–56
    honesty of, 97
    loneliness of, 194–96
    Murray's parody of, 214
    O'Driscoll compared with, 199–201
    scandal about, 192–93, 196
    use of metaphor by, 118
    wit of, 197
    Yeats compared with, 194, 196
    Yeats's challenge accepted by, 194

Larkinesque, use of word, 192
Latin American poetry, 106
Latini, Brunetto, 149
Lawrence, D. H., 271
Learning Human (Murray), 209–12
Leaves of Grass (Whitman), 295
Leavis, F. R., 131
Lenin, 110
Less Deceived, The (Larkin), 193, 194, 195
"Lesson of Baudelaire, The" (Eliot), 301
Levertov, Denise, 327, 328
Lewinsky, Monica, 285
Library Association Record, 193
Library of Congress, 287
"Libretto" (C. D. Wright), 115, 118
Lichtenstein painting, 284–85
life:
    art prevented by, 221
    criticism of, 13, 299
    turned into art, 125–26
life changes, in Glück's work, 100
Life on Earth (Seidel), 81, 87–91
Life Studies (Lowell), 295
"Life Studies" (Lowell), 103
"Lines Composed Over Three-Thousand Miles from
        Tintern Abbey" (Collins), 265–66
"Lines on the Winter Campaign, 1980" (Brodsky),
        250
"Lithuanian Nocturne" (Brodsky), 253–54
loneliness:
    of J. Wright, 178
    of Larkin, 194–96
longing, as Justice subject, 150, 151, 154
"Looking Forward" (O'Driscoll), 204
Lopate, Philip, 308
Lord Weary's Castle (Lowell), 138
"Lost in Translation" (Merrill), 134–35
Lost Son, The (Roethke), 175–76
"Lost Son, The" (Roethke), 176
Lourdes, 230
love, 230, 277
    Glück's encounter with, 104
    in Koch's poems, 185, 188, 189
    in Stallings's work, 293, 294
Love, Susan, 90
"Love Again" (Larkin), 197
"Love Calls Us to the Things of This World"
        (Wilbur), 146
lovelessness, of Larkin, 195, 197–98
"Love Song of J. Alfred Prufrock, The" (Eliot), 302,
        318

Lowell, Robert, 60, 141, 169, 282, 295, 329
    ancestors claimed by, 184
    confessional poetry of, 154, 172
    Glück compared with, 99, 100
    Justice compared with, 148–49, 154
    psychoanalysis as viewed by, 103
    Roethke compared with, 178
    Seidel influenced by, 87
    Walcott influenced by, 23
    Wilbur compared with, 138
Lucretius, 10–11
"Lullaby at Cape Cod" (Brodsky), 248–49
Lurie, Alison, 126, 132, 133
lust, in Hecht's work, 160, 161
"Lycidas"(Milton), 183
"Lying in a Hammock at William Duffy's Farm in
        Pine Island, Minnesota" (J. Wright), 181–82
Lyrical Ballads (Wordsworth), 325
lyric poetry:
    honesty in, 97
    privilege of, 47

McKuen, Rod, 257
Macneice, Louis, 246–47
mad cow epidemic, 73
madeleine, Proust's use of, 125
madness, 96, 138
"Make it new" injunction, 280
"Man Closing Up, The" (Justice), 156
Mandelstam, Osip, 243
Manicheanism, 310–11
"Man Listening to Disc" (Collins), 261
Mann, Thomas, 319
mannerism, 52
"Man Who Married Magdalene, The" (Hecht), 162
Many Loves of Dobie Gillis, The (TV show), 304
"Map, The" (Bishop), 291
"March" (Seidel), 92
"Marina" (Koch's love), 188
marriage, in C. D. Wright's work, 114, 117
Marvell, Andrew, 23, 296
Marxism, 224, 229
Mary Magdalene, 162
mass culture:
    degrading, addictive, 70
    irony and, 262–63
mass murders, twentieth-century, 60, 70
"Master Jeweler Joel Rosenthal, The" (Seidel), 83
materialism, *Howl* and, 308–9
Materialism (Graham), 35
"Matinees" (Merrill), 134–35

Maud (Tennyson), 100

Maule's Curse (Winters), 317

Maurras, Charles, 301

Meadowlands (Glück), 98, 100, 102

    Telemachus in, 101

meaning:

    allegory and, 268

    communication of, 44

    as convention, 43

    rhythm and, 290

    syntax of narrative vs., 80

    Tate's view of, 326

    world's hidden, 46

Mehigan, Joshua, 288–91

Melville, Herman, 317

memory, 125, 136, 230

    water metaphor for, 48

"Men at Forty" (Justice), 155

Mercian Hymns (Hill), 65, 75, 78

Meredith, George, 100

Merrill, James, 125–36

    aestheticism of, 130–31

    Auden compared with, 129

    Augustan Age and, 136

    childhood of, 126, 134

    as comic or Mozartian poet, 126–27

    as decorative poet, 126

    elegance of, 129–30

    fresco painter compared with, 127

    generosity of, 132

    liberality as flaw of, 129

    limits of achievement of, 127

    love of puns of, 127–28

    luxurious poetry of, 126

    metrical repertoire of, 128–29

    money and status of, 126

    snobbery of, 132–33

    Wilbur compared with, 144

Merrill Lynch, 126

metaphors, 222

    of Brodsky, 246

    defined, 146

    of Hecht, 164

    of Larkin, 118

    of Merrill, 125–26, 146–47

    of Milosz, 230

    of O'Driscoll, 202

    of Osterhaus, 287–88

    of Proust, 125

    of Roethke, 174

    in Seidel's work, 93

    of Stallings, 293–94

    translation and, 249

    water, 48–49

    of Wilbur, 146–47

    wit and, 259

"Metaphysical Poets, The" (Eliot), 11, 297, 298

Metaphysical wit, 152–53, 201, 259

metaphysics, 177

    of Justice, 149

    of Wilbur, 146

meter, 145, 327–28

    iambic pentameter, 281, 322

    Merrill's repertoire and, 128–29

"Mexican Divertimento" (Brodsky), 250

middle age, Justice's writing about, 155–56

middle class, 203–5, 222

Midsummer (Walcott), 23

military life, in poetry, 139–40

Milosz, Czeslaw, 60–61, 220–32, 258

    flaw in poetry of, 229

    God as viewed by, 230–31

    importance of dates to, 224

    Norton lectures of, 229–30

    ordinary endowed with significance by, 268–69

    postmodernism of, 221–24, 227, 231

Milton, John, 17, 178, 183, 298–99, 325

mind, *see* inner experience

"Mined Country" (Wilbur), 139

"Minutes" (Stalling), 292

misery, 72

misogyny, of Larkin, 192–93

"Missing Person, The" (Justice), 155–56

"Mister Hanusevich" (Milosz), 229

modernism, modernist poetry, 12, 41, 184, 187,
    246, 321, 326

    alternatives to, 172

    Eliot's understanding of, 296–99

    Imagism, 280

    information withheld in, 25, 27, 33–34

    inner experience and, 35, 69

    Milosz's opposition to, 221–24

    technological change and, 297–98

    theoretical vs. phenomenological encounter
        with, 25–26

    Waste Land as, 295–99

modern poetry, modernness:

    Arnold's definition of, 9–11

    Collins's views on, 269–70

    criticism and, 322–29

    Eliot's views on, 10, 11

    heroism and, 11, 131

modern poetry, modernness (*continued*)
   risk taking and, 12, 13
   twentieth-century obsession with, 322–29
   virtues and vices of, 11–12
   Winters's objections to, 315–17
Moloch, Molochdom, of Ginsberg, 308–9, 311
Monroe, Harriet, 314
Montague, John, 203
Moore, Marianne, 139, 314, 329
morality, 177, 319
   Brodsky's views on, 243
   of Hill's work, 53, 57–58, 60
   of Victorians vs. moderns, 301
Morandi painting, 284
More, Paul Elmer, 312
"More Blues and the Abstract Truth" (C. D. Wright),
   119, 120
"More Light! More Light!" (Hecht), 159–60,
   167
mosaics, in Ravenna, 131
Mother Goose, 176
Motion, Andrew, 192
"Mr. Bleaney" (Larkin), 196
Muldoon, Paul, 292
murder, 61
   in Hecht's work, 159–60
   mass, 60, 70
   in Mehigan's work, 290, 291
Murray, Les, 207–19
   Bunyah legacies in work of, 207
   as character, 207–8
   Frost compared with, 208–9
   Whitman compared with, 208
"Muse of History, The" (Walcott), 18
music, 309
   in Hecht's work, 163–64
   Justice's poetry and, 151–52
   of Stravinsky, 297
"Music of Poetry, The" (Eliot), 302
"MV Agusta Rally" (Seidel), 92
"My Dim-Wit Cousin" (Roethke), 174
Myers, Alan, 250
"My Heart" (Collins), 260–62
"My South" (Justice), 157
Mystery of the Charity of Charles Péguy, The (Hill),
   62–64, 68
mysticism, 269
   in *Howl,* 307, 308–9
   in Roethke's work, 177
   in Simic's work, 106, 111
   of Zagajewski, 238–42

Mysticism for Beginners (Zagajewski), 237, 238–39,
   241–42
myth:
   Glück's use of, 94–97, 100–102, 293
   history as, 62
   of Romantic *poète maudit,* 141
   satire or deconstruction and, 101
   Waste Land and, 300, 301
   see also Greek mythology
My Tokyo (Seidel), 82–83, 87
"My Tokyo" (Seidel), 82–83

Nabokov, Vladimir, 255
naïveté, 19
"Names" (Walcott), 19–20
narcissism, 103, 163, 200
   in Merrill's work, 133
   of Olds, 274–75
narrative, C. D. Wright's interest in, 114–20, 123
Native Realm (Milosz), 225
nature, 323, 324
   in Hecht's work, 164, 165
   in Hill's work, 75–77
   imagination and, 49
   Milosz's views on, 268–69
   in Murray's work, 213
   Orpheus's song and, 164
   in Roethke's work, 175–76
   Wilbur's views on, 146, 147
   Wordsworth's views on, 266
Nazism, Nazis, 108, 217, 218, 232
   in Poland, 223, 225, 226
Nebuchadnezzar, 77–78
neoclassicism, 324
neo-Humanist movement, 312
neo-Romanticism, 174
New Addresses (Koch), 191
New and Collected Poems, 1952–1992 (Hill), 53,
   64
New and Selected Poems (O'Driscoll), 199
New Criticism, New Critics, 56, 106, 152, 189,
   282, 326
Newman, Cardinal John Henry, 71
newness, objections to, 280–81
New Poets of England and America (Hall, Pack, and
   Simpson, eds.), 179–80
New York City, 83–84, 90–93, 186
   centrality of, 185
   Hell of, 88, 91
   as new Rome, 184
New York School poets, 184–91

egotism of, 185
  lack of moderation of, 189
Night Light (Justice), 154, 156
"Night Panic" (Simic), 111
nihilism, 10–11, 299
"1945" (Hecht), 167–68
"1998" (Osterhaus), 285
Nobel Prize, 19, 243
North Ship, The (Larkin), 194, 195
"Norton Anthology of English Literature, The"
  (Collins), 258
nostalgia, as Justice subject, 151, 157
"Nostalgia" (Collins), 261
"Nostalgia and Complaint of the Grandparents" (Jus-
  tice), 157
"Nostalgia for a New City" (Yezzi), 283
nothingness, 89, 289
"No Worst, There Is None" (Wright), 121

"O, Thou Opening, O" (Roethke), 176–77
objective correlatives, 35, 69, 166, 215, 277
objectivity, Justice's technique of, 152–53
oblivion, romance of, 149–50
Oblivion (Justice), 149
obscenity, of *Howl,* 304
obscurity, 25–40
  complexity vs., 40
  of Eliot, 25
  explanations for, 34–35
  of Graham, 26–40
  of Hill, 73
  of Milosz, 221
"Ode to Pleasure" (La Fontaine), 140–41
"Ode to the Confederate Dead" (Tate), 56
O'Driscoll, Dennis, 199–206
  "global-regionalist" perspective of, 203
  in Irish Civil Service, 199–200
  Larkin compared with, 199–201
  work as favorite subject of, 202–4
Odysseus, 100, 101
Offa, King, 65
O'Hara, Frank, 190, 327
  Koch compared with, 184–85, 189
old age:
  in Glück's work, 100
  in Hill's work, 75
  in Justice's work, 156
  in Larkin's work, 197
"Old Fools, The" (Larkin), 197
Olds, Sharon, 271–79
  childhood of, 271

  consolation offered by, 278–79
  egotism of, 275
  father of, 273–74, 277–78
  narcissism of, 274–75
  sex in poetry of, 271–78, 286
"Old World, The" (Simic), 110–11
Olson, Charles, 172, 322, 327, 328
Omeros (Walcott), 20, 22, 23
"One Art" (Bishop), 291
"One More Day" (Milosz), 268–69
One Train (Koch), 189
"Only" (O'Driscoll), 201
On the Banks of the Niemen (Orzeszkowa), 220–21
"On the Farm" (Justice), 157
"On the Great Atlantic Rainway" (Koch), 188–89
"On the Marginal Way" (Wilbur), 143–44
"On the Modern Element in Literature" (Matthew),
  9–11
"On the Porch" (Justice), 157
"On T. S. Eliot" (Glück), 97
Open House (Roethke), 172, 174
opera, 134
Optimist, The (Mehigan), 288–91
"Optimist, The" (Mehigan), 288–89
Orchards of Syon, The (Hill), 66, 76–78
"Orchids, The" (Roethke), 175
"Order of Service, An" (Hill), 59–60
ordinary, the:
  Collins's devotion to, 258, 259, 263–65
  Olds's use of, 275
  optimism and, 288
  significance given to, 268–69
originality:
  Eliot's standard for, 281
  measures of, 280
Orpheus, myth of, 164
"Orphic Calling, An" (Hecht), 163–64
Orzeszkowa, Eliza, 220–21
"Osso Buco" (Collins), 264–65
Osterhaus, Joe, 284–88
Othello (Shakespeare), 58
Ouija, 130, 133
"Out, Out—" (Frost), 290
"Ovid in the Third Reich" (Hill), 53, 60

Pack, Robert, 179–80
painting, 52, 130, 229, 284–85
  Walcott's interest in, 21, 22
Palestine, British massacre in, 217
Palmer, Michael, 34
Palo Alto, Calif., 315

Paradise (heaven):
    of Dante, 76, 88
    in Hill's work, 75–76
    New World as, 21–22
Paris Review, Wilbur's interview in, 141, 144
Parker, Dorothy, 204
Parmigianino, 52
parody:
    in Hill's work, 54–55
    in Murray's work, 214
Partisan Review, 187
Part of Speech, A (Brodsky), 244–46
"Party" (Justice), 155
Patterson, Floyd, 170
peace poets, 140
Péguy, Charles, 62–64, 68
Penelope, 100, 101
Penguin, 244
perception, Graham's views on, 29–30
perfection, of life vs. the work, 194
Periclean Athens, 9
"Peronism" (O'Hara), 185
Persephone, myth of, 39, 94–95, 100
persona, of Seidel, 87
"Phenomenal Survivals of Death in Nantucket"
    (Glück), 99
phenomenological level, 25–26
"Philosophy of Composition, The" (Poe), 326
Picnic, Lightning (Collins), 257
Pinsky, Robert, 305, 328
Pissarro, Camille, 22
Plath, Aurelia, 137
Plath, Sylvia, 137–38, 141, 169
    Roethke's influence on, 175
Plato, 319, 323, 324
Platonic ideal, afterlife as, 149
pleasure:
    Koch's views on, 186
    meter and, 328
    transcendence and, 309
"Pleasures of Peace, The" (Koch), 186
Poe, Edgar Allan, 317, 326
"Poem" (Justice), 149
Poem That Changed America, The (Ginsberg), 303, 305
"Poet, The" (Emerson), 146
Poetics (Aristotle), 323
Poetry, 111
poetry, poet:
    "aria of effect" sung by, 254
    Aristotle's views on, 323–24
    Arnold's definition of, 13

    as calling, 96, 235
    candor in, 96–97
    of discovery, 298
    everything else vs., 200
    Plato's views on, 323, 324
    prose compared with, 243
    reading vs. doing a reading of, 26
    romantic view of, 324–28
    Tate on demands of, 40
    as vocation, 148
Poetry Book Society, 193
poiesis, 323
Poland, 62, 233
    Communism in, 224, 225, 226, 234
    martial law in, 234
    Nazi occupation of, 223, 225, 226
    Solidarity movement in, 234, 237
    Warsaw Uprising in, 226
Polish poets, *see* Milosz, Czeslaw; Zagajewski, Adam
political violence, 60–61, 62
"Pomegranate" (Glück), 94–95
Popa, Vasko, 108
Pope, Alexander, 136, 324
"Poppy" (Hecht), 162
pornography, Larkin's taste for, 192, 196
"Portrait of Tragedy" (Brodsky), 254
postmodern, postmodernists, 10, 12, 326
    Heidegger as inspiration for, 108–9
    humane, 223, 231
    Milosz as, 221–24, 227, 231
"Potato" (Wilbur), 139–40
Pound, Ezra, 172, 280, 322, 326
    ambiguity of, 282
    Eliot compared with, 301
    Hill compared with, 72, 73
    Imagism of, 280
    "Make it new" injunction of, 280
    Waste Land edited by, 300
power, honesty and, 97
Praise to the End! (Roethke), 176
"Prayer" (Olds), 272
Prelude, The (Wordsworth), 48, 49, 136
"Presences" (Justice), 156
"Pressed Duck" (Seidel), 83
"Primer" (Simic), 107
Primitivism and Decadence (Winters), 317
"Prism" (Glück), 105
prizefighting, 170–71
Prodigal, The (Walcott), 23, 24
"Progress" (Mehigan), 289
projective verse, 172

"Promise, The" (Olds), 275–76
Proofs & Theories (Glück), 95–96
prose, poetry compared with, 243
"Prose and Verse" (Eliot), 298
Proust, Marcel, 125–26, 136
"Provinces" (C. D. Wright), 117–18
"Psalm II" (Ginsberg), 306
"pseudo-reference," 123
psychoanalysis, 101–3
psychological dangers, of exile, 255
Pulitzer Prize, 138, 170, 176
puns, punning, 259
    Merrill's love of, 127–28
    in Stallings's work, 292
    of Yezzi, 282
"Pupil, The" (Justice), 151
Purgatorio (Dante), 25

"Quality of Sprawl, The" (Murray), 210
Quest for Reality (anthology), 313
"Questionable Mother, A" (Mehigan), 290
Questions of Travel (Bishop), 295
"Quintets for Robert Morley" (Murray), 215

racism, of Larkin, 192–93, 196
"Rackets" (Seidel), 84
Rademacher, Pete, 170
Radiance (Osterhaus), 284–88
Ransom, John Crowe, 139, 172, 282, 312
    Justice influenced by, 150
    Winters's criticism of, 317
"Rara Avis in Terra" (Hecht), 167
Raskin, Jonah, 304, 306
"Raven, The" (Poe), 326
Ravenna, Christian mosaics in, 131
"reader" vs. "rider" type, 209–10
"Reading an Anthology of Chinese Poems of the Sung Dynasty, I Pause to Admire the Length and Clarity of Their Titles" (Collins), 269
reason, 160, 163, 251, 293, 316, 317
redemption, in Hill's work, 75
"Redress of Poetry, The" (Heaney), 200
reference:
    for courteous poet, 113
    for discourteous poet, 114
regret, as Justice subject, 150, 151
religion, 300
    death of, 268, 269
    sex and, 271, 277
    see also Catholicism, Catholics; Christianity; God

religious poetry:
    of Glück, 103–4
    of Hill, 53–55, 64, 68–71
"Remarks on Colors" (C. D. Wright), 119
remembering, *see* memory
Renaissance, 323
repressive regimes, overturning, 271
Republic (Plato), 323
"Requiem for the Plantagenet Kings" (Hill), 55–56, 69
Revell, Donald, 34
Rexroth, Kenneth, 327
rhyme, 128, 145, 281, 327
    Brodsky's retention of, 248
    in Stallings work, 291, 292
rhythm:
    meaning and, 290
    of *Waste Land,* 301–2
Rich, Adrienne, 179
Rigbee, David, 247
Rimbaud, Arthur, 141
risk taking, 12, 13
Rite of Spring, The (Stravinsky), 297
"Robinson" (Kees), 157
Roethke, Theodore, 170–79
    background of, 170, 173, 174
    Bogan's influence on, 174
    boxing and, 170–71
    death of, 177
    Eliot's influence on, 176, 177
    "greenhouse poems" of, 174–75
    Justice compared with, 148–49
    meaning of poems of, 178
    Pulitzer Prize of, 170, 176
    sensitivity and sentimentality of, 171
    sincerity of, 173, 177, 183
    verse writing course of, 173
    Wright compared with, 170–73, 182, 183
    Yeats imitated by, 177
Romans, ancient, 95, 212
Romanticism, 141, 324–28
    of Ashbery, 41, 45–52
    Winters's criticism of, 316–17
"Romantic Landscape" (Simic), 110
Romantic music, Justice's link with, 151
"Root Cellar" (Roethke), 175
"Round the Point" (Larkin), 194–95
Ruggles, Carl, 151
"Ruins of a Great House" (Walcott), 22–23
Russian language, English compared with, 245, 247, 251

Russian poetry, Russian poets:
    Brodsky as, 243, 245, 251
    Brodsky's views on, 247

"Sacrifice" (Hecht), 168
sadness, Justice as poet of, 158
Sailing Alone Around the Room (Collins), 257
Saint Judas (J. Wright), 179
St. Lucia, 17, 18, 20
St. Petersburg, 255
San Francisco Poetry Renaissance, 304
Sante, Luc, 305
Satan, in Osterhaus's work, 286–87
Satan Says (Olds), 272–73
"Satan Says" (Olds), 272–73
satire, of Larkin, 197
"Saturn" (Olds), 273
Scattering of Salts, A (Merrill), 135
Schiller, Johann Christoph Friedrich von, 19
"Schoolsville" (Collins), 259–60
Schuyler, James, 184–85
Schwartz, Delmore, 184, 187, 313
Scott, Walter, 151
Seager, Allan, 174
"Seasons, The" (Thomson), 190
Seidel, Frederick, 79–93
    childhood of, 89
    Eliot compared with, 84–85
    Lowell's influence on, 87
    as moralist, 93
    persona of, 87
    shifting identities of, 79
    snobbery of, 83
    social interest of, 81–85
    strangeness of, 81, 85
    syntax of narrative in, 80
Selected Early Poems (Simic), 106
Selected Poems (Brodsky), 244
self-assurance, honesty and, 97
self-control:
    sex and, 287
    Winters's concern with, 317–18
self-expression, 316
Self-Portrait in a Convex Mirror (Ashbery), 45–46
"Self-Portrait in a Convex Mirror" (Ashbery), 52
self-scrutiny, 131
"Send No Money" (Larkin), 196
sentimentality:
    Justice's avoidance of, 152
    of Olds, 278
    of Roethke and J. Wright, 171
    of Seidel, 93

September 11, 2001, 93
"September Song" (Hill), 53, 60
"Sestina on Six Words by Weldon Kees" (Justice),
    152
Seven Ages, The (Glück), 95
Sewanee Review, 180
sex, 300
    in Eliot's work, 302
    in Glück's work, 104
    in Hill's work, 57–58
    Howl and, 305, 309
    in Larkin's work, 195
    in Murray's work, 208, 214–15, 216
    in Olds's work, 271–78, 286
    in Osterhaus's work, 285–87
    in Roethke's work, 176
    in Seidel's work, 79, 86, 92
    in Stallings's work, 293
    in Wright's work, 120–21, 124
"Shadow, Hawk, and Dove" (Osterhaus), 287
Shakespeare, William, 17, 73, 142, 168, 176
    Walcott compared with, 21, 22–23
Shaw, Robert Gould, 60
Shelley, Percy Bysshe, 141, 251, 271, 296, 308,
    325–26
    imagination as viewed by, 49–50
"shining the particulars" technique, 116–18
"Short History of British India, A" (Hill), 62
"Short History of the West" (Graham), 34
shrieking, 50
sibling rivalry, 102
Sidney, Sir Philip, 324
"Siesta in Xbalba" (Ginsberg), 306–7
"Significance of 'The Bridge' by Hart Crane; or What
    Are We to Think of Professor X?" (Winters),
    316
Simic, Charles, 106–12
    childhood of, 108
    Heidegger's influence on, 108–9
    literary influences on, 106
Simpson, Louis, 179–80
sincerity:
    Glück's opposition to, 96
    Justice's views on, 154–55
    of Roethke, 173, 177, 183
    of Wright, 180, 183
Sincerity and Authenticity (Trilling), 141–43
"Six Lectures in Verse" (Milosz), 230
snobbery, 211, 270
    of Collins, 263
    of Merrill, 132–33
    of Seidel, 83

Snyder, Gary, 303–4
social class, 203–5, 222, 300
Socrates, 323
So Forth (Brodsky), 244–46, 252
solemnity, of Hill, 59
Solidarity, Solitude (Zagajewski), 234–37, 241
Solidarity movement, 234, 237
solipsism, of Seidel, 86
solitude:
  as Justice subject, 151
  solidarity vs., 234–37
"Somebody's Life" (Hecht), 164
"Some General Instructions" (Koch), 190–91
"Songbook of Sebastian Arrurruz, The" (Hill), 64
"Song of Myself" (Whitman), 318
"Sonic Revelations" (C. D. Wright), 123
"Sonnet" (Wilbur), 142–43
Sophocles, 10
sound, Merrill under the spell of, 128
"Source, The" (Olds), 273
South, the, as Justice subject, 150–51
"Southern Gothic" (Justice), 151
Soviet Union, 229–30
  in Afghanistan, 250
  Brodsky expelled from, 244
  Brodsky in, 243, 244
  Poland occupied by, 225
Spanish baroque, Hill's translation from, 64
"Speak" (J. Wright), 182–83
"Spectacle, The" (Mehigan), 290–91
Speech! Speech! (Hill), 66, 72–76
  obscurity of, 73
Spender, Stephen, 247
Spirit of the Age, 228
Stalin, Joseph, 225
Stalinism, 240
Stallings, A. E., 291–94
Statue of Liberty, 284–85
Stauffenberg, Claus von, 68
Steal Away (C. D. Wright), 114, 122, 123
Steiner, George, 235
Stevens, Wallace, 29, 317, 326
  Ashbery compared with, 41, 45, 50–51
  Collins's work and, 257, 258, 267
  Justice influenced by, 150
Stevenson, Adlai, 184
Stonington, 126
Strauss, Richard, 134
Stravinsky, Igor F., 297
String Light (C. D. Wright), 118
"Study of Poetry, The" (Arnold), 13
"Subway, The" (Tate), 318

suffering, 100, 169
  knowledge gained through, 95
  of Larkin, 197
  of Merrill, 134
  of O'Driscoll, 200
suicide, 96, 310
Summer Anniversaries, The (Justice), 150
Sun Out (Koch), 188
Sunrise (Seidel), 87
Sunset Makers, The (Justice), 154, 157
Surrealism, 41, 106, 108
Swarm (Graham), 34–40
  Christianity and, 37–40
  epigraph of, 37
  notes to, 34
"Sweeney Among the Nightingales" (Eliot), 302–3
Swinburne, Algernon Charles, 296
Symbolism, 222, 326
symbols, 165
  allegory and, 25, 26
  Emerson's views on, 146
  Holocaust as, 274
  inner experience and, 69
"syntax that digests iron and spits out petals," 213
Szymborska, Wisława, 249

"Taking a Walk with You" (Koch), 189
"Tales from a Family Album" (Justice), 150
"Talking in Bed" (Larkin), 196
"Talking Shop" (O'Driscoll), 199
Tate, Allen, 282, 283, 312
  Crane's suicide and, 310
  on demands of poetry, 40
  Hill influenced by, 56, 282
  on meaning of poetry, 326
  Roethke as viewed by, 170
  Winters's views on, 318
technological change, modernism and, 297–98
Telemachus, 101
"Telemachus' Dilemma" (Glück), 101
television, 82–83, 304
"Television Was a Baby Crawling Toward That
  Deathchamber" (Ginsberg), 308
Tempest, The (Shakespeare), 142
Tenebrae (Hill), 54
Tennis Court Oath, The (Ashbery), 42
Tennyson, Alfred, Lord, 100, 231, 295
  Eliot's objection to, 296, 298–99
"Thames at Chelsea, The" (Brodsky), 247
"Thanksgiving" (Koch), 186
Thank You and Other Poems (Koch), 188–89
"Them and You" (O'Driscoll), 204–5

theoretical level, 25–30
    defined, 26
    in Graham's work, 26–30, 35
therapeutic language, of Merrill, 135
therapy, poetry writing as, 139
These Days (Seidel), 82, 87
Things of This World (Wilbur), 142–43
"Thin Man, The" (Justice), 155
"This Couple" (C. D. Wright), 116
Thomas, Dylan, 209
Thomson, James, 190
"Thousand and Second Night, The" (Merrill), 134–35
"3 Poems About Kenneth Koch" (O'Hara), 190
"Thrush" (Glück), 104
Thucydides, 10
Thwaite, Anthony, 193–94
"Thyme" (Stallings), 292
Tiepolo's Hound (Walcott), 21–22, 23
time:
    Ashbery's views on, 46
    tragedy of passing of, 266
Tin Drum, The (Grass), 215
"Tintern Abbey" (Wordsworth), 49, 266, 267
Tiresias, 97, 101
"Toads" (Larkin), 197, 199
"To L. E. Sissman" (Hecht), 166
"To Marina" (Koch), 188
"To My Twenties" (Koch), 191
"Tony" (Merrill), 132–33
"To One of the Dugout Nine" (Osterhaus), 285–86
"To Psychoanalysis" (Koch), 191
"Tornfallet" (Brodsky), 252
"To Satan in Heaven" (Justice), 153–54
"To Stammering" (Koch), 191
totalitarianism, Zagajewski's views on, 234, 236
"To the Hawks" (subtitled "McNamara, Rusk, Bundy") (Justice), 154
"To the High Court of Parliament" (Hill), 68
To Urania (Brodsky), 244–46, 254–55
"To William Cobbett" (Hill), 67
"To You" (Koch), 189
"Tradition and the Individual Talent" (Eliot), 281, 301
Traherne, Thomas, 34
transcendence, 327, 329
    Howl and, 306, 309
Transcendentalism, 146
transcience, as Justice subject, 150, 151
transformation, 108–9
    imagination and, 49–50
    longing for, 46

translation, 64, 140–41
    of Brodsky, 244–50, 255–56
    censorship compared with, 245
Translation of the Gospel Back into Tongues (C. D. Wright), 114–15
Transparent Man, The (Hecht), 164–65
Treatise on Poetry, A (Milosz), 222, 225–28
"Treatment" (C. D. Wright), 115–16
"Tree Rings in the Surface of the Butcher's Block, The" (Osterhaus), 286
"Tremayne" (Justice), 157–58
Tremble (C. D. Wright), 123
Tremor (Zagajewski), 233, 237–38
Trilling, Lionel, 96, 141–43, 145
    Howl as viewed by, 303, 309–11
Trinidad, 18
Triumph of Achilles, The (Glück), 95
Triumph of Love, The (Hill), 66, 69–73, 75
    biblical epigraph of, 71
    "LAUDA!" in, 72, 76
Troubled Thoughts, Majestic Dreams (O'Driscoll), 199
truth, 165
    Glück's views on, 95–96, 98
    honesty and, 97
Tsvetaeva, Marina, 243
Tuckerman, F. G., 313, 318
"tup," use of word, 58
25 Poems (Walcott), 18
"Twenty Sonnets to Mary Queen of Scotts" (Brodsky), 249
"Two Cities" (Zagajewski), 234
typewriters, Olson's praise for, 328

"Ugly Sister" (Larkin), 195
"Underneath (Calypso)" (Graham), 38
"Underneath (9)" (Graham), 34, 38–39
"Underneath (Upland)" (Graham), 34, 38
"Undressing Justine" (Milosz), 220–21
United States, 233
    Augustinian moment of, 184
    Brodsky's remaking of life and career in, 244, 255
    poetry as minor pursuit in, 235
    Vietnam War and, 250
universe, childhood of, 89
Unrepresented World, The (Zagajewski), 233, 236
"Untold Cynicism of Poetry, The" (Zagajewski), 239
"Untrustworthy Speaker, The" (Glück), 102–3
"Up Jack" (Wilbur), 140
Urania, 253–54

"Vague Memory from Childhood" (Justice), 157
"Variations on a Text by Vallejo" (Justice), 148, 150, 156
"Variations on a Theme from James" (Justice), 153
Varieties of Metaphysical Poetry, The (Eliot), 298
Vaughn, Robert Boardman, 149
Venetian Vespers, The (Hecht), 165–66, 167
Venice, 165–66
"Venus" (Seidel), 92
Very, Jones, 313
"Via Funari" (Brodsky), 254
Victorian England, Victorians, 9
    Eliot's views on, 11, 296–99
    moderns compared with, 301
"Victoria's Secret" (Collins), 261–63, 266
Vietnam War, 250
"Villa Basque, The" (Osterhaus), 288
"Vindaloo in Merthyr Tydfil" (Murray), 209
Virgil, 17
"Vision of Dame Kind," 269
Vita Nova (Glück), 98, 100, 103
vocation, poet as, 148
Voice at 3 a.m., The (Simic), 110–12
"Votive Candles" (O'Driscoll), 202

Waking, The (Roethke), 170, 176–77
"Waking in the Blue" (Lowell), 138
Walcott, Derek, 17–24, 207, 213, 295
    abstract ideas of, 22
    ambivalence of, 19–20
    Brodsky translated by, 246
    cosmopolitanism of, 24
    elevated style of, 22–23
    epic ambition of, 20
    landscape of, 19, 20–21
    Lowell's influence on, 23
    painterly quality of, 21, 22
    self-imposed responsibilities of, 18
"Walking Across the Atlantic" (Collins), 258–59
Walking to Sleep (Wilbur), 143–44
"Wall, The" (Justice), 152–53
Walton, Izaak, 257
Ward, Edna, 137
"War of the Worlds, The" (Seidel), 93
Warsaw, occupied, 222
Warsaw Uprising, 226
Wars of the Roses, 57–58
Washington, University of, 170
Waste Land, The (Eliot), 176, 295–303
    Madam Sosostris in, 299–300, 301
    as modern classic, 296

as modernist work, 295–99
music and rhythm of, 301–2
Tiresias in, 97, 101
Winters's views on, 315
"Water-Gardening in an Old Farm Dam" (Murray), 212–13
water metaphors:
    in Ashbery, 48–49
    in Wordsworth, 48
Wave, A (Ashbery), 45
"Weather Permitting" (O'Driscoll), 201
"Weed Puller" (Roethke), 175–76
Weimar, 159, 160
Wendell (painter), 130
Wescott, Glenway, 314
Wesley, John, 71
West Indian Federation, 18
"What Calls for Thinking" (Graham), 34
Wheeler, Susan, 80
"When Lilacs Last in the Dooryard Bloom'd (Whitman), 141
"Whether Moral Virtue Comes by Habituation" (Hill), 66
"Which But for Vacancy" (Graham), 34
"White" (Simic), 109
White Buildings (Crane), 315
Whitman, Walt, 45, 79, 141, 295
    Howl influenced by, 305
    Murray compared with, 208
    Winters's views on, 313, 316, 318
Whitsun Weddings, The (Larkin), 193, 295
"Whitsun Weddings, The" (Larkin), 192
wholeness, Romantic longing for, 46, 49
"Why Ralph Refuses to Dance" (C. D. Wright), 119, 121
Wilbur, Richard, 137–47, 179
    Brodsky translated by, 246
    Hecht's essay on, 163
    Jarrell's review of, 138
    Lowell compared with, 138
    military life of, 139–40
    Paris Review interview of, 141, 144
    Plath's meeting with, 137–38
    poetic gifts of, 139
Wilde, Oscar, 130
Wild Iris, The (Glück), 95, 103–4
will, personal, extreme exercise of, 96
Williams, William Carlos, 322
Wimsatt, William Kurtz, Jr., 282
Winters, Yvor, 123, 153, 310, 312–21, 326
    as autodidact, 314

Winters, Yvor (*continued*)
 background of, 314
 Crane as viewed by, 315–17, 319
 form as viewed by, 318–21
 irritating qualities of, 312–13
 provincialism of, 314–15
 U.S. literary map redrawn by, 315
wit, 189
 of Collins, 258–59
 of Justice, 152–53
 of Koch, 189, 191
 of Larkin, 197
 Metaphysical, 152–53, 201, 259
 of O'Driscoll, 201
 relationship of punning to, 259
 of Zagajewski, 240–42
"Witch of Endor, The" (Hecht), 168
"Woman in Heat Wiping Herself, A" (Olds), 274
wonder, of J. Wright, 178
Wordsworth, William, 12, 111, 131, 136, 141, 325
 Ashbery compared with, 48
 Collins's work and, 257, 265–67
 imagination as viewed by, 49
 Roethke compared with, 175
 Winters's poor treatment of, 313
work:
 of O'Driscoll, 199–200
 as O'Driscoll's subject, 202–4
"World, The" (Milosz), 223–24
World War I, 63
 in *Fredy Neptune,* 215, 217
World War II, 187
 in *Fredy Neptune,* 217, 218
 in Hecht's work, 167–68

in Jarrell's work, 140
Milosz in, 225
in Wilbur's work, 139–40
Wright, C. D., 80, 113–24
 formal experiments of, 119–20
 narrative interests of, 114–20, 123
 "shining the particulars" technique of,
  116–18
Wright, James, 170–73, 178–83
 background of, 170, 173, 179
 boxing and, 170–71
 crisis in development of, 179–80
 "deep image" poetry of, 172, 181–82
 revulsion against "technical skill" of, 178
 Roethke compared with, 170–73, 182, 183
 sensitivity and sentimentality of, 171
 sincerity of, 180, 183
Wyatt, Sir Thomas, 313

Yale Younger Poets series, 170
Yeats, William Butler, 100, 177, 203, 306, 323
 Larkin compared with, 194, 196
Yezzi, David, 282–84
younger generation, ingratitude of, 69

Zagajewski, Adam, 108, 233–42
 flight from politically engaged poetry by, 234
 mysticism of, 238–42
 poetry as calling for, 235
 solidarity vs. solitude and, 234–37
 wit of, 240–42
Zeitgeist, 320–21, 322
"Zielinski, Adrian," 224–25
"Zone of Silence" (Milosz), 232